JIM O'B

FROM A TO Z
A BOXING MEMOIR
FROM ALI TO ZIVIC

LIMITED EDITION

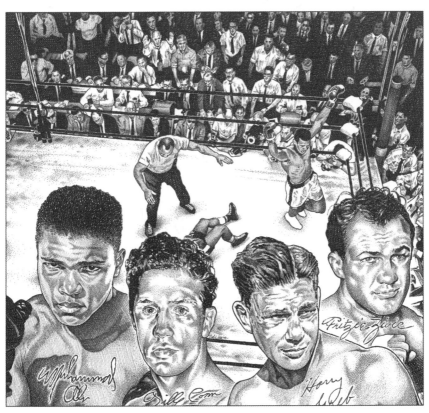

Artwork by Bob Weaver

*"What's the sense of fighting
if you can't fight dirty."*
—Fritzie Zivic

Merry Christmas 2016
to Pat,
With best wishes
from our friend
Hedly Hanna

Jim O'Brien
PhD (English) '64
Osher Adjunct Professor
2012 - 2016

2

Jim O'Brien

A special thanks to Tim Conn and his mother Mary Louise Conn for offering their time, patience and stories through the years, especially in 2016 when I called upon them so many times. I was always comfortable in their company and you couldn't help but smile and laugh when they shared memories of life with Billy Conn. It wasn't all roses or, as the French like to say, it wasn't all sunshine, lollipops and rainbows. But it seems like it was a wonderful ride, like the Sky Rocket at Kennywood Park.

—Jim O'Brien

Published by James P. O'Brien — Publishing
P.O. Box 12580
Pittsburgh PA 15241
Phone (412) 221-3580
E-mail: jimmyo64@gmail.com
Website: www.jimobriensportsauthor.com
First printing, September 2016
By R.R. Donnelley of Pittsburgh Printing
Typography by Cold-Comp

ISBN 978-1-886348-27-1

All autographs in this book are reproductions. Some stories are reprinted with permission.

Cover artwork by Bob Weaver

Graphic design Cathy Pawlowski

Books By Jim O'Brien

COMPLETE HANDBOOK OF PRO BASKETBALL 1970–71
COMPLETE HANDBOOK OF PRO BASKETBALL 1971–72
ABA ALL-STARS
PITTSBURGH: THE STORY OF THE CITY OF CHAMPIONS
HAIL TO PITT: A SPORTS HISTORY OF
THE UNIVERSITY OF PITTSBURGH
DOING IT RIGHT
WHATEVER IT TAKES
MAZ AND THE '60 BUCS
REMEMBER ROBERTO
PENGUIN PROFILES
DARE TO DREAM
KEEP THE FAITH
WE HAD 'EM ALL THE WAY
HOMETOWN HEROES
GLORY YEARS
THE CHIEF
STEELERS FOREVER
ALWAYS A STEELER
WITH LOVE AND PRIDE
LAMBERT
FANTASY CAMP
STEELER STUFF
PITTSBURGH PROUD
IMMACULATE REFLECTIONS
A WINNING WAY
GOLDEN ARMS
FROM A TO Z

To order copies of these titles directly from the publisher, send $29.95 for all editions. Please send additional $3.75 to cover shipping and handling charges per book. Contact publisher regarding availability and prices of all books in Pittsburgh Proud series, or to request an order form. Some books are sold out and are no longer available. You can still order the following: Doing It Right, We Had 'Em All The Way, Hometown Heroes, Glory Years, The Chief, Lambert, Fantasy Camp, With Love and Pride, Immaculate Reflections and Golden Arms.

Contents

5

Acknowledgments

I believe I decided I had to write this book after the first time I visited Mary Louise Conn in her room at The James P. Wall Home for the Aged that is operated by The Little Sisters of the Poor in the Brighton Heights section of the North Side in Pittsburgh.

She was such a delight and her late husband Billy Conn was the light-heavyweight champion of the world and came close to claiming the crown for heavyweight champion that was worn with such glory by Joe Louis. Mary Louise and her son Tim were so helpful and generous with their time, and Tim pointed me in the right direction more than once.

Doing this book reminded me of the many wonderful folks I met along the way during my sports-writing career and it was fun to reflect on those times. I have many people to thank for their support through the years.

My list of patrons, fortunately, is a long one: Rich Barcelona of Bailey-PVS Oxides LLC, Suzy and Jim Broadhurst and Jeff Broadhurst of Eat'n Park Restaurants and Parkhurst Dining Corp., Bob Buzzelli of Mellon Bank of New York, Dan Koller of Allegheny Valley Bank, William Campbell of Intuit, Inc., Don Carlucci of Carlucci Construction, Ken Codeluppi of Wall Firma Inc., Armand Dellovade of A.C. Dellovade, Don DeBlasio of DeBlasio's Restaurant, Mike Fabio of Prader-Willi Syndrome Association of Pennsylvania, Steve Fedell of Ikon Office Solutions, Jim, Barbara and Ted Frantz of TEDCO, Inc. Frank B. Fuhrer Wholesale Company, Wayne Fusaro Pancreatic Cancer Research Fund, Thomas B. Grealish of Henderson Brothers, Lou Grippo of The Original Oyster House, James S. Hamilton, Hoddy Hanna of Hanna Real Estate Services, Timothy M. Heim of HHM Insurers, the late Elsie Hillman, Sy Holzer of PNC Bank, Huntington Bank, Dave Jancisin and Derek Jancisin of Merrill Lynch, Bill Johnson of H.J. Heinz, William Kammerer, Tom Keane, Dave King of Nicklas King McConahy, Dan R. Lackner of Paper Products Company, Domenic Laudato of Pittsburgh

Asphalt Company, Mike Lee of Lee Construction Inc., David J. Malone of Gateway Financial, Jack Mascaro of Mascaro Construction, Robert F. McClurg, Nancy and Pat McDonnell of Atria's Restaurant & Tavern, John R. McGinley Jr. of Eckert Seamans, Clark Nicklas of Vista Resources, Inc., John Paul of Highmark, Pittsburgh Section of Society of Mining Engineers, Glenn Porter and Richard Gresh of PPG Public Parking Inc., Steve Previs of Knight Capital European Ltd. in London, Clifford Rowe of P.J. Dick Corporation, Andy Russell of Laurel Mountain Partners, Robert Santillo and Dan Rains of McCarl's, Bohdan W. Stone, Rich Dietrick and Rob Meredith of Morgan Stanley, Tom Sweeney of Compucom, Robert J. Taylor of Taylor & Alsko Law Offices, Thomas J. Usher former CEO and Chairman of U.S. Steel Corp., Western Pennsylvania Caring Foundation, Sam Zacharias of Gateway Financial, John Zanardelli of Asbury Heights,

Others who have worked with me: Chuck Belliotti, Joan and Tom Bigley, Dale Blaha of Altany, Lloynd & Lindquist, Inc., Dan Bartow of Legends of the North Shore, Ann and Art Cipriani, Dave and Frank Clements, Ralph Cindrich, Todd Cover, Dr. Patrick J. DeMeo, Kevin Joyce of The Carlton, Gregory L. Manesiotas, Dennis Meteny, Linda and Frank Meyer, George Morris, Andy Ondrey, Jim Roddey, Linda and Frank Sam, Len Stidle, Barbara Stull and Kim Ravenda.

I want to thank the following individuals for their loyal support: Tony Accamando, R. Everett Burns, Renny Clark, Ray Conaway, Tony Ferraro, Dr. Freddie Fu, Bob and Frank W. Gustine, Jr., Mike Hagan, F. Edwin Harmon, Donald J. Hastings, Dee and Wayne Herrod, Karen Horvath, Jeff James, Carl R. Moulton, Retired Pitt Chancellor Mark Nordenberg, Ron Parfitt, Joseph Piccirilli, Pittsburgh Tribune-Review Multimedia, Matt Polk, Rob Pratte of KDKA Radio, Charlie and Steve Previs, Joe Reljac, Arthur J. Rooney Jr., John Rooney, Patrick J. Rooney, Patrick J. Santelli, Fred Sargent, Rich Snebold, Dick Swanson of Swanson Group, Ltd.

Special assistance has been given to me by Debbie Brookfield of Intuit, Debbie Keener of Reed, Smith Shaw & McClay, Dan Hart, Burt Lauten, E.J. Borghetti, Sean Duffy, Kelly Bird, Jim Duratz, George Gojkovich, Ted Harhai, Russell M. Livingston, Keith Maiden, Dr. Haywood A. Haser, Heinz History Center and Western Pennsylvania Sports Museum, Joe Landolina, Pete Mervosh, Sharon and Alex Pociask, Joe Pohl, Bill Priatko, Tom Anderson, Gerald Smith, Matthew Eapen and Emily Churchman.

My last book, Golden Arms, had the official blessing of Bishop David Zubik, and we'd like to extend that ad infinitum.

This book is also dedicated to the many patrons who have passed on, and without whose support in the early stages this series would not have been possible. So this is in memory of Bill Baierl, Mel Bassi, Aldo Bartolotta, Rudy Celigoi, Ed Prebor, Steve Previs Sr., Art Rooney Sr., Fred Fetteroff, Vince Scorsone, Miles Bryan and Bill Tillotson.

Bruce McGough of RR Donnelley Pittsburgh Printing shepherded this project from start to finish. Denise Maiden and Cathy Pawlowski of Cold Comp Typographers came through with their "whatever it takes" attitude.

I had an outstanding proofreading team that included Bruce McGough, Tom McGuire, Jack Sega, Mike Hagan, Roger Glunt, Ed Lyness, Art Humphreys, Bill Vizza, Dallas Frey and Pat Santelli. They made sure I dotted all my i's.

There is scarce mention here of two local boxing champions of recent vintage, Michael Moorer of Monessen and Paul Spadafora of McKees Rocks, because this is a memoir and I never met or spoke to these fighters, and was not a fan of either. I think the toughest guy to ever come out of McKees Rocks was Clem Smarra.

Introduction
I miss that speed bag

I never learned how to hit a speed bag properly until I turned 70. It happened one day during the winter of 2013 when I was working out on my Silver Sneakers pass at the South Hills Jewish Community Center (JCC) in Scott Township, a suburb about eight miles south of Pittsburgh.

Fritzie Zivic lived in Scott in his retirement years and he would have been proud of me. I visited his wife Helen there after he died to talk about him. Myron Cope's first home after he got married was in Scott Township and he was in a senior retirement residence in the same community called Concordia of the South Hills when he died. When Cope was a kid, he spent time learning the manly art of self-defense and liked to talk about his boxing days.

In between, Cope spent a lot of time in poor health at the nearby St. Clair Hospital where a friend of mine, Robert Terrell, an attendant, looked after him, and a friend of ours, Joe Gordon, the former publicist of the Pittsburgh Steelers, looked in on him just about every day of the week.

It was a good neighborhood for me because Jack Riley, the original general manager of the Penguins, and one of his star players, Pierre Larouche, lived nearby. I went to their homes to interview them. They were the best story-tellers of the Penguins of the past.

I saw a guy in the gym at the JCC making the speed bag hum and I asked him to show me how he did it. He said he was Irish and he was happy to help a fellow Irishman, even if I wasn't reminding anybody there of Billy Conn.

I picked up on it right away and quickly realized that it wasn't as difficult to do as I had always figured.

It felt good to make the racket I was making. Rat-a-tat-tat, rat-a-tat-tat. People started paying attention to what I was doing. That black bag was making a lot of noise.

"Were you a boxer?" someone who was on a nearby treadmill walk wanted to know.

I just smiled and didn't respond. After a brief spell, I said, "What do you think?" And I winked.

Few other people in the workout area ever used the speed bag. Or the heavy bag that hung from the ceiling nearby. The heavy bag wasn't as much fun to hit. It was difficult to make any noise, except for a dull thud. And it hurt the hands to hit it too much. That was not the case with the speed bag. I asked my wife Kathie if she wanted me to show her how to do it, but she wasn't interested. "No, thanks," I think she said.

I also skipped rope at the JCC. I did my best to do it the way I'd seen Sonny Liston and Muhammad Ali do it, crossing the rope, twirling it alongside my right leg, doing it backwards. I hummed "Night Train" as I did it, like Liston who played a vinyl record on a 45 rpm music box. I wasn't bad but I didn't remind anyone of Sonny Liston or Muhammad Ali either. I didn't even remind me of me when I skipped rope when I was 15.

I had been mistaken for a boxer only once before, probably 40 years earlier, when we were driving near Syracuse on our way to visit my Kathie's college roommate, Sandy Allenson, at her mother's home in upstate New York.

I was taking a leak in the men's bathroom and a guy two urinals away was checking me out, causing me a bit of nervousness. Then he said, "Were you a boxer?"

I told him I wasn't. "You look like a boxer I once saw in Syracuse," the man said.

When I got outside, I told Kathie what the man had said. She was hardly impressed. "How come no one ever thinks you're an architect or mistakes you for something intellectual like that?"

I had no idea.

Every time I'd come to the South Hills JCC I'd do a turn or two on the speed bag, and get the attention of the room.

There was a guy there named Rich, an old-timer who liked to lift barbells and liked to talk about boxing. So he liked to talk to me.

Then I came in one day and the speed bag was gone. The heavy bag was gone. And, before long, Rich was gone.

A staff trainer named Bonnie Livingston told me that too many members had complained about the noise I was making. I used to go there a few times a week. Now I hardly go there at all.

I wanted to get a picture of me working on the speed bag. I thought I'd use it when I got around to writing a boxing book.

Well, I've done it. I feel competent about the challenge of writing a book about boxing. I think I have known enough Pittsburgh boxers and some great boxers who came here to fight, and some I met along the way while working in Philadelphia, Miami, New York and Pittsburgh, all good fight towns once upon a time. Muhammad Ali, who was the same age as me, died while I was working on these stories. He's a big part of this book because he was the most fascinating fighter I ever met, and covering his first fight with Joe Frazier for the heavyweight boxing title was the No. 1 sports event that I covered in my career.

I have been thinking about this for a long time. When I finally adhered to Myron Cope's advice from 60 years earlier and sat down and started writing, I discovered that it was easy to do. As easy as making that speed bag bounce back and forth. Hope no one complains.

When I told Roy McHugh, who had turned 101 that year, that I finally got around to writing the book, he said, "No one will buy it."

He sounded like my wife when he said that.

When I told him I was enjoying doing it, he said, "How old are you?" When I told him I would be 74 in August, he said, "Well, you're still young. If you enjoy it, then do it."

While I was in the home stretch of writing this book, I paid several visits to the Greb-Conn Boxing Club, located in the rear basement of the Royal York Apartments in Oakland, on the other side of the building from where the Park Schenley Restaurant was last located before it closed.

I watched the young fighters working out, an equal mix of white and black boxers, about a dozen of them. I wanted to ask them all the same question: Why are you here?

I saw some heavy bags hanging from the ceiling, but I didn't spot a speed bag. Michael McSorley, a good-looking boxing buff who operates the gym and trains fighters, told me it had been broken. I was disappointed about that. I wanted to work on the speed bag for a while, to show the young men what I could do. None of them knew me and I wanted their respect so that they knew I recognized all the faces of the famous boxers plastered on the walls of the gym. I knew something about boxing and the world they were in.

Hope you agree.

Following the first Conn-Louis fight, William G. Nunn, the father of the famous Steelers' scout Bill Nunn Jr., wrote in *The Pittsburgh Courier*:

"For our money, Joe Louis is still the greatest champion ever to grace the ring. He proved tonight that he had it in him. With the chips all down...with the cards stacked against him...with 50,000 white folks pleading for Conn and 5,000 Negroes praying for Joe to win...the winner and still champion, Joe Louis...Thank God!"

Alonzo Johnson
Writer and boxer exchange low blows

"You gotta sit down and start writing."
—Myron Cope

Have you ever heard of a professional fighter from Rankin named Alonzo Johnson? He was a pretty fair heavyweight boxer, ranked as high as No. 5 in the Top Ten in *The Ring* magazine and he lost a disputed split decision fight to Muhammad Ali when Ali was an up and coming contender named Cassius Clay.

Clay was booed in his hometown of Louisville over the decision. You can still see a vintage video of the fight on the Internet, but it's not worth viewing. It wasn't much of a fight.

That fight by the way was Clay's first with a ranked pro fighter and his first on national television. It was on the Gillette boxing series. Teddy Brenner, the matchmaker at Madison Square Garden, put the fight together for television.

I met Myron Cope and Alonzo Johnson in the same aisle of a locker room on the campus of the University of Pittsburgh in my teenage years. I can still see the dark blue metal lockers and the wooden bench that ran between them. It was in Fitzgerald Field House, also known as the Pitt Field House. The locker room was in the basement of the building.

The meetings came five years apart. Both occurred during the Pittsburgh Golden Gloves Boxing Tournament, sponsored by the *Pittsburgh Post-Gazette* for the benefit of its Dapper Dan Charities. I was 14 when I met Myron Cope for the first time and 19 when I met Alonzo Johnson.

Cope was a talented young sportswriter for the *Post-Gazette* and the Golden Gloves was his best annual assignment. Al Abrams, the sports editor and featured columnist at the newspaper, never gave Cope any choice assignments, not wanting anyone to outshine his own star

ALONZO JOHNSON

Rankin heavyweight lost a decision to Cassius Clay in Louisville in Clay's first fight on national television on July 22, 1961. It can still be seen on YouTube.

in the city's morning newspaper. Cope would later leave the paper to pursue a more satisfying and rewarding career as a free-lance writer and drew assignments from some of the top magazines in the country such as *The Saturday Evening Post, True* and *Sports Illustrated.*

Anyone who did proper research and checked sports page clippings from that period would be able to recognize how much better a writer was Cope compared to his contemporaries. Most of them wrote in a style that needed decoding to understand. They would call a hockey puck a "black biscuit," Saturday would be "the Sabbath," a night game would be "an arc-light tilt," New York was "the Gotham," and its Giants' football team "the Maramen."

When Cope told Abrams he was leaving the paper to pursue a career as a free-lance writer, Abrams said, "You'll starve." That's the same thing that Jim Boston, the business manager of the Steelers, told Mel Blount when the Pro Bowl defensive back said he'd retire from the Steelers rather than accept a meager raise.

Cope and I both loved boxing and covering the Golden Gloves. It was my favorite event of the year back then.

Johnson was a fine fighter from Rankin who had been a Pittsburgh Golden Gloves champion, boxing for the Lee Moore A.C. in Braddock. He went on to become one of the top-ranked heavyweight fighters in the country. I was 19 when I was introduced to Alonzo Johnson.

Both meetings served me well, though the one with Johnson took some time to develop into a winner.

Cope was carrying a small portable typewriter at his side when I spotted him in the locker room in the winter of 1956. I had just started, at the age of 14, as the sports editor of *The Hazelwood Envoy,* a bi-weekly tabloid in my hometown. I filled two pages of that newspaper with stories and my reflections on the local sports scene every two weeks. It didn't seem like a big deal at the time, but it blows my mind now to think that I was responsible for filling two pages of a newspaper so often at such a young age. I never missed a deadline.

* * *

I wrote about the Glen-Hazel Boys' Club, located in a hous-ing project at the peak of Glenwood and Hazelwood. Cy Obremski, who worked at the Jones & Laughlin Steel Mill by day, coached amateur boxers at night in a recreation building at the center of the housing project. Fighters came from all over the city to be tutored by Obremski. He knew his stuff and, best of all, he looked like a fight guy.

His assistant was Renaldo "Babe" DiGiosio, who looked even more like a fight guy. It was once said of Yankees' outfielder Hank Bauer that he had a face that looked like a clenched fist. The same could be said for Babe DiGiosio. I went to the Glen-Hazel Boys Club as a kid to learn how to box and take care of myself. I had no intention of continuing to compete in boxing. I just wanted to survive on the streets, which could be mean from time to time. It was a good idea to know how to box as a young boy in the streets of Glenwood and Hazelwood. Obremski looked after me and never over-matched me. One time, when I was in against a much better boxer, Johnny Robinson, who was smaller than me, I ducked his first punch and when I raised my head I came up under his chin and struck it with the top of my head. He went down, and I threw a punch against air to make it look like I had actually punched him. Sonny Liston might have called it "a phantom punch." No mat-ter, he was counted out and, fortunately, we never fought again. Johnny Robinson became a minister, and was lucky to survive having his throat slashed by some local rogue. Didn't I say those streets could be mean?

My wife Kathleen can be mean, too. When I related my KO story of Johnny Robinson, she responded by saying, "It's a wonder you didn't kill him with that head of yours. He must have thought he got struck by a bowling ball!"

Obremski's team won the Golden Gloves team boxing title 11 out of 12 years in one stretch, and after I no longer covered them, they extended that to 17 of 19 team titles. They were the Yankees of Pittsburgh amateur boxing.

The Post-Gazette gave the Golden Gloves a great deal of publicity in those days. They would devote the top third of a page to thumbnail pictures of the participating fighters for weeks in advance of the tournament. That's when newspapers knew how to promote their own promotions. The pictures were less than an inch wide and about one-and-a-half inches deep.

I remember outstanding fighters such as Carmie Price of Ambridge and Raybon Stubbs of East Liberty, Emil Brtko of the North Side, Johnny Morris of Pittsburgh and Jack Rogers of Uniontown. There was a fierce fighter from The Hill named Cephus Huff. He shaved his head clean and he was a mean-looking dude. The Glen-Hazel Boys Club boasted such fighters as Eugene Tippett, Carl Jordan, James T. Gilliam and Jimmy Gilliam, King Williams, Pat Deasy and Augie Broudy. Johnny Eubanks from East Liberty, and Don "Toro" Smith and Bob Baker from The Hill would later fight some top-ranked heavyweights. The early fights in the Golden Gloves Tournament were held at the South Side Market House and the championship fights were held at the Pitt Field House and later the Civic Arena.

Cope was only 5 feet, 5-3/4 inches tall at best, but I was smaller than he was at the time. I think he liked me better when he could look down at me when he was speaking. I introduced myself and asked for his advice. "Mr. Cope, what do I have to do to become a writer?" I asked him.

Before you read this next line, call up your best Myron Cope voice imitation and it works better.

"Kid, you gotta sit down and start writing!" Cope came back in a bellow. Say that again in your best Myron Cope voice and I guarantee you'll get a chuckle.

"Nice meeting you, Kid," he continued and kept moving to get to some boxers for interviews. I'd catch up to Cope on many occasions as a young man for more advice. I always admired his writing and his work ethic and he was kind enough to suffer my constant inquiries through the years. He was a great role model.

His words to me that night at Fitzgerald Field House may be the best bit of advice I ever got in the writing game.

Every year, at some point in February or March, I remember what Cope said. I know that if I am going to get a book out in time for the holiday season I better get started, I better sit down and start writing. I think of Cope's advice, and I think of it coming in Cope's voice, and I smile and sit down at the computer.

My pal Pat Santelli sent me a card that I keep posted behind my computer. It reads: "The difference between a successful person and a non-successful person...A successful person continues to do things he doesn't want to do."

And there's another card next to it that reads: "Inspiration is the act of drawing up a chair to the writing desk."

* * *

I smile when I think of my two meetings with Alonzo Johnson. Those two meetings came ten years apart.

I met Alonzo Johnson the first time when I was 19 and a sophomore at the University of Pittsburgh. That was in 1961. I had just been named the sports editor of *The Pitt News*, the first non-senior ever to hold that position. I felt pretty good about myself. I was still writing a column for my hometown newspaper, and was about to give it up to concentrate on my college work.

Cy Obremski introduced me to Alonzo Johnson. He was a handsome fellow, full of himself. He had fought Cassius Clay before he changed his name to Muhammad Ali. They had gone ten rounds in Clay's hometown of Louisville with Clay getting a controversial decision.

You can call up images from that fight at Freedom Hall on the Internet these days, one of the miracles of the high tech age. I had never seen footage of that fight until 2010 and it turned out that it wasn't much of a fight. The two fighters mostly pawed at each other and held onto each other like they were trying to keep their footing on an ice rink. Clay was booed during the fight and after the decision was announced and that was in his hometown.

"Jim, I want you to meet Alonzo Johnson," began Obremski. "He is the fifth-ranked heavyweight fighter in the world. He fought Clay."

Johnson just smiled proudly at Obremski's proclamation and I was excited about meeting a boxer of such regard. He was probably the best boxer out of Pittsburgh, along with heavyweight Bob Baker, since the glory days of world champions Billy Conn and Fritzie Zivic.

"Alonzo, I want you to meet Jim O'Brien," said Obremski. "He's the sports editor of our local weekly, *The Hazelwood Envoy*."

Johnson just smirked. "Big fuckin' deal," he said. And he turned on his heels and strutted away.

I was crestfallen. I stood there stunned for a moment, as if Johnston had struck my chin with a left jab. He had me wondering what I had done to rate such a response from a world-ranked fighter. Obremski could see the disappointment in my eyes. "Why'd he say that?" I asked Obremski in a bit of a plea.

"Don't let it bother you, Kid," Obremski said. "He's just full of himself these days. Get over it."

(Johnson finished up as a fighter with a string of losses and his final record was an undistinguished 22-19 won-lost legacy. He's in his mid-80s if he's still around.)

Fast forward to 1971. I am working as a sports writer for *The New York Post*, then the largest circulation afternoon newspaper in the country. I got the boxing beat at the paper when Vic Ziegel gave it up to work as the night sports editor. He had succeeded the legendary Lester Bromberg on the boxing beat.

Bromberg and Milt Gross, the lead columnist at *The Post*, both used to whisper their questions when they were interviewing athletes so the sportswriters for the morning newspapers couldn't get the same information. Bromberg not only whispered, but there were times he whispered in Spanish.

I sat near Gross at ringside for the first Muhammad Ali-Joe Frazier fight at Madison Square Garden on March 8, 1971. It was billed as "The Fight of the Century" even then, and it's even bigger 45 years later. I had one of the four best seats in the house.

Ali had follow-up fights that same year, following his defeat by Frazier, with Jimmy Ellis and Buster Mathis at the Houston Astrodome. I covered both fights.

There was a lot of boxing activity in the lobby of the hotel in Houston that was headquarters for the first fight. It was done to boost interest in the fight and to help sell tickets. There were boxing rings set up here and there and there was boxing equipment everywhere one looked.

I was walking through the lobby one day when Ali's trainer and corner-man Angelo Dundee sidled up next to me. Dundee was a delight for writers. He loved to talk and he offered great stories and insights into his fighters. I had first met him in 1969 when I went to work at *The Miami News*. He and his brother Chris, who promoted the fights at the Miami Beach Convention Center, took a liking to me.

For one thing, I was a big boxing fan. For another, I was from Pittsburgh. The Dundees were originally from Philadelphia, and they knew Art Rooney and Barney McGinley, who had promoted fights in Pittsburgh while owning the Pittsburgh Steelers in the National Football League.

I had spent a lot of time at the Fifth Street Gym on Miami Beach that was overseen by the Dundees. Ali trained there in the early days of his boxing career. The joint was full of fight people, interesting characters, exiles from New York and Cuba. The Dundees had taken me into their arms and were of considerable help to me when I covered boxing matches on Miami Beach. They introduced me to everyone in the fight game. The times I spent with the Dundees and with Muhammad Ali and many other great boxers are some of the best times of my sporting life.

The Dundees remain two of my favorite people in sports, ranked close behind Art Rooney in my personal ratings. Chris and Angelo are gone now. I would call Angelo on occasion in recent years and reminisce about the old days. "You were the new guy in town and you liked boxing,"

Angelo would tell me. "So we liked you and took you under our wings. You were good for boxing."

So Angelo Dundee gets my attention in the hotel lobby in Houston. "How do you like this?" he asks, looking around the lobby at all the boxing-related activity.

"Come with me, I want you to meet someone," he says. So he's got me headed toward a corner of the lobby where there is a heavy boxing bag hanging from a steel apparatus. There is a boxer banging away at the heavy bag. His ebony body is glistening from the sweat his pounding at the heavy bag has produced.

I recognized him. It was Alonzo Johnson. Dundee got Alonzo's attention and he was positively beaming. He never looked better. Alonzo Johnson was as handsome as Muhammad Ali in their heyday. The introductions were reversed this time around.

"Alonzo, I want you to meet Jim O'Brien," declared Dundee, as if he were ring announcer Johnny Addie. "He covers Ali's fights and he's with *The New York Post*, the largest evening newspaper in the country."

Johnson just smiled. He seemed pleased to meet me.

"Jim, I want you to meet Alonzo Johnson," said Dundee. "He's Muhammad Ali's sparring partner."

I couldn't help myself. "Sparring partner?" I repeated. "Sparring partner?" I stretched two two-syllable words into two four syllable words for dramatic effect. Then I said "Big fuckin' deal." And I walked away.

Dundee came chasing after me. "What the hell was that all about?" he asked, almost incredulously, his dark eyes bulging as they often did.

"If you have time, I'll explain," I said. He nodded, and I told him my Alonzo Johnson story.

"For god sake, Jim, you don't hold a grudge for ten years," declared Dundee.

"You do," I came back, "when you're Irish and you're from Pittsburgh!" I could have added, "and you're from Hazelwood," but Dundee wouldn't have understood what that was all about. To me, that's one of the great comeback stories in boxing.

Muhammad Ali
Some personal memories of Ali
from a Pittsburgher's time with him

Muhammad Ali was the most fascinating figure I ever knew in the world of sports. Ali attracted attention—some good and some not so good—but you couldn't take your eyes off him.

He was handsome as all hell, had a great sense of humor and timing—in the ring and with a microphone at his mouth—and was different from most fighters, most athletes, most human beings.

Some still hold it against the man because he refused to report for military service when he was drafted. We were the same age and I wasn't thrilled about going into the U.S. Army when we were in a war in Vietnam. But I went and am grateful I was sent to Alaska and not Vietnam. I was one of the lucky ones.

I started my military duty at basic training in Louisville, Ali's hometown, in November of 1964.

Now, on a day such as Memorial Day, I am pleased and feel good that I can stand up and be counted when they ask who was in the military service. But I am not Muhammad Ali, or Cassius Marcellus Clay as he was called before he embraced the Muslim faith.

I never knew if he was honest about all that, or just an actor on a world stage. Whatever it was, it made him a compelling figure. For a writer, a man such as Muhammad Ali was a gift from the gods, whomever they might be.

It was easy to write stories about Muhammad Ali, and I was in Miami and New York at the right time, to meet Muhammad Ali, to be embraced by Chris and Angelo Dundee, who mentored Muhammad Ali and brought him along in the international boxing world. Those connections served me well.

At age 28, when I was a wunderkind at *The New York Post*, one of only two sportswriters on the staff who were not

Jewish, I was assigned to the boxing beat. My boss knew I had covered boxing in Miami in addition to the Dolphins, and he knew I had some knowledge of the fight game.

I had gone to a gym as a youth in Pittsburgh to learn how to box, not to box competitively, but to be able to take care of myself in a sometimes rough neighborhood in Glenwood and Hazelwood. The Glen Hazel Boys Club won 11 of 12 team championships in the Pittsburgh Golden Gloves back then in the '50s and '60s.

That was the best event I covered when I was the sports editor of *The Hazelwood Envoy* from age 14 to 19 when I became the sports editor of *The Pitt News*.

He was called Cassius Marcellus Clay when he came to Pittsburgh for the first time. He celebrated his 21st birthday a week before he knocked out Charlie Powell, a former pro football player, in the third round at the Civic Arena. That victory came on January 24, 1963.

Ali taunted Powell prior to the fight. He said, "You're old. You're an old man, Charlie Powell." So Charlie's brother, Art, a terrific wide receiver for the Oakland Raiders, got upset and he wanted to hit Ali.

Angelo Dundee interceded. "He's just kidding," he assured Art Powell. "We're trying to sell tickets."

Dundee, looking back on that night, recalled, "The place sold out. It was Pittsburgh in the middle of winter (late January) with ice on the streets, and it was sold out. Muhammad did that. Muhammad attracted people."

Before Ali fought Sonny Liston, he called him "a big ugly bear." Said Dundee: "there's never been a better salesman in the profession."

His birthday party when he was still Cassius Clay was held at the Sherwyn Hotel, which is now the building that serves as the main part of the Point Park University complex in downtown Pittsburgh. He recognized local sportswriter Myron Cope sitting in the first row. Cope had written a national magazine piece about Clay, a story that earned some journalism acclaim for Cope, like one he would do later on Howard Cosell, who teamed up with Ali on television like Abbott and Costello and Martin and

Lewis to lighten up things during a challenging period in our nation's history.

This was when blacks were protesting the way they were treated and demanding that their civil rights be respected. There was turmoil in the country, nasty confrontations and college kids trying to find their way in life.

When Cope, a diminutive journalist at 5-6, caught Clay's attention at the press conference on his 21st birthday, Clay called him "Mickey Rooney" and that broke up the house. Clay became Muhammad Ali and he dodged the draft and he was barred from boxing, and was in exile in that regard for three and a half years. He fought Jerry Quarry in his first fight upon return to action.

It was at that point that I replaced Vic Ziegel as the boxing writer at *The Post*. Ziegel had decided to take a fling as a night sports editor and I was fortunate to grab the assignment at the right time and the right place. Ziegel was a funny fellow, in person and in print—a rare parlay even for a bettor, and regarded Babe Ruth and then Muhammad Ali as the greatest sports figure ever.

Ali's next fight was with an Argentinian brute, Oscar Bonavena. I shared a room with Angelo Dundee one night a week before the fight. This was at the Loew's Midtown Motor Inn, a modest hotel in the heart of Manhattan. I was sitting on one of the two beds in the room when Dundee, sitting on the bed nearest to the door, took a call from Hank Stram, the head coach of the Kansas City Chiefs. You remember stuff like that.

I was in a privileged position. Dundee liked sports writers and he liked Pittsburgh and the Rooneys, the Steelers' owners who had been in boxing promotion. My time in Miami covering Chris Dundee's boxing shows on Miami Beach served me well.

Ali was to go for a run the next morning in Central Park. His entourage would accompany him. I remember his masseur, a black Puerto Rican named Luis Saria, knocked on Ali's door at the hotel early the next day.

Ali shouted, "I'm off today!" And we all dutifully, and gladly, retreated to our respective rooms.

"You don't tell Ali what to do," said Angelo Dundee. "He calls his own shots. He does what he wants to do."

That often leaves a trainer talking to himself and questioning his role and the responsibility of the boxer.

A week later, I came back to the hotel on the afternoon of the fight to see Dundee and Ali, and check out the scene. Ali and his corner-man and cheerleader Drew Bundini Brown got into a long black limousine outside the hotel on Eighth Avenue and drove off. Ali's younger brother, Rahman Ali, originally named Rudolph Valentino Clay, was with them. They could have walked to the old Madison Square Garden from there. I figured they were on their way to the still new Madison Square Garden at 33rd Street.

I walked up the street two blocks and went down a stairway to the Eight Avenue Subway. There was a commotion on the platform at the bottom of the stairs and I heard Bundini Brown shouting, "Muhammad Ali has arrived! He is a man of the people!"

There was Ali and Brown and his familiar entourage on the platform causing all kinds of commotion. What a sight!

Imagine what it must have been like to be a straphanger, standing in the midst of an already mobbed train just after five o'clock and seeing Muhammad Ali get on the train. Ali loved to do stuff like that, and his followers encouraged his showmanship. He liked showing up in Harlem unannounced at a playground, to get down with his people, as he often put it.

I got on the train with the Ali party. I was hoping it was the "A" train so I could use a headline like "Ali Takes the 'A' Train to Work." But it was not the "A" train. So much for that. I couldn't make a reference to the song made famous by Billy Strayhorn and Duke Ellington.

I took notes on the activity on the train. When we got to the Garden and were ready to enter the Media Entry at the backdoor of the sports arena, Ali extended his right arm toward the top of the door and held it open so his pals could get in without proper credentials and tickets of any kind. "I've got to look after the people!" Ali shouted to a gathering crowd, fending off security guards with his free hand.

The fight wouldn't start for a few hours, and I retreated to Penn Station under the Garden and took out my portable typewriter and sat down on a bench and began to write a story. I remember a bum coming over to see what I was doing. He would be called a homeless person today. He moved on, unexcited about what I was doing.

When I was covering a big sports event, I was always a bit nervous, hoping I could come up with something special, something different, something no one else had. And I had mine before the fight even started. I wrote what is called a "sidebar"—a sidelight to go with my main piece—about how Ali got to the Garden that evening. I was the only member of the media to witness Ali's excursion. This was on December 7—Pearl Harbor Remembrance Day, ironically enough. It was 1970.

I sat in my ringside seat like a cat that had just swallowed a canary. I couldn't wait to see the next day's *New York Post*.

It wasn't a great fight. Bonavena had a plodding style that frustrated Ali and Ali struggled at times. Ali didn't look like the Ali of old. Some boxing writers and pundits wrote him off after that weak showing. Ali won by a TKO at 2:03 of the 15th round.

This fight was a warm-up for Ali to fight Joe Frazier on March 8, 1971, again at the Garden. It was the first time two undefeated boxers would fight for the heavyweight title. It was billed as "The Fight of the Century," and it more than lived up to its billing. It wasn't the greatest fight of the century, but it was definitely the greatest fight scene of the century.

Frazier won the 15-round fight on a decision. It remains the most important sports event I ever covered. Being one of four writers from our paper who covered the New York Knicks when they won their first NBA championship in 1970 is second, followed by covering the Steelers when they won their fourth Super Bowl in 1980.

Boxing was my favorite sport to write about because there were so many colorful figures associated with the sport. They were always available for interviews. That was then; there's little to draw interest in boxing these days.

I had one of the best seats in the house. At 28, the same age as Ali, I was the youngest sportswriter at ringside. The seats directly behind me sold for $100, which might not get you in the building these days.

Joe Frazier, Muhammad Ali and Arthur Mercante, a great man who was the referee, are all dead now. All the people who were sitting near me are gone. Nat Fleischer, the editor of *Ring Magazine*, was on my left side, and Milton Gross, our main columnist at *The Post*, was a few seats away to my right. My bosses, unbelievably enough, executive editor Paul Sann and sports editor Ike Gellis, sat in the seats between Gross and me. Neither took a note; they were not writing about the fight. Larry Merchant, our columnist, was not seated at ringside. He had to be steaming. Nearby were Burt Lancaster, Frank Sinatra, Lorne Greene, Jack Kent Cooke, the owner of the Lakers and Kings who promoted the fight, and movie mogul Darryl F. Zanuck. They are all gone.

I still have my Muhammad Ali wristwatch, with a figure of him and his name spelled out instead of numbers 1 through 12 on its face. You can count the letters and space in his name and it comes out to 12. I once showed it to Buster Mathis before Ali fought Jimmy Ellis in Houston, and he got excited when I told him that there were 12 letters without a space in his name. I don't know if there has ever been a Buster Mathis watch.

I have souvenirs from that fight, programs, media handouts, a plate and plaque and tickets. I have a ticket for a closed-circuit showing of Ali's first fight with Sonny Liston from the screening at Syria Mosque on the Pitt campus. I paid $8 for it which was $3 more than it originally cost. Best of all, I have my memories of Muhammad Ali. He died at age 74—scary stuff if you are turning 74 in a few months—but his legend will live on forever. He was and is The Greatest.

Angelo Dundee
Boxing's best ambassador
who was in every sportswriter's corner

The 5th Street Gym was a school house for young boxers and young sports writers alike. You went there to learn about boxing from one of the best in the business, Angelo Dundee, kid brother of Miami Beach boxing promoter Chris Dundee.

Both had protuberant eyes and they could look into the heart and soul of boxers and sports writers alike. Their doors were open to anyone who could help them sell tickets to the next fight in town.

I was as fortunate as Cassius Clay to find that gym before he became Muhammad Ali. I had learned a lot about boxing at the Glen-Hazel Boys Club in my hometown in Pittsburgh, but I got my graduate degrees at the Dundees' 5th Street Gym and at Gil Clancy's Gym in Manhattan.

I would meet and get to know Jimmy Ellis, Luis Rodriguez and Al Jones in Miami and Emile Griffith and George Foreman in Manhattan, as well as many easily forgotten fighters.

The Dundees and Clancy could not do enough to make every sports writer who walked into their respective gyms feel welcome and a valued ally. The Steelers offices were like that when Art Rooney Sr. was alive. No more.

Art Rooney liked sports writers and would have liked to have been one, but the pay was better to own the team. Today, sports media at the Steelers' complex on the South Side are monitored by interns when they are talking to the players, and kept behind boundary lines whenever possible. There are even rules about what they are permitted to do.

Angelo Dundee was one of the most affable and cooperative people I ever dealt with in sports, right up there with Art Rooney Sr. and Art Rooney Jr. He could make your day and he often did. He introduced me to the boxing world, the champions and greats, and the supporting cast, the colorful underside of boxing.

Young kids from all over the country, dreaming of being boxers, dreaming of being champions like Clay or Ali, climbed those steep wooden stairs to the second-floor 5th Street Gym. It was above a pharmacy. The stairs creaked when you stepped on the dark boards.

"Most of them arrive broke," said Angelo Dundee on a Thursday, December 12, 1975, when I was working at *The New York Post*. I had first met the Dundees in the fall of 1969, when I came to Miami to work for *The Miami News*, covering the Dolphins, boxing and whatever else (even jai alai and alligator wrestling) sports editor John Crittenden suggested.

It was my first full-time job on a daily newspaper and I stayed one year before moving on to New York for the next nine years. I could have gone to Chicago, Dallas, Albany or Detroit, but I decided New York was best. There were two of every sports team in The Big Apple.

But I stayed in touch with Angelo Dundee and he appreciated that. His brother ran the business end and Angelo was the trainer for many of the boxers in the gym, champions and prospects alike. "We give them rent money for a week, some food money, and tell them they gotta get a job," said Angelo.

"They want to know where Ali dresses, where he works out, if he hits this bag or that bag. Some of them know his record by heart." Then, imitating fight guys as cast in Hollywood, Angelo looked toward the ring in the center of the room, blinked his eyes a few times and added with a shrug, "I tell 'em dis is da same ring and all!"

As long as Ali was alive, boxing would remain alive. "Every boxer ought to send a part of their purse to him," said Paddy Flood, a fight manager in Manhattan.

* * *

Madison Square Garden had a fight card the following night, a promising card topped by a 10-rounder matching unbeaten and untested Duane Bobick of Bowlus, Minnesota, against Randy Neumann of New York's Cliffside Park. Bobick was seeking his 33rd straight victory.

ANGELO DUNDEE

CHRIS DUNDEE

Cornerman Angelo asks
Jimmy Ellis to pace
himself.

Dundee was a pure delight in
boxing circles; seen here with
Sugar Ray Leonard.

Bobick's brother, Rodney, two years younger at 23, was in the ring during our visit to the 5th Street Gym. "He's cruder than his brother, but he's coming along," said Angelo.

Rodney was a beefy, slow-moving fellow, and he was sparring with another overstuffed plodder in a blue sweat suit. "They're both clowns," observed a veteran trainer. Rodney threw one right that took a lunch break on the way to the head of his opponent.

"One of the reasons he's down here," volunteered Angelo, "is because he's on a one-year suspension back home in Bowlus. He broke up a bar there."

Sitting nearby was Rodney's young wife, Mary, who appeared to be several months pregnant. "I wonder how they get by?" asked my wife Kathie, who was making the rounds with me.

Kathie was with me because we were on vacation. We had gone to the Bahamas, but got bored after two days of white sand beaches and ultra-blue ocean water. So we cut short our stay in the Bahamas, and went to Miami, where we had lived in 1969, and took up residence at a hotel on Miami Beach. The water tasted better, so did the salads.

Bobick's wife wanted Ali's autograph in the Wilfred Sheehy book on Ali, but Ali was not in Miami at the time.

Angelo obliged her. "Here," he said, scrawling some words on a blank page in the front of the book. "This is exactly how he'd sign it himself."

* * *

I knew I was back in my element when veteran trainer Lou Gross gave me the business as soon as I walked into the 5th St. Gym.

"You've gotta get off the basketball beat, and get back to boxing," growled Gross, the self-labeled "internationally known boxing trainer," when he saw me. "That basketball is a dying sport." That's an interesting twist on sports economics. That's what people had been saying about boxing since David & Goliath.

It was business as usual for the Dundees that day. Chris was constantly on the telephone. He had a wrestling show that evening, and something was going wrong with it, and he was upset with somebody because Jose Napoles' name was misspelled on the marquee out front.

Angelo was arranging pictures and paintings of the champions he'd produced on the wall behind his desk.

Chris' son, Mike, managed Elisha Obed, who a month earlier won the world junior middleweight title, and Mike was raving about Obed, the first boxing champion to come out of the Bahamas. So was Moe Fleischer, who trained Obed. Fleischer, 74 at the time, used to work at eight different fight clubs in the New York area back in the late '40s. He had gotten his second wind in Miami.

He used to book fights at St. Nicholas Arena, Eastern Parkway Arena and Ridgewood Grove, among others, and claimed to have put Rocky Graziano, Billy Graham, Sandy Saddler and Jose Torres in some of their early four-rounders.

Later at lunch at Puerto Sagua, a restaurant that featured Cuban cooking and was frequented by the fight gang, we were joined by Hank Kaplan, a retired marine biologist who was a highly-respected ring historian. He spent several hours every day working on his boxing records, and wrote an occasional piece on pugilists he'd seen and knew well. The conversation turned to the Ali-Frazier fight in Manila. "Over the last three rounds of that fight," said Kaplan, "Ali was the greatest heavyweight fighter who ever lived. No heavyweight fighter ever threw more punches per minute than he did that night. He was moving like a featherweight."

All heads nodded at the round table. Some bunch. But beautiful guys. Hopefully, they would always be in business.

Budd Schulberg in *Ringside*:

"Old fighters don't fade away, they just slowly die in front of our eyes."

Al Jones
Saved me from buying
a smoked ham in Homestead, Florida

The man wanted to sell me a smoked ham. I had no idea where he got the ham. He held it out for me to check out. It was about an eight to ten-pound ham, tightly wound with dark string. I didn't inspect it too closely. I was instantly sold on it. I didn't want to upset the seller.

This was in a bar/restaurant in Homestead, Florida, nearly 40 miles south of Miami, just before one travels into the Florida Keys.

It was in the winter of 1969, but it was hot in South Florida that day, with temperatures in the low 80s. Yet the man was wearing an olive green jacket, fitting him as tightly as the string on that ham. It was an Army field jacket with first sergeant's stripes on the sleeves. He wore one of those hats with cotton-lined ear flaps and another flap in the back of the head, the kind I had worn a year earlier during a 10-month stint in Alaska that completed my two-year tour of duty during the Vietnam War.

I had spent those last ten months at Fort Greely, the Army's Cold Weather Testing Center, so I recognized the green gear. I had to give up mine when I left the military. I always wondered how some soldiers came home with their garb.

I was scheduled to meet Al Jones, the house heavyweight boxer in the Fifth Street Gym stable back in Miami. He frequently fought on cards of Chris and Angelo Dundee on Miami Beach. I had told Al I'd like to see him in his old neighborhood. Get some local color.

I heard many of his boyhood friends, who flooded his dressing room after victorious fights on Miami Beach, picked avocados and strawberries for a living back in Goulds. Princeton, where Jones was born, was near Goulds, a community named for one of the town's early businessmen. A man named Lyman Gould cut down trees and turned them into ties for the railroad that ran through the town.

As the man was in my face, pressing me to buy the smoked ham, I questioned the wisdom of my decision to go to the region where Al Jones grew up like few others in the neighborhood. I was the only white man in the dimly-lit bar/restaurant. The man could have sold me anything, including his winter jacket. We were the same height, about 5-8, but he was barrel-chested and looked tough as nails, tougher than me, I figured.

He had my attention, for sure. His tattered fatigue jacket bore the bald eagle sleeve patch of the 101st Airborne—knowledge gained from my ten months at the U.S. Army Hometown News Center—and the name JOHNSON printed on a white strip across the left side of his chest.

Just then, thankfully, Al Jones, who was 28, came in the front door with an attractive woman at his side. Jones' 6-6, 200-some pound body was outlined by the afternoon sun that shone brightly through the open door, turning him into a silhouette. He was a magnificent specimen. He introduced the woman as his girlfriend. I forget her name. She was not my main concern at the time.

"Leave the man be, Sarge," barked Al Jones when he saw my predicament. "Don't go selling him something!" The man backed away as if Jones had jolted him with a right-handed jab.

I had my wallet in hand, and was relieved that I didn't have to cough up some more money on my visit to Homestead. That community was named for homesteaders who had settled there.

I was making $200 a week in 1969 as a sportswriter at *The Miami News,* the afternoon newspaper. I was the highest paid guy on the staff, next to sports editor John Crittenden. Art Grace, who covered the horse racing scene, was making $175 a week after 17 years on the staff. I never thought at the time that Kathie and I were getting by on $40 a day, supplemented by some steady free-lance writing. Crittenden had responded to a request for a photo of former University of Miami basketball star Rick Barry by offering me a job on his staff off my work as the editor of *Pittsburgh*

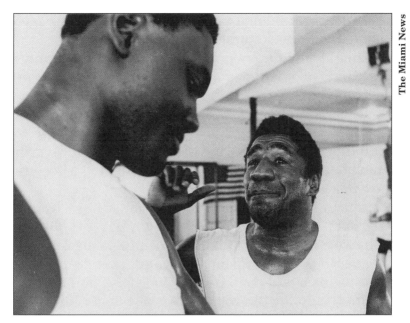

Al Jones, at left, gets an earful from Luis Rodriguez, one of the boxing champions at Fifth Street Gym.

Muhammad Ali, right, then called Cassius Clay, approaches street entrance to the 5th Street Gym on Miami Beach back in late '60s.

Weekly Sports, a tabloid that also helped launch the careers of Beano Cook, the co-publisher, and Bob Smizik.

I should have known I was in for a challenging day when I arrived in Homestead about 15 minutes earlier. I pulled into a parking slot in front of the restaurant/bar—I don't recall the name of the place—and saw about six or seven black men rolling dice against a wall near the front door. Judging by the hooting and hollering, I heard upon stepping out of my car, these guys were having a good time. Money was changing hands.

Then I did a real smart thing. I must have been nervous. I managed to lock my keys in my car. I've done that maybe twice in my entire life. Bad timing. One of the men recognized my predicament and came over to offer help. He told me he could open my car door for a dollar. I gladly gave him the dollar. He got a wire coat hanger and slid the hooked part down the side of the window on the driver's side and had the door open in an instant. A cop with an appropriate instrument for such problems couldn't have gotten into my car any faster.

I figured the guy had lots of practice. We had guys in my hometown of Hazelwood, back in inner-city Pittsburgh, who could do that just as skillfully and as fast.

Then I went inside, not aware that I would be accosted by a guy in winter military garb with a smoked ham in hand.

But that's the boxing world. You are bound to meet some interesting one-of-a-kind characters. I always prided myself in going to places others didn't dare to go. When I was 19, I once went to the Aurora Club, a late-night bar in the black community of Pittsburgh's Hill District in the company of the Steelers' Hall of Fame running back John Henry Johnson and got a good story out of it. Once again, I was the only white guy in the joint.

* * *

Al Jones was born in Princeton, Florida on July 20, 1940 and grew up in Goulds, about midway between Miami and Homestead. The Dundees labeled him "The Goulds Terror," but the nickname didn't gain popular use. Al Jones was anything but a Terror.

Goulds is a bad neighborhood, with lots of bums and pan-handlers. Someone reported to the police that some-body dug up a newly-planted plant in his front yard and tried to sell it for $5 around the neighborhood. Goulds has a high crime rate: on a scale of 1 to 100 (with 1 low crime rate) Goulds grades out at 91. The national average for similar communities is 41.

Al Jones was a good guy, a friendly fellow, and that was one of his problems in the fight game. He had sparred frequently with Cassius Clay at the Fifth Street Gym, as had Jimmy Ellis, a proud pugilist who would become, like Clay—to be known later as Muhammad Ali—heavyweight champion of the world. Jones also sparred there with Willie Pastrano, a light-heavyweight champion trained by Angelo Dundee and Lou Gross.

Boxers, with Ali the exception, usually had real jobs to support themselves. Joe Frazier worked in a Philadelphia slaughter house. Jimmy Ellis was a cement finisher. Al Jones had several jobs. He worked as a bouncer at a night club in Goulds, as a meat packer and, best of all, as a mor-tuary assistant. Boxers always had interesting stories to share.

Jones lost his debut outing and then won 33 bouts in a row and when he retired he had a pretty good record, 33-3-3, but he had had brittle hands, much like a Pittsburgh heavyweight named Bob Baker in the '50s. Jones was a lefty and he broke his left hand four times, as bad a fracture the fourth time as fight club physician and fan Dr. Ferdie Pacheco had ever seen. Jones couldn't continue against Tom Prater and thus a promising career came to an end.

He had come back after retiring a first time and was heading toward a title fight when he lost to Prater. There are many stories like the Al Jones story in the boxing world. He looked for a while like a solid contender. He had the body and ambitions, but he wasn't up to the challenge.

My boss at *The Miami News*, John Crittenden, liked Al Jones and he liked him enough to be critical of his lifestyle and training habits. "He had too many excuses," wrote Crittenden in his column. Jones was the kind of boxer that left Chris Dundee, the promoter, and Angelo Dundee, his manager and trainer, in tears too often. He blew big opportunities; he blew the big time.

Crittenden believed Jones needed motivation. Angelo Dundee talked about "finding the right button" to do that. Crittenden wrote of Jones: "He needs to learn to keep his composure after being hit, instead of backing off and looking for a way out. He needs to throw a series of punches, instead of trying to do all of his work with one-shot lefts. Just once, I'd like to see him step out of a clinch and sock somebody, instead of spending so much time pulling up his pants."

Dr. Pacheco, who enjoyed talking to sports writers, wrote a book called *Tales from the 5th Street Gym—Ali, the Dundees, and Miami's Golden Age of Boxing.* I bought it at a Barnes & Noble Book Store inside Madison Square Garden, when Kathie and I were killing time between sessions of The Big East Basketball Tournament in 2010. The names were all familiar to me from my days in Miami.

I had to smile when I saw the name of Eddie Talhami, a Miami-based boxer and regular at the Fifth Street Gym. Angelo Dundee liked to play tennis and he knew I liked to play tennis. He told me that Talhami had been a public parks champion in Miami and that I should play him. So we played. I was losing early points, I think, because Angelo had told me how good of a tennis player Talhami had been.

After a while, I realized I was better than Talhami. He wasn't that good at all. Angelo Dundee had put me on. He put it into my head that Talhami was a top-notch tennis player. If he had been, he would have killed me. I'm sure it was a tactic Dundee had employed in boxing. He had the last laugh.

* * *

My main beat at *The Miami News*, during my one-year stint there before moving to New York for nine more years, was covering the Miami Dolphins in the final year of the American Football League. And boxing was my beat on Miami Beach, mostly during the winter months when tourists were in town looking for sports, entertainment and gambling at the horse and greyhound tracks, or the jai alai frontons.

Miami was an action town.

The Dolphins went 3-10-1 in 1969 under head coach George Wilson. The Dolphins fired Wilson and hired Don Shula away from the Baltimore Colts just before I left town for New York. The Dolphins went 10-4 the next year and would go undefeated (17-0) in 1972 and win the Super Bowl. They are the only team in NFL history to go undefeated and untied in a season.

John Crittenden and Edwin Pope, the sports editor and featured columnist of *The Miami Herald*, were outstanding writers and mentors. There was a late-night spot called Julie's Pad near the Herald Building overlooking Biscayne Bay that housed both dailies.

I went to Julie's Pad a few nights to spend time and talk to Pope and Jack Mann. Sometimes we were there till 2 a.m. It was like night school. Mann had revolutionized the sports writing business in an earlier stint as sports editor of *Newsday*, a Long Island afternoon newspaper. Mann and Larry Merchant, the man most responsible for me getting hired by *The New York Post* a year later, had stressed good insightful writing at their respective newspapers. Merchant came to *The New York Post* after serving as the sports editor of *The Philadelphia Daily News*. Mann liked to talk and I liked to listen. Larry King, who hosted a local radio talk show, came by now and then. Yes, that Larry King.

Homestead is 40 miles from downtown Miami, about a 50-minute drive on US 1. I traveled that way a few times before with my wife Kathie, and once with my mother Mary O'Brien in the back seat, marveling at the magnificent scenery, especially when we soared across long bridges above the Atlantic Ocean. We traveled to Key West. I wanted to check out some of the favorite watering holes, such as Sloppy Joe's, where writers such as Ernest Hemingway and Tennessee Williams once held court.

Ernest Hemingway

Tennessee Williams

I have visited the homes or bars where other writers, such as Tom Wolfe in Asheville, North Carolina, or Pat Conroy of Beaufort, South Carolina. I have spent time in Chicago with Frank Deford and Buzz Bissinger, and Studs Terkel and Scott Turow when they appeared at book festivals on Printers Row in The Windy City. I like to walk where they have walked and talk where they have talked. I thought something good might rub off on me.

I read in his book "Chronicles" that Bob Dylan used to do that, visiting the homes of famous people he admired and those who influenced his song writing.

I covered about five fights featuring Al Jones during my year in Miami, starting with his victory over Cleveland Williams on May 20, 1969. I also saw him fight Charlie Polite, Giant Jack O'Halloran—he was a hulking 6-8—and Henry Clark, all pretty fair fighters.

In his book, Dr. Pacheco wrote that Al Jones was the kind of prospect that boxing managers dream about.

"Chris Dundee almost fainted when Al Jones walked into the 5th Street Gym," said Dr. Pacheco. "Alan Jones was six feet six inches tall and was muscular perfection on a huge scale. He had come of his own accord. He wanted to fight for the heavyweight championship of the world.

"There was one hitch. He was sweet natured. There was not one spark of aggression in his huge body. He was walking personification of Ferdinand the Bull. You can't teach a pacifist to be mean. No matter what you did, Al Jones smiled."

I had seen a similar personality in James T. Gilliam, who won the heavyweight title of Golden Gloves competition in Pittsburgh and New York while a member of the Glen-Hazel Boxing club in my hometown. He lacked the killer instinct. He left boxing to work as a front counter clerk in a post office in Mt. Lebanon and later became a minister with his own church in Bethel Park.

His son, Armon Gilliam, was just like his dad. He was 6-9, 235 pounds and managed to play 13 seasons (1987-2000) as a power forward in the NBA, and was the best paid pro athlete ever in Pittsburgh, if one of its best-kept secrets in the sports world. He didn't have a mean bone in his large body. I helped him with his writing efforts at local libraries. He died at age 47 after playing in a pick-up basketball game at LA Fitness in Collier Township. His viewing was the strangest I'd ever attended. We were ushered out of the church without an opportunity to offer our condolences to members of Armon's family. His father, I later learned, was suffering from Alzheimer's disease and didn't make sense in conversation.

Jim O'Brien

Armon Gilliam, who died at age 47 after playing in a pick-up basketball game, was survived by his parents, Alma and James T. Gilliam. An ordained minister, Rev. Gilliam was a Pittsburgh and Eastern Golden Gloves heavyweight champion in the '50s.

*   *   *

Chris Dundee got his brother Angelo to train Al Jones to be a fighter. He had Lou Gross, one of the trainers at the gym, to watch after Al Jones to see that he behaved properly, and didn't wear himself out with women who were drawn to him like moths to a bright light. Jones was a good-looking guy, darker than Ali, but with a sunny personality. Al Jones beamed like a light tower.

Dr. Pacheco said Al Jones had an "amicable face."

Jones was supposed to get a big money match with contender Jerry Quarry, and one in South Africa against Ali, but neither bout came to fruition, and Jones' chance to get into the big-time went up in smoke. He dropped out of a fight with Leotis Martin that might have led to a big bout, saying he had a bad cold. "If Al Jones gets a head cold," griped Angelo Dundee, "for him it's Hong Kong flu."

Chris Dundee estimated that Jones would have made a half-million for fighting Quarry and a million if he got a title fight. Neither happened. Boxing is full of stories of could have been and might have been. Remember Terry Malloy, as played by Marlon Brando in the movie "On the Waterfront," crying to his brother about his lost shot at the big-time. His brother Charlie was played by Rod Steiger.

"You don't understand, Charlie, I coulda had class. I coulda been a contender. I coulda been something, instead of a bum, which is what I am, let's face it."

That movie won the Academy Award as "best picture" in 1954.

*   *   *

I first became aware of Al Jones on Monday, May 6, 1969, after I had been in Miami just over two months. I had already covered spring baseball, some ABA activity with the Floridians, alligator wrestling, horse racing at Gulfstream and talked to Ted Williams, the new manager of the Washington Senators, and to Sid Solomon, the owner of the St. Louis Blues of the National Hockey League. There was much to like about writing sports in Miami.

Here's the story I wrote that day for *The Miami News*:

At noon yesterday Apollo 10 and Big Al Jones were both pronounced set to go. "He's in great, great shape," said trainer Lou Gross of Jones, who is scheduled to go against Cleveland (Big Cat) Williams in a 10-round heavyweight bout on the Beach tomorrow night. "He'll have no excuses if he blows this one."

The gym was jammed with bodies, but the biggest of them all was absent, namely Big Al Jones. It was the Sabbath, it seems, and Lou Gross declared it a day of rest. "I laid him off today," said Gross, a glint in his eyes. "He's just right already, and I don't want to mess with him."

So Jones is ready physically. How about mentally? People point to their heads all the time when they're discussing Al Jones.

"I think he's in the best frame of mind," answered Angelo Dundee, his manager, "and the best shape he's ever been in."

"He's got a clear mind," said Gross.

Okay, so the countdown began yesterday at Cape Kennedy and Chris Dundee's home on the Beach.

There's a chance the three astronauts' wives aren't the only ones not sleeping well these nights. Chris Dundee, the promoter, looks like a guy who always sleeps with his eyes open, one at least, like a cartoon alligator. When Chris is concerned, he gets no rest at all. "Sleeping pills do me no good," Chris complains.

The last time Chris carded Big Al Jones, the kid came down with a head cold. The Dundees diagnosed his head ailment otherwise. Chris was called on the phone that Sunday night in November and told by Big Al that he couldn't go through with his bout with highly-rated Leotis Martin—the biggest bout of the 25-year-old boxer's career.

The Dundees had a falling star on their hands. It killed Chris at the gate, and Angelo at the heart. ("It just took the wind out of my sails," he said. "I was all keyed up for it.")

Jones promises it won't happen again. "I'll be there," he says. Hopefully, he doesn't have a draft blowing through an open window in his bedroom.

The Apollo 10 mission is intended to clear the way for a future flight to land on the moon. There's not much difference between the flight and the fight tomorrow. If Jones gets by Williams, he can go all the way up, says Angelo Dundee. This was a moon shot for Al Jones, too.

"If he wins," said Angelo, "he's ready for faster company. Jones wants good company. He wants rated fighters. Cleve's been with tougher guys."

The way Angelo envisions the fight—or war, as he prefers to call it—Williams, who has 55 knockouts to his credit, will try to bomb Jones out right away.

"Jones will be doing the same thing," he says. "I believe in big guys trying to get lucky early."

He said Jones will have to keep Williams off balance, keep him moving, get him tired. "If he lets Williams get set," added Angelo, getting pop-eyed for emphasis, "and he unloads...Al Jones is outta there. Remember, though, Jones is a left-hander and he figures to give this guy ulcers coming at him that way."

Coming or going, southpaw Jones gives guys ulcers, especially guys like Angelo and Chris Dundee.

Al Jones needed a job
to stay out late

John Crittenden wrote a column in *The Miami News* in early 1970 about how boxers such as Al Jones had real jobs in their lives. "In December (1969) when Al Jones had his driver's license renewed, he finally had the occupation line on the license changed from 'driver's helper' to 'professional fighter.' Jones is 26 years old, ranks fourth among the world's heavyweights and has been fighting professional since 1964, but only recently, it seems, did he decide it was full-time work."

"When Al Jones first started," Angelo Dundee said, "I was always afraid he'd hurt himself lifting things. He was a helper on a furniture mover's truck." Then he got another job, but it was no safer. Jones became a bouncer in a bar in Goulds, the South Dade town where he lived.

"You got your clothes tore off you," Al said, "and you tore somebody else's clothes off. Sure, the place was rough. People got killed there—what else could be worse? But I loved it in those days—there was a time when I would jump up from the dinner table and go out and fight. Now a guy practically has to throw a punch at me to make me fight. I don't want a split lip anymore."

If the job was dangerous, Crittenden continued his inquisition, why didn't Jones quit?

"I told you that I was younger then," Al laughed. "It was the only way I could get to stay out at night. If I hadn't been working, my Mama would have made me come home at dark." Jimmy Ellis of the same 5th Street Gym on Miami Beach said he didn't remember his cement-finishing days as the worst of times. "You're out there in nice weather sometimes," he told Crittenden, "in a tee shirt and work pants, the wind blowing, seeing the people walking by. It's better than looking at a machine all day."

He was asked what he would do if he lost to Joe Frazier in an upcoming bout. "I won't jump out no windows," said Ellis. "I can always go back to the cement. It's a living."

Cleveland Williams
Gentle giant builds a boat in a bottle

Serenity is not something normally associated with the world of boxing. But it fit in the case of Cleveland "Big Cat" Williams, a world-ranked heavyweight fighter from Houston.

He was a big man in his hometown. He was 6-4, 220 pounds and packed quite a punch, but he was no match for a younger Muhammad Ali, who knocked out Williams in his fifth title defense of the year on November 14, 1966 at the Houston Astrodome.

I heard about Cleveland Williams and what I remembered the most was that he had taken a bullet in his abdomen from a policeman during a traffic stop on a highway near Houston, and that he had the wounds to prove it, like medals of courage that showed just above his black boxing trunks when I first met the man in the flesh.

I knew about his bullet wounds the way I knew that Bob St. Clair, a lineman for the San Francisco 49ers, ate raw meat. It said so in the bio sketch on the back of St. Clair's bubble gum card, the kind I collected and memorized as a boy back in Hazelwood. Stuff like that stays with you, especially if you were the sports editor of your hometown tabloid at the age of 14.

Now I was sitting on a metal chair, up close and personal with Williams in a dressing room at the Miami Beach Convention Hall on May 20, 1969. There were bright lights bordering the giant mirror in front of him. Showgirls put on their makeup and checked out their skimpy sequined costumes in front of those mirrors for the variety show hosted by Jackie Gleason for many years (1952-1970). The theater inside the hall is now named after Gleason, one of the greatest entertainers of our time as a comedian, actor, composer and music director.

This scene with Williams in the dressing room was what made reporting on boxing so different from covering other sports on a major league level. Chris Dundee, who promoted fights on Miami Beach, had brought me, then a rookie sports reporter for *The Miami News*, to the dressing room to meet and talk to Cleveland Williams.

Williams was less than an hour away from entering the ring, hearing a critical crowd rooting for a hometown favorite, and taking blows to that belly and his face, which was swollen in some places from old war wounds.

Williams was going to box Al Jones, a 6-6 left-handed heavyweight who was a popular pugilist for fight fans in South Florida. Jones built up quite a record (26-1-1 after losing his debut fight) boxing mostly in Miami Beach and was regarded as an up-and-coming contender. Williams was to be another notch in his belt. Williams was now mostly "an opponent" for such boxers.

"I knew he was slow, and I thought I could handle him," Jones told me over the telephone a few days before the fight.

Williams flashed a slight smile when he was introduced to me. He talked to me, and answered my questions, but his main concentration was on a boat he was building inside a bottle. His hands were taped tightly with white adhesive tape, and he was less than an hour away from ducking Jones' right-handed jabs, yet he was talking to a local writer. His thick fingers were free of the wrappings, and he maneuvered them to manipulate the materials inside the bottle. It looked like a discarded wine bottle and may have been just that.

That's what I loved best about the boxing beat. People in boxing wanted you to talk to their fighters. They wanted all the publicity they could get. Boxing was a tough profession. Promoting boxing and paying the bills was even tougher, according to Chris Dundee.

Just as I was about to sit down to write this story, I was unpacking some boxes in the basement of a new home I had moved into less than a month earlier, in June of 2016. I found a photo of my mother as a little girl that was somehow placed within a bottle she had given me.

I was always fascinated by how that was done, and here was Cleveland Williams working on such a ship. He told me he had been at it for about five months. He was building a schooner, and it was done with thin slats of wood, small sticks really, pulled upright with thread-like string. Williams worked on his ship and talked to me, always with a slight smile.

He also pointed to the hip where a bullet was still lodged from an altercation with a highway trooper back on November 29, 1966. According to a *New York Times* report, Williams was stopped in his car on a highway outside Houston because the policeman said Williams was speeding

Richard Goldstein's story said the police reported that Williams resisted arrest and in a scuffle that followed the policeman's .357 magnum went off. The bullet went into Williams' stomach, ripped across his intestines, and lodged in his right hip.

Williams underwent four operations to repair the damage to his colon and he lost his right kidney in the process. He also spent some time in jail. When he returned to fight in Houston less than two years after the incident, he was given a standing ovation "like no other athlete in Houston sports history," according to a *Houston Post* report.

He lost 60 pounds during his recovery. He built himself back up to his fighting weight by tossing 80-pound bales of hay on a farm in Yoakum, Texas that was owned by his manager, Hugh Benton.

Al Jones scored a TKO in the eighth round of a 10-round battle with Wiliams that night on Miami Beach.

Williams died at age 66, just a few days after he was struck by a car on a street in Houston. It took a speeding car to stop Cleveland Williams for good.

That fight against Ali was notable in many ways.

Williams had knocked out 51 of his previous opponents while building up a record of 65-5-1, yet he was a decided underdog to the champion Ali, who was nine years younger and at his prime. The crowd of 35,460 was the largest crowd for an indoor fight in the history of the sport.

"Big Cat," as he was called, had an interesting background. He was a native of Griffin, Georgia. He worked in a pulpwood mill at the age of 13 and began boxing a year later. He won his first four fights and when the local boxing officials found out how young he was they barred him from boxing until he turned 18.

One of his big wins was against Ernie Terrell, but he was knocked out twice by Sonny Liston.

In the fight at the Houston Astrodome with Williams, Ali introduced the Ali-shuffle for the first time, to the amusement of most fans and the scorn of old-line boxing officials.

Ali floored Williams four times before the fight was stopped at 1:08 of the third round. Williams was never a contender after that.

He tried a comeback when he was in his 40s, but it was short-lived. Richard Goldstein wrote that Williams was seen traveling with a cardboard suitcase that was held together by an electrical cord. It brought to mind the boxing line...the bigger they are the harder they fall.

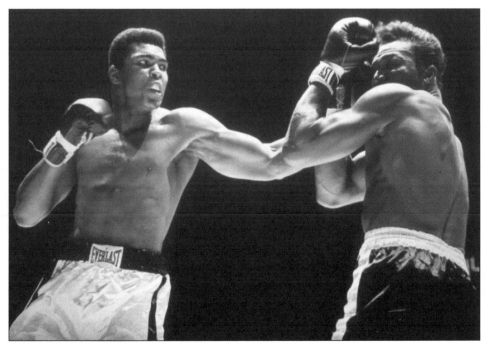

Cleveland Williams was overwhelmed by Muhammad Ali in 1966 title fight.

Lou Gross
One of the guys who made
the 5th Street Gym so fascinating

L ou Gross scanned the scene at the 5th Street Gym on
Miami Beach and blanched. What he saw made him
close his eyes.

Men in motion, in various phases of training, filled
the second-story loft. "Lookit those guys," snapped Gross,
nodding toward trainers in sweat-damp T-shirts who were
showing their fighters what to do next.

"They don't know what it's all about," said Gross. "They
think they're trainers. They're shoemakers!"

Fight manager and trainer Angelo Dundee, standing
nearby and taking it all in, shook with laughter. "That's
what he calls 'em," cried Angelo. "Shoemakers!"

"It's a phrase of our own," explained Gross, a phrase-
maker who's a syndicated boxing columnist and free-lance
boxing trainer, and one of those characters who exists to be
enjoyed, by other writers, if not other trainers.

As I took notes on what Gross was giving me, I knew he
was going to get himself into trouble with the other trainers. They'd be tossing the next day's *Miami News* to the
gym floor in disgust, and giving Gross the silent treatment
the rest of the day. Maybe the rest of the month.

"Ain't he beautiful?" Angelo Dundee declared. "He's a
Runyonesque character. There ain't many of them left."

A New York columnist named Damon Runyon
wrote about all these Broadway characters—that's what
Runyonesque comes from—and they were captured in a
still popular musical called "Guys and Dolls."

The 5th Street Gym was itself a variety show, just like
the Jackie Gleason Show that shared the Miami Auditorium
with boxing shows promoted by Angelo's older brother,
Chris Dundee. It was a setting full of colorful characters,
guys who were eager to talk to sportswriters. No one ran
and hid like they do in the locker rooms of pro basketball,
baseball, hockey and football teams.

*   *   *

Boxing does not have a built-in constituency, or season ticket holders. Every show has to be sold to the public. It has to be promoted. The Dundees got that; so did Lou Gross. Plus, Lou Gross wanted to get some ink for himself, to make him semi-famous.

Lou Gross was a guy with plenty of opinions, and he'd shake out his gym bag of words in haberdasher fashion, blending show biz and boxing notes in a column which appeared in several local weekly tabloids and also a sheet in his native Chicago, called *The Referee.*

"I'm not a great writer," said Gross, with a rare hint of modesty, "but I get the message across. I've got good information. I know who's who and what's happening. I write like a Walter Winchell." And maybe Damon Runyon, too.

He was also familiar with Grantland Rice and Ernest Hemingway. At 59, he was familiar with their works. Personally, he preferred Hurley to Hemingway.

Hurley? Yes, Jack Hurley, a tough boxing trainer who also wrote a fight column in Chicago many years earlier. "He was a boost and blast writer," said Gross. "I've been doing it for 38 years. But I try to help everyone out."

He would mention Eddie Talhami, a local light-heavyweight whom he trained. One of Gross' neat literary devices was to include his fighters in good company, e.g., from one of his columns: "...Jimmy Ellis can be seen boxing at Beach's 5th St. Gym with Eddie Talhami, a boy with a lot of class..."

He also dropped in lines about local restaurants he frequented and sometimes ate for free.

*   *   *

When word seeped down the long stairway from the 5th Street Gym to a shop below that Lou Gross was calling certain trainers "shoemakers," the man in the shop below was upset. After all, he was a shoemaker by trade.

"Don't call them shoemakers," the man scolded Gross one day. "They're not good enough to be called shoemakers."

One of the so-called shoemakers upstairs was equally indignant and disturbed by the damning phrase. That shoemaker made Gross out to be a heel.

"He's a publicity hound!" said the same trainer, talking about Gross, then pointing toward the writer's notepad, he advised, "You can put my name down on that. Gross is a good cut man, but he's nothing in the gym. He just wipes sweat off fighters, he never says nothing helpful to his man."

When these remarks were repeated to Lou Gross he got defensive. "I got a reputation," he said, "for making champions." When he said something with conviction like that, his eyebrows would come together expressively, then he'd blink a few times, punctuating his thoughts in the dot and dash manner of his boxing and entertainment column.

Gross was quick to tell you how he took over as trainer for Willie Pastrano when he was on the comeback trail and four or five fights later Willie was the light-heavyweight champ of the world.

Angelo Dundee was the man who put Pastrano under Gross' care. "I'm not thin-skinned," Dundee said, driving his Chrysler Newport along 5th Street one afternoon with a sportswriter riding shotgun. "Else I'd ask Lou what the hell's going on. He don't mean no harm when he says stuff like that.

"You have to understand," Angelo went on to say, "Lou Gross is a firm believer in himself. He believes he's the best damn trainer there ever was."

A few months earlier, Dundee asked Gross to take over the training of Big Al Jones. "Lou's been a good luck charm," Angelo would tell anyone who asked about the switch. "He was good for Pastrano, who knows?"

Outside the dressing room after the fight at Miami Beach Convention Center Hall the previous Tuesday night, the purple onion above Cleveland Williams' right eye hadn't stopped swelling yet, and already Lou Gross was polling people for their opinions on the Gross-trained Jones, who won by a TKO in the 8th round.

"Don't he look brand new?" asked Gross, sliding his eyes around. "Howdya like the new Al Jones?"

Better than the new Cleveland Williams, for sure, and, hopefully, he would last longer than the new *Saturday Evening Post.*

"He followed our plan," said Gross. "We wanted to chop him down...slowly...slowly."

* * *

Lou Gross not only learned how to write from Jack Hurley, but also how to train fighters. Gross got enraptured when he recalled his 11 years with Hurley.

"He was one of the toughest and roughest trainers ever," said Gross. "You got total respect in those days."

Dr. Ferdie Pacheco, who works corners as a cut man for the heck of it, said, "Gross goes back to the Neanderthal days of boxing. Less psychology, more brute strength. Maybe that's what Al Jones needs, a no-nonsense guy."

Gross gives you the inside story on Al Jones. "I was told Jones would be trouble," he said. "I treat him like a silk glove. If a fighter listens, you don't chew him out. But you must be firm."

Watching Gross at work with Jones was a lesson in headmastermanship. Sometimes Gross spoke softly, but then he would switch to his crackled demagogue-ese. "Sit down!" he'd snap. "Okay. Get a shower now."

Some insist that Lou Gross stood in front of a full-length mirror at his Miami Beach home, pulled in his ample paunch, and shadow-trained.

One of his fighters found him a comic sight, outlined against a snowy hill in the Catskill Mountains one time. Willie Pastrano was made to run in the rain, carrying an umbrella, in Manchester, England by Gross, and told to run 40 minutes without stopping two days before another fight, observed that, "not until I saw Lou Gross against the snow, did I realize how much he looked like a penguin."

That should have given the shoemakers something to snicker about.

Luis Rodriguez
One of the stars of
The 5th Street Gym

From *The New York Post*
December 4, 1971

L uis Rodriguez entered a ring for the 119th time in his professional boxing career the other night at Convention Hall on Miami Beach. There was a roar when his name was announced. He is much loved by his fellow Cubans and he, in turn, loved them.

Rodriguez remains one of Chris Dundee's best draws. Chris can count about 4000 or so for every show which has Rodriguez as the headliner. All that's required for Rodriguez is an opponent.

Chris doesn't look too hard to find a fighter who can lick Looie. He hasn't lost on the Beach in 25 fights. In all, he's lost only 11 times, with one draw, so he still has a winning smile.

Some shouted Looie's name aloud when he beamed in acknowledgment of those cries. *"The former middleweight champion of the world...,"* intoned the ring announcer, as announcers will. This is Looie's calling card; he's been trading on it for eight years now.

Rodriguez is ring-worn, to be sure. He weighed 168 pounds for this fight, when he should have weighed 155. Boxing is his whole bag, however, his life, and it always has been. "This is my job; this is my work shop," he once told me at the 5th Street Gym, where he trains. He enjoys the gym more than any fighter I have known.

"A challenger must always be ready," he said when I was working the boxing beat in Miami in 1969.

Angelo Dundee trains Rodriguez, one of his favorite fighters for many reasons. "He came to the United States for a fight (a 10-round decision over former welterweight champion Virgil Atkins at Miami Beach) and he never went back," said Angelo Dundee.

In 1963, Rodriguez won the world welterweight title on a unanimous decision over Emile Griffith in Los Angeles. Seventy-nine days later, Griffith regained the title on a split decision at Madison Square Garden in New York. Griffith took away his title, but not the memory.

"Luis beat him, but that's the way the world goes," said Dundee. "Luis understood that better than anybody."

The two met again in 1964, with Griffith winning on points at Las Vegas. "I got a lot of TV fights by always being ready, and always being available," said Rodriguez

That's where Davey Hilton, his opponent this night at Miami Beach, had first seen Rodriguez. "I seen him fight Griffith on TV," said the washed-up fighter. "Geez, that's pretty long ago, but he's still a tough old fighter."

* * *

Rodriguez remains a man of courage and pride, a man of honor.

Looie won't listen to those who suggest he should retire. He enjoys fighting; it's that simple. He loves the roar of the crowd.

They all do. That's what drives them back to the gyms and the grind of road work. Floyd Patterson is well-fixed, but he was lost outside the ring. Now Carlos Ortiz is on a comeback. He, too, has money. Joe Frazier is at the peak of his career, but he has been advised to quit because of the beatings he has suffered even while winning.

Frazier will have none of that talk. "I want to be alive and stay young," says Frazier, "as much as possible. I can't wait to get back and fight again."

Rodriguez was angered when asked by the local fight commission to submit to an extensive physical exam before his last fight. He bristled when sportswriters implored him to retire.

Looie says they are young, that they know nothing about boxing, and that they are trying to make a name for themselves. Someday, indeed, they may not attack an assignment with the same vigor as they do now, or write as well as they may now, yet they, too, will resist retirement, as we all will. Then maybe they will understand why Rodriguez resents their views. One difference, however, is that they can't get hurt.

"His pride is hurt," said Angelo Dundee, his trainer and the kid brother of promoter Chris Dundee. "He's a former champion of the world. He belongs with the great ones. He's a boxer's boxer. Everyone says, 'Stop, stop!' Everybody's being the judge and the jury."

When would Angelo tell one of his fighters that he's finished? "I never say," answered Angelo. "I learned early in my career not to do that. I like to keep my fighters as friends. I told one once to stop and he never talked to me again.

"You just can't tell a man to stop. You're better off with doing it gradually, with some grace. There's a proper way to let a guy go out—with some style."

Dundee wouldn't say how, but there are subtle ways. Davey Hilton, for instance, couldn't hurt your mother-in-law. He never hits back. He came from Canada and he absorbed 10 rounds of punches for a payday.

Hilton had a cauliflower ear to attest to his being a boxer, but that was about it. There have to be draft-dodgers across the border with more fight in them.

"Why didn't he fight back?" cried Chris Dundee, a promoter who wants his money's worth. "He could have taken him. I can't understand Hilton—but I'm glad for Looie's sake."

I'm sad for Looie's sake.

* * *

Luis Rodriguez died July 8, 1996 at the age of 59 at a hospital on Miami Beach. He had undergone kidney dialysis for the previous two years.

His career record was 107 wins and 13 losses with 49 knockouts. He twice beat champion Benny "Kid" Paret, who would later die of injuries suffered in a bout with Emile Griffith.

"He was the Marvin Hagler of his time," said boxing historian Rick Encinosa. "Luis fought and beat the top fighters he faced. He didn't shy away from any opponent."

FORMER CHAMPIONS—Heavyweight Jimmy Ellis tells welterweight Luis Rodriguez that a fighter must use his head. This is a scene from the 5th Street Gym in Miami Beach.

On why Floyd Patterson continued to fight Talking to writer Gay Talese:

"Well, first of all, I love boxing. Boxing has been good to me. And I might just as well ask you the question, 'Why do you write?' Or, 'Do you retire from writing every time you write a bad story?'"

When I was going through my scrapbook for 1971, I discovered a clipping from a story I wrote two days after I wrote the previous story on Luis Rodriguez. It reminded me of what a wonderful career I enjoyed as a sportswriter. I covered a press conference at Mama Leone's Restaurant in Manhattan where Jackie Robinson was hailed by *SPORT* magazine as the "Man of the 25 Years." He was accompanied by former Dodgers teammate Pee Wee Reese. This story appeared in *The New York Post* on Tuesday, December 7, the anniversary of Pearl Harbor.

Here's who were present to be honored in their own sports:

Jim Clark, auto racing; Kareem Abdul-Jabbar, college basketball; Rod Laver, tennis; Vince Lombardi, coach; Rocky Marciano, boxing; Bob Mathias (Kiski Prep grad), track & field; Gale Sayers, pro team rookie; Don Schollander, swimming and diving; John Unitas, pro football; Doak Walker, college football. That's quite a lineup. It would have been better if a few other honorees could have been there: golfer Arnold Palmer; jockey Willie Shoemaker and baseball's Willie Mays, hockey's Gordie Howe.

Courtesy of University of Louisville

Judge Dwayne Woodruff, a graduate of the University of Louisville and a generous donor to its athletic programs, had chance to meet Muhammad Ali at a campus event in Ali's hometown.

Larry Merchant
He hired sports writers
who could actually write well

L arry Merchant changed my life. You may know Merchant as the eloquent story-teller and tough-talking interviewer from the HBO boxing series. He retired from that post in 2013 after 35 years at ringside. At age 85 in 2016, he was living with his wife Patricia Stich, an actress with movie and TV credits, and doing some writing at his home in Southern California.

I know him better as the sports editor and columnist for the *Philadelphia Daily News* back in the early '60s, when I was a student sports editor of *The Pitt News*, and even better when he became a columnist for *The New York Post* in the late '60s.

Larry Merchant was responsible for me being hired by *The New York Post* in the winter of 1970. That was a major development in my career. I remain grateful.

I had just been hired by Conde Nast Publications on Madison Avenue to be the editor of *Street & Smith's Basketball Yearbook*. I held that post for 23 years and continued to contribute to the magazine as an emeritus editor for another eight years. I had also been hired in 1970, but had not yet reported to work, at *The Detroit Free Press*.

I was at a Knicks' basketball game at Madison Square Garden after coming to New York to meet with Conde Nast executives. Merchant spotted me at the press table at courtside. "I hear you're going to Detroit," he said. "Why are you going there? You'll get lost in the Midwest."

"No one has offered me a job here," I replied.

"Hold on a minute," said Merchant. "I'll be right back."

He went up into the stands at the Garden to see his boss, sports editor Ike Gellis, and touted my candidacy for a staff opening.

He came back and took me to meet Gellis who told me that he had offered the position to Sandy Padwe of *The Philadelphia Evening Bulletin,* and Padwe was going to let him know if he was accepting the position or not. "If he turns us down," said Gellis, "you get the job."

Just like that. I knew Sandy Padwe. He was a Penn State grad, just a few years ahead of me, and he had been writing for a wire service in Pittsburgh when we first met. He also was one of our original writers when Beano Cook, the Pitt sports publicist, and I started an irreverent tabloid called *Pittsburgh Weekly Sports* in the fall of 1963.

We kept that paper going for nearly five years and, thanks to Beano, we had approval to use stories by the best writers in the business. We simply subscribed to their newspapers and picked up whatever was appropriate for a Pittsburgh readership. Merchant was one of our contributing writers. All our writers got a free subscription to *Pittsburgh Weekly Sports,* often instead of the $2.50 stipend we had promised. That was good for three months' worth of papers. That's how Merchant was aware of my work.

The great Red Smith, then at *The New York Times,* asked Beano why we didn't use his stuff, and we were happy to oblige him, a Pulitzer-Prize winning sports columnist. Beano Cook introduced me to the best sports-writing in the country and the writers themselves.

Padwe went to Philadelphia before we had published many issues of the paper. Thankfully, he turned down the offer from Ike Gellis. I apologized to the folks at *The Detroit Free Press*—they had given me my choice of three different combinations of teams, pro and college, for me to cover—and instead accepted the job offer from Ike Gellis.

Not only was I going to the Big Apple—where there were at least two teams in every pro sport—but it made sense because it would make it much easier for me to serve on the side as the editor of *Street & Smith's Yearbook.* I also had other writing and editing opportunities in New York.

Two New York-based sports attorneys, Steve Arnold and Marty Blackman, had gotten me the post at *Street & Smith's* and also one to be the editor for *The Complete*

Handbook of Pro Basketball and a book called *ABA All-Stars*. I was a busy boy—at age 29—in New York. Arnold and Blackman represented some of the top sports stars in town and were among the early sports agents.

I had worked at *The Pittsburgh Press* on city-side as an intern, with a *Wall Street Journal* scholarship, during the summer of 1962, and as an intern at *The Philadelphia Evening Bulletin* during the summer of 1963. Beano Cook had a hand in getting me hired at both places. The summer at *The Press* was great. I got to write stories for every section of the paper, including a front page story on a prison riot at Western Penitentiary and on the op-ed page next to columns by Jim Bishop and Robert Ruark. During my junior and senior years at Allderdice High School, I worked as a copy-boy in the classified ad section of *The Press*. That's how I got my foot in the door in the first place and made sure I got to know all the writers.

I worked the over-night shift in Philadelphia and hardly ever got to do any writing. It didn't compare to my experience in Pittsburgh.

Even so, it was not a wasted summer. I went to Philadelphia in the first place because it had the best collection of sports writers this side of New York. Merchant was there, and he had hired Stan Hochman, Sandy Grady and Jack Kiser. George Kiseda, who came out of Monessen to write for the *Pittsburgh Sun-Telegraph*, was there at the *Bulletin*. Kiseda might have been the best basketball writer ever and he was even better covering City Hall. George Esper of Uniontown was writing in Philly for the Associated Press and would become its Vietnam correspondent. Hugh Brown covered the Eagles and Ray Kelly and Bill Conlin covered the Phillies and they were all kind and generous with encouragement, though Conlin did complain to me once about the fact that I was getting paid $95 a week as an intern, about enough to pay for my monthly apartment rental in Rittenhouse Square.

Hochman, who has died, wrote a column about Merchant when he retired from HBO about how Merchant had put together a great staff in Philadelphia. "He wanted us to inform them, entertain them and, once in a while, surprise them," wrote Hochman.

The Daily News had a columnist and boxing writer named Jack McKinney, who was one of the best in the country on the boxing beat, and also had a popular night-time sports talk show on the radio.

McKinney would do anything to get a story. He once went into a cage with lions, he jumped out of an airplane, he drove a racing car at a local track, and sparred with Sonny Liston. "I saw fear in Liston's eyes," wrote McKinney of the experience. "It was fear that he was going to kill me."

I went to boxing shows in Philadelphia, which was a good fight town in those days. I saw world champions such as Harold Johnson and Joey Giardello introduced in the ring before local fighters went at it. There was an amateur fighting in Philadelphia at the time who was the Golden Gloves heavyweight champion in 1962, 1963 and 1964 named Joe Frazier. That's right, "Smokin' Joe" Frazier.

Philadelphia was a great sports town. I went to Phillies' games at Connie Mack Stadium and recall going to Shibe Park, perhaps for a soccer game. This was all before we were introduced to Rocky Balboa from the "Rocky" movie series. Today, there are statues of both Balboa and Frazier in Philadelphia.

Merchant was just as fearless in his own way as any of those guys. He was from Brooklyn, which helps explain something about his swagger. He is 5-4½, about the same size as Myron Cope and Roy McHugh, but walks tall. Some boxers tried to intimidate him. Some threatened to choke him. Among those he clashed with were Mike Tyson, Oscar de la Hoya and, more recently, Floyd Mayweather Jr. He responded to Mayweather giving him a bad time—"you don't know shit about boxing"—by saying, "I wish I *were* 50 years younger and I'd kick your ass!" That was a big hit on YouTube. Merchant was often quoted as saying, "I wish I *was* 50 years younger and I'd kick your ass." I didn't think Merchant would resort to poor grammar, no matter how mad he might be, and viewing the incident on my computer proved me right.

Check this out on your computer. It's funny.

Merchant shared the mike at ring-side with Jim Lampley, who called the fight, and Max Kellerman, the boxing analyst. Merchant provided stories and memories and marvelous essays off the top of his head.

I learned so much from the likes of Larry Merchant. He and Vic Ziegel and Pete Hamill would often meet at the Lion's Head bar/restaurant on Christopher Street in Greenwich Village.

Larry Merchant

I lived on Long Island and was not part of their inner-sanctum. I was told Norman Mailer might stop by, as did Jimmy Breslin, Arthur Daley and Frank McCourt. It was an Irish pub, but Hamill, Breslin, Daley and McCourt were the only Irish guys in that group. I came to the conclusion while writing this book that I was never one of the boys. I was too competitive, even with guys on the same staff, and never teamed up on a story.

Breslin, a terrific writer, once told the owner of the Lion's Head, "There's nothing better than going to a bar and lying to your friends."

I have not seen Merchant in over 35 years but I swear he looks the same except for the all-white hair. Those luminous blue eyes still sparkle. He has a great smile. His real name was Larry Kaufman. Like Myron Cope, he was encouraged to change his name for his newspaper byline, so it didn't sound so Jewish. Kaufman, in German, means merchant. I never knew that until Roy McHugh, at age 101, told me so in the summer of 2016. I have always gotten smarter by keeping company with older sportswriters.

Joe Frazier vs. Muhammad Ali
Boxers for breakfast in New York

Don King, Muhammad Ali and Joe Frazier were among my favorite sports personalities. They always had something to say, and especially in the case of King and Ali. They provided provocative, lively, often amusing banter. They were good copy, as writers liked to put it. Frazier was merely genuine, sincere, honest, hard-working and more comfortable in the ring. He let his punches do the talking.

But King, Ali and Frazier were a little difficult to digest for breakfast. Lox omelets or mushroom omelets and a Bloody Mary go down fine at 9 a.m. and you couldn't ask for a better atmosphere than could be found in the Rainbow Room on the 65th floor of the NBC Building in Rockefeller Plaza. My Johnny Carson suit never seemed to fit better. But King, Ali and Frazier for breakfast...forget it. Too much Hollandaise sauce for one day.

The hard sell was already in gear for the third fight. Referring to fight fans, Ali said, "The fools still think that chump can beat me." So they would do it again, and the money numbers would be impressive as usual.

* * *

This time it would be on October 1, 1975 in Manila, or September 30, if you would be watching on a closed circuit telecast of the fight at your favorite movie theater. (Does that mean you can see it earlier if you stay at home?)

To induce some to travel to Manila for the fight, there were huge posters everywhere depicting the sights of Manila, and there were four young beautiful women from that country standing behind Ali and Frazier as the two exchanged meaningless, often childish barbs. That's show biz boxing style, folks.

One got the impression that even Frazier found Ali's antics amusing, and recognized that they would help

66

Photo courtesy of Chicago Bulls

Don King, Mike Tyson and Walter Payton cross their hearts upon hearing The Star Spangled Banner being played at Chicago Stadium.

International News

Sugar Ray Robinson improves his record to 26-0 with decision over Fritzie Zivic, the former welterweight king, in a 10-round non-title bout at Madison Square Garden on October 31, 1941.

promote the sale of tickets and make him more money. Then there were the times, too many, when Ali's banter slipped into bad taste, when he got too personal, and downright demeaning, and Frazier's eyes would narrow and he would bristle.

Frazier knew better than to get into a verbal exchange with Ali. No one could meet that challenge. "I'm not gonna get all worked up," said Frazier. "I'm not gonna make too much noise. I'm not going to be branded with that sort of image."

Yet Ali persisted in waving a toy gorilla in the face of Frazier, saying it was Joe's conscience, that it reminded him of Joe, and again that he was going to hold onto it until they fought again. "Hang on to it, right," responded Frazier. "Right on!"

Think about that scene. Do you think Jerry Quarry, the so-called "White Hope," would have gotten away with such bad behavior?

He would have been pilloried in newspapers and on TV and radio reflections about the fight for suggesting Frazier was a gorilla.

Ali would interrupt Frazier when he did attempt to speak, throw mock punches over Frazier's forehead, and go on and on, demonstrating unreal spark for any man at that hour of the morning. Frazier frowned and smiled, alternately, and kept his cool most of the time.

* * *

Portraying Frazier as the outsider, as usual, Ali suggested he would be fighting in his country, that he was the favorite son in the Far East. "Everywhere's your home country," said Frazier.

"That's right," countered Ali. "Just ask those pretty girls."

"They're not gonna be in the ring with you," shot back Frazier.

Ali assailed Frazier in many ways. Ali pointed out that he had fought 41 rounds in the previous year, compared to eight rounds for Frazier, and that he was in better shape as a result. Frazier said he had gotten all the proper work he needed at his gym in Philadelphia.

King, with his electrified silver and gray hair teased high over his head, sat between the two boxers and kept quiet, rather unusual behavior for him. He was wearing a black tuxedo, and playing the humble role, probably because an announcement was made at the affair that the New York State Athletic Commission had issued him a promoter's license in New York just the day before.

King did announce that he would promote a fight between the winner of this fight and George Foreman at Madison Square Garden, if he could get some sort of tax break.

"Foreman massacred Frazier," Ali reminded everyone, "and he could beat Frazier every day of the year. And I can beat Foreman every day of the year. Yet the people still want to see me fight Frazier. I don't understand."

Ali was at the 9 a.m. press conference on time, or at "9 a.m. sharp," as the invitations read. Frazier didn't show up until 9:45. His timing was perfect. Ali's voice started to fade around 9:43. "Was he getting nervous?" Frazier wanted to know.

"He doesn't have to worry about me showing up. I'll be in his face all the time when we get in that ring."

*　*　*

Ali won by a decision over Frazier in "The Thrilla in Manila," which was rated as one of the best fights in boxing history. It was the third and last of their fights. Ali took away $9 million and Frazier $5 million. It can still be seen on the Internet.

*　*　*

A week after the Ali-Frazier press conference, I received a call from Connie Hawkins. He had called me earlier, as promised, when he jumped from the ABA to the NBA and signed to play for the Phoenix Suns. I had an exclusive on that. Now, six years later, he was calling to tell me wanted to return to his hometown to play for the New York Knicks. Hawkins had come out of Bedford-Stuyvesant. He started his pro career playing for Archie Litman's Pittsburgh Rens of the American Basketball League, and then for Gabe Rubin and Jason Shapiro's Pittsburgh Pipers of the American Basketball Association.

Alas, the Hawk never got to fly for the Knicks. He liked to say, "I was Dr. J before Dr. J." When I was on the nominating committee for the Basketball Hall of Fame, I put together an endorsement package with comments from top NBA coaches and players to support his candidacy and Hawkins was elected to the Hall of Fame.

Former NBA Commissioner David Stern was the league's attorney when Hawkins and his attorneys, Roz and David Litman of Pittsburgh, sued the league in 1969 for keeping Hawkins from playing in the NBA. "I never saw attorneys argue for their client with the passion of the Litmans, and they won their case," said Stern.

George Von Benko

THE HAWK AND ME—Connie Hawkins of Brooklyn, called Pittsburgh his second home because of the way the Litman Family looked after him. Author Jim O'Brien got The Hawk into the Basketball Hall of Fame.

Pat Deasy
Died the week before Muhammad Ali celebrated his 70th birthday on January 17, 2012

They were reminders of how I got started writing about boxing and the heights to which it carried me. Deasy and Ali were both Golden Gloves champions in their early days, and Pat would be pleased to be mentioned in the same sentence as Ali.

Deasy was 72 when he lost his bout with cancer, that insidious disease that has stolen family and friends from many of us. He was from my hometown of Hazelwood. We both played for the Hazelwood Steelers, a sandlot football team, in our early teens, and we both learned to box at the Glen-Hazel Boys Club in the local housing project.

I had no designs on boxing competitively, but if you were a young man in Hazelwood in those days it was a good idea to know how to box. It was a matter of survival on the streets. I boxed at recreation centers around the city with a Glen-Hazel team. I made my debut at the Warrington Recreation Center, 329 E. Warrington Avenue in Beltzhoover.

Pat Deasy was a clean-cut good-looking young kid. His body was always sculpted to the bone. He looked hard and he played hard, and he knew how to box. He was generous with his grin.

Deasy first fought under the names of Johnny "Pat" Hopkins and Babe DiGiosio because he was too young to be fighting in the local amateur ranks, so he borrowed birth certificates from friends who were a bit older. Hopkins was a guy who played drums in a local band. I remember Renaldo "Babe" DiGiosio, a trainer for the Glen-Hazel Boys Club, who had the perfect mug for a boxing movie. DiGiosio put his right hand on my left shoulder a lot to get my full attention and told me about boxing and boxers. I didn't know that Deasy had borrowed Babe's name for some of his outings until I attended Pat's viewing at the

71

John D. O'Connor Funeral Home on Second Avenue in Hazelwood, directly across the main street from St. Stephen's Catholic Church where we were baptized, received first communion, were confirmed and, in time, married our girlfriends.

David O'Connor, who was the funeral director, following in his father's and grandfather's footsteps, had all my books on display in a glass case in his office. It is my Hazelwood Hall of Fame. David, who had been a good football player in his day, was battling a brittleness in his bones caused by cancer—multiple myeloma, but he had been fighting the good fight. He sent me encouraging notes.

I covered the Glen-Hazel Boys Club in the Pittsburgh Golden Gloves competition. The team, coached by a steelworker at J&L named Cy Obremski, won the team championship 11 out of 12 years in one glorious stretch during the '50s and '60s, and continued to win team titles after I was no longer covering them. I knew Cy's son, Jerry, a nice kid.

The Golden Gloves Boxing Tournament was my Super Bowl from the time I was 14 till I was 19 and served as the sports editor of *The Hazelwood Envoy.* There were fighters from The Hill District and Homestead who journeyed to the Glen-Hazel Boys Club to fight for Obremski. King Williams and Eugene Tippett of Homestead were both top-notch boxers. The team that represented Pittsburgh against the East at Madison Square Garden was made up mostly of fighters from the Glen-Hazel Boys Club.

"It's really the Glen-Hazel Boys Club versus The East," wrote Cope in one of his columns. The team traveled by train to New York's Penn Station.

Muhammad Ali, then known as Cassius Clay, celebrated his 21st birthday in Pittsburgh. I was there, as was Myron Cope and KDKA-TV's Bill Burns and WWSW's Joe Tucker, at his birthday party at the Sherwyn Hotel which is now David L. Lawrence Hall of Point Park University at the corner of Wood Street and the Boulevard of the Allies.

Clay was fighting Charlie Powell on January 24 at the Civic Arena and would kayo Powell in the third round. Powell played pro baseball and pro football, five seasons as a defensive lineman for the San Francisco 49ers and two seasons with the Oakland Raiders. His younger brother, Art Powell, was a great wide receiver for the Oakland Raiders.

Clay had met Myron Cope in his hometown of Louisville when Cope interviewed him for a story in a national magazine. It's a story that has appeared in several "Best Sports Stories" collections. Clay was then known as "The Louisville Lip" because he loved to make outrageous claims and spouted his own poetry to entertain the media.

That day at the Sherwyn Hotel, Clay kept referring to the diminutive Myron Cope as "Mickey Rooney" and that drew laughs from everyone. Especially Cope.

I wish I could have been in Louisville for Ali's 70th birthday. Famed basketball coaches Rick Pitino of Louisville and John Calipari of Kentucky were invited. I spent ten weeks at nearby Fort Knox, Kentucky when I was inducted into the military service in 1964, and later covered many ABA games and all-star events at Freedom Hall involving the Kentucky Colonels. Ali appeared at halftime at one of those games, as I recall. I have a card somewhere acknowledging that I am a member of the Kentucky Colonels, not the team but the honorary group.

When I appeared at PirateFest at the David L. Lawrence Convention Center in mid-January of 2012, I met a nephew of Pat Deasy, and he told me Pat was not doing well. So I was not surprised when I saw his obituary in the *Post-Gazette*. Another of Pat's nephews, Joe Deasy, resides in Munhall.

I went to Hazelwood for Deasy's viewing on a Sunday afternoon to pay my respects and to renew my acquaintance with boyhood schoolmates. The place was packed. Pat Deasy was a popular guy. I remember him as a tough kid, but well behaved and, according to observations by his family that afternoon, he never had a bad word for anyone.

He excelled as a boxer, winning the Golden Gloves lightweight title in 1959 and 1960, and being named the outstanding amateur boxer in Western Pennsylvania. He lived on Gloster Street and he graduated from St. James High School in the city's West End and boxed in the military service.

In his later years, he could be seen running the streets of Pittsburgh—I caught him in action a few times when I'd pass in my car—and he ran in 35 marathons, including the Boston Marathon.

He also survived a stabbing at a service station in his community. He was honored there as "a Hazelwood hometown hero."

I met Pat Deasy's family at the funeral home. There were shamrocks and Irish sayings on banners throughout the room. St. Patrick was pictured on the memorial cards that were at the sign-in station. Pat was proud to be Irish, and fought a few times billed as "Irish" Pat Deasy.

There was an album on display and I was pleased to see that it contained clippings of stories I'd written about Deasy and the Glen-Hazel Boys Club in *The Hazelwood Envoy* alongside of clippings of stories Myron Cope had written in the *Post-Gazette*. It's an honor to share space with Myron Cope in any album.

Better yet, there was a program from a fight show that was held on the grounds behind the nearby American Legion post on August 16, 1956.

That was four days before my 14th birthday. I became the sports editor of the local weekly when I was 14.

For me, perusing this program was like an archaeological find. My father wasn't much of a sports fan. He never took me to see the Steelers or the Pirates or the Hornets play, or any college sports events. In fact, the only sports event I remember attending with him was that fight show behind the Legion that summer night in August of 1956.

I studied the program. There was a slip of paper pasted into the fight lineup with Pat Deasy's name on it because, as the note explained, he was too young to fight under his own name.

Right below his name was a match-up featuring Augie Broudy of the Glen-Hazel Boys Club against Cephus Huff of the Kay Boys Club in The Hill. This was a light-heavyweight bout. I remember that bout so well, for the best and worst of reasons.

It brought back some special memories, some good, some not so good, but I had to smile just the same. Augie Broudy lived at the top of Sunnyside Street, just up the hill from my house. In fact, my father was born in a home on Sunnyside Street back in 1905.

Augie was a friend of my father, one of his drinking buddies. Augie was drunk most of the year, but sobered up to fight now and then. Cephus Huff was one of the meanest looking fighters I ever saw. He had a shaven head and his black head glistened under the overhead lights. Picture Rubin "Hurricane" Carter. He split Broudy's ear open early in the three-round fight, and Broudy was bleeding profusely. The referee halted the action briefly to check Broudy's bloody ear. That's when my father stood up from his seat, in the first row in the second section from the ring, and exhorted Broudy to continue to box. "C'mon, Augie, hang in there!" he hollered.

That's when Broudy's father stormed by and swore at my father, exhorting him to "sit the fuck down and shut the fuck up." I was startled by the exchange, I still recall. And that's my best memory of being at a sports event with my dad. Sorry, I don't have any of those warm- fuzzy being- with-dad-at-a-ballgame-peanuts-and-cracker- jack stories I loved when Phil Musick wrote them. One of his good friends and boyhood neighbors told me, however, that those stories were pure fiction.

I later learned that Augie Broudy was a homosexual. I always knew his brother was a homosexual. He used to stroll Sunnyside Street with a white poodle in his arms. I didn't know about Augie in this regard until one day when we were sitting next to each other on bar stools at the Munson Hotel, a flop house at the corner of Second Avenue and Glenwood Avenue, not far from the Glenwood Bridge. As I was talking to Augie, he put his right hand on my left thigh and began stroking it. I reprimanded him, and told him not to do that, and he stopped. And smiled. I left the bar soon after. The subject never came up again.

When I worked in New York, I remember that boxing champion Emile Griffith was thought to be gay. He worked as a milliner in a women's hat-making factory. Benny Paret made fun of Griffith in this regard, and called him a "homo" in several pre-fight interviews. Griffith was incensed by Paret's taunting. When they fought, Griffith went after Paret in a rage and never stopped punching him. Ruby Goldstein was criticized for not stopping the fight sooner. Paret died from injuries suffered in the onslaught.

I went to Miami in 1969 to cover the Miami Dolphins in their final season in the American Football League, and the sports editor was excited when I also expressed an interest in covering boxing. John Crittenden loved boxing, but none of the other guys on the staff shared his passion for the sport.

So I covered boxing matches that were held on a bi-weekly basis on Miami Beach during the winter when the town filled up with tourists from the North, especially the East, spending the winter in a warmer climate.

There was lots of action in Miami in those days, with football, spring training for baseball, jai alai, greyhound racing and thoroughbred racing. You could bet on anything and everything. You couldn't do that in most states back then.

Chris Dundee promoted the fights and his kid brother, Angelo Dundee, trained many of the fighters in the Fifth Street Gym. One of Dundee's prize young fighters was Cassius Clay. Jimmy Ellis, Willie Pastrano, Ralph Dupas and Luis Rodriguez were in his stable and they all won world titles as well.

I loved to go to the Fifth Street Gym. It was full of characters, trainers and fight people from New York and Philadelphia. They all had stories. Non-stop stories. The trainers who thought they were the real deal called the wannabes "plumbers" and "shoemakers." Local plumbers and shoemakers resented that. It was a great training ground for a young writer.

The Dundees took a liking to me. They knew Art Rooney and his partner Barney McGinley, who promoted fights in

Pittsburgh, and they figured if I knew those guys I had to be all right. The Dundees had spent some time in the fight game in Pittsburgh, which was once a big fight town.

"You were interested," Angelo Dundee told me in May 2010 when we spoke on the telephone, "so we took you under our wings and taught you something about boxing. We loved writers who loved boxing. Hey, we were in business to promote boxing at Miami Beach." I left Miami after a year and went to work at *The New York Post* for the next nine years. I covered all sports for the afternoon tabloid, and in my second year there, I was assigned to the boxing beat. Lester Bromberg, the long-time boxing scribe, had retired, and his replacement, a wonderfully gifted writer named Vic Ziegel, surrendered the beat soon after assuming it because he wanted to become the night sports editor.

I lucked into that assignment, along with the Monday Night Football beat I had come by the year before. That was in September of 1970 when I covered a game featuring Joe Namath and the New York Jets against the Browns in Cleveland and all the Monday Night games in that first season.

I'm more amazed by my good fortune now than I was then, not being able to comprehend how big a deal it would become. I got to know Howard Cosell because of both boxing and Monday Night Football.

On March 8, 1971 I had one of the four best seats in the house, sitting in the press row at ringside, for The Fight of the Century. Smokin' Joe Frazier defeated Ali in a 15-round bout that is still considered the greatest fight in boxing history.

It's the most significant sports event I ever covered, and I traveled with the Knicks and Nets when they won titles in the NBA and ABA, and with the Pittsburgh Steelers when they won their fourth Super Bowl in six years back in January of 1980.

This 2016 Super Bowl was the 50th and I covered eight of them, the first in 1970 when I was still with *The Miami*

Golden Gloves Open

| Ron Straight | Tony Guido | Gene Thomas | Regie Schultz | Jack Matesic | Rege Mc |
| Pastorius A C | Luvara's Gym | Luvara's Gym | Aliq. CIO | Willow Club | Willow (|

| Dick Blackson | Milo Trkulja | Don Smith | Hen. Layrusky | Al Gibson | Cleve F |
| Aliq. CIO | Aliq. CIO | Moore A C | Aliq. CIO | Turtle Creek | Moore |

| Len Obremski | Rich Baker | Carl Jordan | Geo. Coleman | R. Edmonds | Harry |
| Glen Hazel | Glen Hazel | Glen Hazel | Canonsburg | Aliq. CIO | Aliq. (|

These fighters are part of the huge cast slated for action this week in the

'onight on Southside

| ldy Moore | Roy Norris | John Taylor | Henry Culver | Tom Stoy | Ron Measel |
| oore A C | Pastorius A C | Pastorius A C | Luvara's Gym | Wash., Pa. | Aliq. CIO |

| Anastasiu | Mitch Robinson | Terry Irwin | R. Washensky | Geo. Pettiford | Babe Di Giosio |
| irtle Creek | Turtle Creek | Frankstown A C | Frankstown A C | Turtle Creek | Glen Hazel |

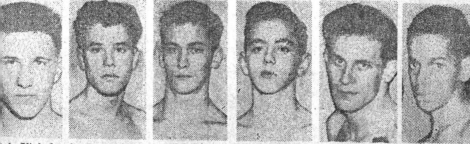

| ob Utchel | S. Ragghianti | Paul Francis | Ron Francis | Ossie More | Ed Thompson |
| nkstown A C | Willow Club | Willow Club | Willow Club | Steubenville | Steubenville |

Gloves tournament, which gets under way tonight at Southside Market House.

79

News. It's hard to believe that 46 years have passed since then. Joe Frazier died from cancer on November 7, 2015 at the age of 67. That, too, brought back the excitement of that special night in New York at Madison Square Garden. I was in the midst of some of the greatest sports writers of all time, including Pulitzer Prize winners Red Smith, Arthur Daley and Dave Anderson of *The New York Times,* great writers such as Norman Mailer, Budd Schulberg and William Saroyan, and the great sports artist Leroy Neiman. There were also the likes of boxing legends Joe Louis and Billy Conn, Gene Tunney and Jack Dempsey, celebrities such as Frank Sinatra, Burt Lancaster, Diana Ross, Lorne Green, Jack Kent Cooke and Darryl F. Zanuck.

I remember my stomach hurt after watching Ali and Frazier pummel each other from start to finish. Ali spent the night in a New York hospital and he was passing blood from the blows he'd taken in the kidneys.

That all began, of course, from covering fights involving the Glen-Hazel Boys Club. I checked out that program from that fight night in August of 1956 from cover to cover. I saw so many familiar names, people who had a positive influence on me as a kid, like the local pharmacists and an eye doctor. My eye doctor was cross-eyed which always fascinated me.

That program pointed up the dramatic difference between Hazelwood then and now, how it has gone from being a vibrant community to a ghost town. There were 14 physicians listed on one page in the program. Now there are none with a local address. UPMC has a small satellite medical unit there now. There were seven or eight social clubs and now there is one, the Hungarian Club was hanging on by the threads when I wrote this, and closed its doors for good in 2014, and moved to East Eighth Avenue in Munhall. There was a Chinese laundry man who belonged to the Hungarian Club in Hazelwood and now, I'm told, the majority of members are black.

There was an I LIKE IKE ad in the program. I counted 120 businesses that bought space in the program. The ones that read "Compliments of a Friend" were paid for by local bookies and numbers writers. Most of the buildings that housed those businesses have disappeared from the local landscape. There might be as many as ten or twelve businesses in the one-mile stretch these days.

Good people remain in Hazelwood and many of them turned out to pay tribute to Pat Deasy, still a hometown hero. It was good to see them. I'm glad I was there. I was blessed to grow up in that town.

PAT DEASY
A Hometown Hero

From Budd Schulberg in *Ringside*:

"We had a wave of great Irish fighters— from John L. Sullivan and Gentleman Jim Corbett to the 'Toy Bull Dog' Mickey Walker and the brash, nimble and brave Billy Conn. As the Irish moved up into the mainstream, there was less economic need to use the prize ring as their way out and up."

Carl Jordan
He was revered by young men in The Hill District

The things I remember most about my visit to see Carl Jordan at his relatively new home on Webster Avenue in the Crawford Square section of The Lower Hill was that his wife Gladyts was lying on the couch watching TV when I arrived and that she was still lying on the couch when I left four hours later. She never moved. She did wave to me when I took a chair. Great bladder.

And, yes, that's the way Gladyts spelled her name.

"That Gladyts, she likes her TV," said Jordan as I was preparing to depart. "She likes that couch, too."

Then, I also recall, there was a severe dent on the left side of his head, just above the ear, a scar parting what remained of his dark-brown hair. He told me some bad guys wanted to get his son, Carl Jordan Jr., over a matter of illegal drugs, and settled for beating up his dad instead.

There is a pedestrian tunnel that leads from the Oakland side of the Bloomfield Bridge to the sidewalk on the right side of the bridge. That's where the hoodlums trapped Carl Jordan and struck him on the side of his head with a blunt instrument. This was a man who once slipped punches with the best of them, but he was old now and had nowhere to escape harm.

Jordan was still a tough guy, however, and he survived this assault. I visited him on June 14, 2005, according to my handwritten notes on yellow legal pads. He died of natural causes two years later on June 4, 2007.

I was thinking about the Glen-Hazel Boys Club that ruled Pittsburgh amateur boxing in the late '50s and the '60s and I thought about some of the fighters I had known. Carl Jordan came to mind. I looked up the name in the phone book and found it and called him to see if I might be able to talk to him.

He was living in a nice neighborhood. This area was known as "Jews Hill" back in the 19th Century, when many Jews lived there. They're gone now, as are the Italians and Lebanese that lived in what is now a predominantly black community. Tony Bartirome and Bobby DelGreco grew up here to become players for the Pirates.

Goldstein's and Bubbles & Sherman were great delis on Forbes Avenue, closer to The Bluff and Duquesne University that I visited back in late '50s and early '60s. A sporting goods store was in the same strip.

The Aurora Club, a late-night club, was located between Forbes Avenue and Webster Avenue, and there were popular jazz clubs often frequented by both John Henry Johnson and Bobby Layne of the Steelers. Art Rooney Sr. used to go up there to see Gus Greenlea, a numbers kingpin. They both backed the Pittsburgh Crawfords of the Negro Baseball League. There is still a ballfield up there named for Gus Greenlea.

When I showed up at Jordan's door, in a section of the Lower Hill, just above Consol Energy Center, that was completely rebuilt a decade or so earlier, Carl Jordan recognized me from my days of covering the fight club. Of course, he was also expecting me.

"You still got that little boy's face," he said with a smile. "Thank you for thinking about me."

It reminded me of how one of his contemporaries, Roy Jefferson, the best player on Chuck Noll's first Steelers' team in 1969, had greeted me at a golf outing after we hadn't seen each other for nearly 40 years.

"You're old now," Jefferson said, "but I can still see your face in there, like it was when you were around the team."

I guess it's like when you go to your high school reunion and you find yourself talking to one of your former classmates. For a while, you are not sure who you are talking to, then the face from their student days emerges, like the images shift back and forth on the TV series about long unsolved cases called "Cold Case."

I also visited the son, Carl Jordan, Jr., a former Pittsburgh Golden Gloves champion like his father, who was cutting hair at his barber shop on Federal Street on Pittsburgh's North Side. It was called "EZ Cuts." It's still there, but Carl Jordan Jr. doesn't work there anymore. The younger Jordan has had his challenges in and out of the ring.

The barbers and patrons were cutting up and it looked like a scene from "Barber Shop" with Carl Jordan Jr. in the same role as Cedric the Entertainer.

When his dad died, Carl Jordan Jr., 46 at the time, talked about him with Colin Dunlap of *The Post-Gazette*:

"He'd give junkies money. He'd invite them into the house and feed them something. It would make me mad and, like, they were taking advantage of him. But, man, that's just the way my dad was. If he had one dollar to his name he'd give it to someone instead of spending it on himself." It doesn't seem right that it was some junkies who put that serious hurt on his head in that dark tunnel leading to the Bloomfield Bridge.

I saw Carl Jordan as a young boxing prospect work out at the Glen-Hazel Boys Club and box in the Golden Gloves at the South Side Market House and at the Pitt Field House. He showed me some scrapbooks. I recognized those end-to-end head shot photos of all the Golden Glove entries that appeared annually before the *Post-Gazette* sponsored Dapper Dan Golden Gloves Tournament.

He mentioned teammates such as Leroy Scales, James T. Gilliam, Jimmy Gilliam, Eugene Tippett and Augie Broudy, and other Pittsburgh area boxers such as Alonzo Johnson, Johnny Eubanks and Bob Baker.

"They said Bob Baker had bad hands," said Jordan, "but, to me, Bob didn't train properly. I saw him fighting on TV once. I forget who he fought, but he wasn't in shape and he was panting like mad. He quit punching."

When Billy Conn's name came up, Jordan said, "I always thought if he stayed a light heavyweight he'd have been better off." Conn abandoned his light-heavyweight title, and moved up to fight Joe Louis. He lost twice to Louis. But those were his best paydays. And he became most famous for those two fights.

"I remember when I was boxing that Billy Conn and Fritzie Zivic would be introduced before the bouts would begin, and the crowd would cheer them."

He mentioned that Tippett, who had been a promising young fighter, had to retire from the sport when he was diagnosed with an aneurism in the brain. "He could box good and he stayed in shape," Jordan said of Tippett. "He could have been a good one."

Jordan had praise for Carmie Price of Ambridge, Carl Daniels and Ronnie Weisen of Glen-Hazel Boys Club. He mentioned Bernie Stein and Ray Cercone.

He spoke expansively about Tommy Shaffer from Uniontown. "He beat me twice," said Jordan. "He'd be in your face; he'd be right there." Shaffer came back home after serving in the U.S. Army in Korea for several years. He had 256 fights as an amateur and 56 pro fights against some high-ranked competition. He went 38-0 and won the all-Army middleweight title and won the Pennsylvania amateur title six times. He took great pride in running his own boxing club and helped in the development of several "name" fighters. He was paid tribute by both Sugar Ray Leonard and Muhammad Ali for his contributions to the world of boxing. He died at age 81.

Carl Jordan mentioned Augie Broudy, who lived on the same street as I did in Glenwood, and Charles "King" Williams of Homestead. "They could fight big when they were in shape," he said. "Yes, they could fight."

Alonzo Johnson came up for discussion. "He was a tough guy, a slick fighter," said Jordan. "He should have stayed a middleweight. He was better looking than most boxers. He took care of himself; the girls liked him. He fought for the Lee Moore A.C. out of Braddock."

I mentioned Art Betts, who ran the Ammon Recreation Center for years. "He was a good man and helped a lot of people here," said Jordan. "He was one of the baddest asses on The Hill. Bettis was like a dad to all of us. He taught me how to high-jump."

Jordan was pretty good, too. He represented the 147-pound division when he went to New York as part of

Pittsburgh's Golden Gloves team in 1952. Myron Cope covered that action and accompanied the Pittsburgh team to New York. "Cope was my guy," said Jordan. "He gave me lots of good ink." Jordan fought as a pro from 1952 to 1958, and didn't fare that well. He got married in 1956.

Jordan said his own father used to box as "a masked marvel" at traveling carnival shows so Carl learned to box at an early age, around 7.

"My dad was one of the baddest guys," said Jordan. "He pulled that hot steel in the Pittsburgh mills. He died of lung cancer."

Jordan worked at several positions for the Pittsburgh Board of Education. He was a hallway monitor for a long time. "I was friendly with Willie Stargell," said Jordan. "He was upset about some things he found in Pittsburgh. He didn't like it for quite a while. He was ready to leave. Roberto Clemente talked him into staying here. And Willie became the first black to be captain of the Pirates. Everybody loved Pops. Me and Willie got to be good friends.

"Some of my heroes were Jesse Owens, Joe Louis and Jackie Robinson. I wanted to be a baseball player. I played all sports at Fifth Avenue High School. We were always doing something. I even took fencing lessons. When I was boxing, I tried to fight like Joe Louis."

Charley Burley was a great fighter from The Hill that Jordan looked up to. "He used to come around the gym when I was learning how to box," said Jordan. "When I was a kid I used to run into him on the street. He'd jab you lightly in the chest. He'd say, 'Hey, Kid, you want to go a few rounds?' Ol' Charley Burley. People would respond to what he'd say by saying, 'Yeah, Champ.' And Charley would come back, 'I'm gonna drop a bomb on you.'"

When I was doing research for this chapter, I came across an obituary for Carl Jordan on the Internet. It said he died at age 71 and that he had been married to Gladyts for 49 years. They had 11 children, 38 grandchildren, 28 great-grandchildren and lots of nieces and nephews.

I had to smile. At last, I understood why Gladyts was lying on the couch for so long when I visited the Jordans. She was happy just to be left alone.

It also reminded me that Carl Jordan had managed to give me the names of all his children. He and Gladyts had four boys, Carl Jr., Otis, Benjamin and Tony, and seven daughters, Sandra Lee, Lisa, Carletta, Duretha, Janey, Kimberly and Vicki or Victoria. His mind had to be working fine just to come up with that list. "I wasn't going to bring my kids up like my parents did," he said. "I wanted to have a strong family. I kept my nose clean and I didn't go to jail. There are a lot of great people up here helping other people."

He credits Cy Obremski, his boxing coach at the Glen-Hazel Boys Club, for keeping him on the right track. "People asked me what I thought of Mr. Cy," he said. "He came and got me. I was his baby. Before him, I'd ask my previous coach to wrap my hands, and he'd say, 'Don't bother me, kid.' It wasn't that way with Mr. Cy. I first boxed at the South Side Market House in 1949. I fought against the Glen-Hazel Boys Club. He said, 'Come and fight for me. He gave me shoes and he wrapped my hands. I felt like a professional fighter. I was voted the outstanding trophy. He kicked me out of workouts if I was acting up, or behaving like a clown. I had trouble in school early on, fighting in the hallways when I was in eighth grade, acting crazy. Mr. Cy calmed me down. I wanted to make my mother happy. When I finally became a fighter she became a Jehovah's Witness. I'm glad I played sports. Sports kept me out of trouble.

"When I went into the Pitt Field House to fight I felt like I was Joe Louis. I met Carmen Basilio, the great fighter. When they said, 'Carl, you're fighting in here,' I tried my best to be worthy of that. In 1956, when I was 22-years-old, I turned pro. I got to spar with Carlos Ortiz. Charlie Daniels helped me a lot. I had 50 pro fights and I won about half of them and lost about half of them. When you're making $40 for a four-rounder, it's a hard way to make a living. Mike Bazzone took me to New York and I made some decent money there, maybe $300 to $400 for a fight.

"The Hill is getting better. We need a supermarket up here. We chased away businesses and have only ourselves to blame. Kids were going into stores and stealing stuff. Now we've got some nice houses like this one and the neighborhood is looking better." It also says something about the man that he had managed to stay married and keep his family intact. He deserves a gold belt for that.

WTAE Radio

Myron Cope interviewed boxing champion Carmen Basilio of Oneida, New York on his WTAE Radio Sports Talk Show. Pittsburgh Golden Gloves amateur champion Carl Jordan enjoyed meeting both of them.

"Show me a hero
and I'll write you a tragedy."
—**F. Scott Fitzgerald**

Bill Hillgrove
He grew up in Garfield, the hometown of Harry Greb

Bill Hillgrove has one of the most familiar and respected voices in the Pittsburgh sports media. He has been the voice of Pitt basketball since 1969, the voice of Pitt football since 1970 and was hand-picked by owner Dan Rooney to be the voice of the Steelers in 1994.

His family was living in Lawrenceville when he was born in 1940, but he grew up in neighboring Garfield. His dad Bill was a big fan of Lawrenceville's own Fritzie Zivic and his brothers—four of the five were professional boxers— but was also familiar with the legend of Harry Greb, one of the all-time greatest boxers who called Garfield home.

"My dad said Harry Greb was one of the toughest fighters ever," said Hillgrove. "When I was six or seven years old, back around 1947 or 1948, my dad showed me the yellow-brick house where Greb grew up. It was on Millvale Street near Broad Street, just an average Pittsburgh home.

"They tore it down and built Tom's Market there. I was into sports at an early age and I remember reading that the great Gene Tunney, whose only loss was to Greb, said it was the toughest fight he had ever been in. They fought five times and Tunney won four of them. It was supposed to be a great series of fights.

"As Garfield goes," said Hillgrove, "Greb was the biggest celebrity ever to come from there. Frank Gorshin would be next. He lived on Kincaid Park extension, a short half-block in the exclusive section of Garfield. He moved to Stanton Heights and went to Peabody High School and then Carnegie Tech (now Carnegie Mellon University). The third guy, who isn't as well-known but should be, is Jim Sinegal. He's the co-founder and former CEO of Costco."

Sinegal, 80 years old in 2016, went to St. Lawrence O'Toole Elementary School and Central Catholic High School and Helix High School in LaMesa, California.

Gorshin was an actor, comedian and impressionist and best known for his role as "The Riddler" in the Batman TV series. He is buried in Calvary Cemetery in my hometown of Hazelwood, same as Greb and another Pittsburgh boxing champion Billy Conn.

Competing for fourth place on all-time Garfield Guys list would be Bill Hillgrove, the popular Pittsburgh sportscaster, or the late Phil Musick, a sports columnist with *USA Today* and the *Pittsburgh Post-Gazette* and *Press*.

"I don't know how I got talked into it, but I served as emcee once at a sports banquet at Western Penitentiary, and Billy Conn shared the dais with me," recalled Hillgrove when we spoke on July 20, 2016. "The prisoners were talking to each other and they weren't paying us a damn bit of attention. I gave Billy Conn a great buildup as an introduction. He stood up and said, 'Thank you,' and sat back down and didn't say another thing. He wasn't going to try and get their attention.

"There's another story I know about Billy Conn," Hillgrove continued. "He and his wife were shopping at a grocery store in Squirrel Hill when a young guy tried to rob the store. That guy, who was 21, picked the wrong place and the wrong time to do that. Conn tackled him and the guy squirmed out of his jacket and ran without it. The cops found his driver's license in the pocket of his jacket, and captured him later.

"I asked Billy once what kind of punch he delivered to the would-be crook. 'I gave him my old bread and butter punch,' Conn came back, 'an overhand right to the jaw.' That did it. Conn was 73 at the time.

"I know Conn was one of about five boxers from this area who were world champions from 1939 to 1941. I heard his father-in-law, "Greenfield Jimmy" Smith, was a pretty tough guy himself and fought with Bill at a baptism of Billy's son, Tim.

"I knew a boxer named Art Swiden, who was a bartender. He fought some contenders. He could make them look bad. Another boxer bartender was Pete Zivic, who tended bar at Fritzie Zivic's place at 39th and Butler Streets.

Bill Hillgrove is flanked by author Jim O'Brien, left, and Fran Fisher, Bill's broadcasting counterpart at Penn State for many years.

Dick Groat, left to right, Bill Hillgrove and Adam Walker were guests at the Good Guys Luncheon at Atria's Restaurant & Tavern in McMurray in the spring of 2016.

This guy came in the bar and said, 'Fritzie Zivic was a great fighter, but his brother Pete was a bum.'"

The bartender said he didn't think the visitor ever met Pete Zivic. He bet him $10 that he'd never met him. "I know," said the bartender, "because I'm Pete Zivic." The visitor pushed a $10 bill to the bartender.

"I remember Bob Baker was going to be our next champion, but he broke his hand several times and that shortened his career. I remember fighters from East Liberty named Johnny Eubanks and Johnny Morris," added Hillgrove.

Eubanks posted a 16-2 pro record, but retired after getting knocked out in 11 rounds by Wilf Greaves at the Enright Theater in East Liberty. There was another fighter named Reybon Stubbs at that time (mid-50s).

"We had a guy in Garfield who fought named Billy Neumont," said Hillgrove. "He was real character. Everybody knew him.

"One day, Billy comes out of Cavanaugh's with his buddy, this little guy they called 'Sweet Joe.' That's all I knew him by. Neumont asked 'Sweet Joe' if he wanted to go for a ride, and they jumped into a fire truck sitting there at the curb and took off. Billy tried to make a 90 degree turn from Penn Avenue onto Atlantic Avenue just past St. Lawrence O'Toole Parish Church and made about 45 degrees of it. They ran the firetruck straight into the church. He and 'Sweet' Joe jumped ship and ran away. These firemen, who were from Penn Hills, were really hot about the damage done to their pride and joy. The parish priests weren't too happy, either. Billy joined AA and helped reform a lot of drunks.

"My dad was a Lawrenceville kid and he told me that when Fritzie fought in New York, the guys in Lawrenceville would charter a train and it was one rolling party up and back."

Roy McHugh on Billy Neumont:

"His main job was gyping gypsies"

92

Harry Greb
The greatest fighter
to come out of Pittsburgh

Harry Greb was one of the greatest boxers in history. He grew up in Pittsburgh, and was before my time, but his name always comes up when old-time boxing fans reflect on the past.

Bert Randolph Sugar, a friend in my New York days and a legitimate boxing historian, rates Greb as the third best boxer in his book *"The 100 Greatest Boxers of All Time."*

Sugar Ray Robinson is No. 1, followed by Henry Armstrong. Fritzie Zivic of Lawrenceville tore up Armstrong in a bout in New York, but Zivic, who lost a rematch, didn't make the listing. Jack Dempsey is No. 4 and Benny Leonard is No. 5. Joe Louis is No. 6, Muhammad Ali No. 10. Billy Conn No. 41.

Greb was also regarded as one of the toughest and dirtiest fighters from his era, to be followed in that respect by Fritzie Zivic. Greb would bite ears—and you thought that started with Mike Tyson against Evander Hollyfield—thumb opponents in their eyes, and scrape the laces of his gloves across their eyes, and throw low blows. They were also two of the busiest boxers in history.

Greb, who was called "The Pittsburgh Windmill," "The Iron City Express" and "Wild Tiger" and some less flattering names in his day, fought more recorded fights than all but two boxers in ring history. Greb fought 299 times and won 264. He was knocked out twice, once in his first year as a pro and once when he broke his arm throwing a punch.

He reigned as middleweight champion from 1923 to 1926. He grew up in Garfield. His father, Pius Greb, was German and his mother, Dorothy, was Irish-German, the same as my mother. His real name was Edward Henry Greb. He changed his name to Harry when he began boxing. He was a right-handed puncher, 5-feet 8 inches tall, and he fought weighing anywhere from 142 to 170 pounds.

He lived the good life, was known to frequent night clubs and had an unusual training regimen. He was famous for visiting whore houses in red-light districts before his fights, often on the eve of his fights. Most boxers were advised to avoid sex the week of a fight because it was thought to weaken them. Greb believed it turned him into a tiger.

His black hair was always plastered down and he liked to dress like a champion. He looked terrific in a black tuxedo.

He enlisted in the Navy soon after the U.S. entered World War I in 1917.

His most famous fight was against Gene Tunney, who was called "The Fighting Marine." In 1922, Greb went up against the favored and undefeated Tunney in Madison Square Garden for the American light-heavyweight title. Greb swarmed all over Tunney at the opening bell and bloodied his nose 40 seconds into the first round. Greb won a 15-round decision. It was the only defeat in Tunney's 63 pro fights.

He fought Tunney four other times and lost twice with two no-decisions, and the series is considered one of the best in boxing history. Greb had a lot of fans behind him when they fought the third time in Cleveland.

Tunney described Greb in his autobiography called *Arms for Living:*

"Few human beings I have known have fought each other more savagely or more often than Harry Greb and I. The first of the five is for me an enduring memory, a memory still terrifying.

"In the first exchange of the fight, I sustained a double fracture of the nose which bled continually. Toward the end of the first round my left eyebrow was laid open four inches. In the third another cut over the right eye left me looking through a red film.

"All five of our fights were of that order of savagery. My showing became better from one to the another—and in the last bout I beat Harry as badly as he had beaten me in the first."

HARRY GREB
The Pittsburgh Windmill

Chester L. Smith, the sports editor of *The Pittsburgh Press* wrote:

"Greb was inclined to be moody, sometimes truculent and in the ring willing to use every weapon, fair or foul, that he owned. His penchant for rough tactics got him into many a jam, and once he summed up himself by saying, 'Prize fighting ain't the noblest of arts, and I ain't its noblest artist.'

"Some reporters found him unspeakably rude, others took time to understand the young man and soon began to think he was okay. A typical lead on the Greb fight would run this way:

"They tossed pop bottles, rocks and pigiron at Harry Greb as he left the ring last night. Maybe if Harry had kept his thumb out of his opponent's eyes long enough to let him get his bearings it would have been a different story."

Greb and Tunney were both inducted into the International Boxing Hall of Fame in 1990. That was the charter class and it was comprised of Henry Armstrong, Carmen Basilio, Ezzard Charles, Billy Conn, Bob Foster, Joe Frazier, Kid Gavilan, Emile Griffith, Jake LaMotta, Joe Louis, Rocky Marciano, Archie Moore, Carlos Monzon, Jose Napoles, Willie Pep, Sugar Ray Robinson, Sandy Saddler, Jersey Joe Walcott and Ike Williams,

I used to enjoy talking to the late Kelly Harrington, one of the city's biggest sports fans, and a former football player at North Catholic High and Villanova University, when he and his sister Ena ran Tessaro's Restaurant on Penn Avenue in Bloomfield. Harrington was a Harry Greb fan.

Harrington had a classic framed photo of Greb in one of his fights in the center of the backbar. Tessaro's is famous for offering one of the best burgers in town. It lost its host, however, when Harrington died in 2009, at age 57, of a stroke soon after he was diagnosed with non-Hodgkins lymphoma. Greb and Zivic and Conn are still in framed photographs in many watering holes and restaurants in the East End.

Greb went up against some of the best battlers of his era, including Tunney, Mike McTigue, Tommy Loughran, Mickey "The Toy Bulldog" Walker, Battling Levinsky, Mike Gibbons, Tiger Flowers, Johnny Wilson, Frank Klaus, Gunboat Smith, Al McCoy and every one of the near-champions in three weight classes up to the heavy-weight division, where he was considered a serious challenger for Jack Dempsey's crown. But those two never fought.

A boxing writer named James R. Fair once wrote of him, "He is as fast as sin and indestructible as rawhide, Greb was seldom knocked down, but when he was he bounced up off the canvas like a jealous stallion, charged with the ferocity of a rattlesnake and clubbed you silly with as hateful a pair of hands as the prize ring has ever seen."

That was a sample of sports-writing in those days.

Cuddy DeMarco, one of the finest fighters never to win a title, said of Greb: "He was the greatest fighter of his time—better than Dempsey, Tunney, Mickey Walker—all real champs."

Fritzie Zivic's brother Jack, summed up Greb this way: "Toughest, smartest and most durable fighter I ever saw." Zivic was talking about a man who participated in 299 fights and lost only 8. That's not counting the ones he had in the street, including one with Henry Armstrong one night after they'd fought in the ring and went out drinking together afterward and got in an argument.

Greb had a tragic ending. He died on October 22, 1926 at the age of 32 after an operation to repair his nose in the aftermath of an auto accident near Atlantic City. He went off the road in his car. I have read that the doctor had a surgical instrument pierce a blood valve in Greb's head. When he was operated on, it was discovered that he had sight in only one eye and had fought the last part of his career that way. He had suffered a detached retina in a fight in 1921 against Kid Norfolk and was back in the ring a month later. He fought for five years half-blind.

Only a few insiders knew he was blind in his right eye and had less than half sight in his left eye. He fought in

100 fights like that. He couldn't recognize people in the street if they were ten feet away.

Greb's real weakness, however, was women.

"Women mean more to me than anything on earth," he once said when he retired. "If I can't see them, I can't love them, so I'm hanging up my gloves."

Harry Greb of Garfield in formal attire.

Jack McGinley
The silent partner

"God be with you now."

His name was always listed second in the Steelers' administrative directory, right after Daniel M. Rooney, president. His name is John R. McGinley, vice president. His friends, and they are many and devoted, call him Jack, or Jack Sr. Most Steelers fans are unaware of him. He liked it that way. He was the ultimate silent partner.

The Steelers have never had photos of their officials in their annual media guide, so few people even know what Jack McGinley looked like. That was OK, too. This was a man comfortable in himself and with his coterie of family, friends and the good fathers from the clergy ranks.

"I'm not that interested in getting my picture in the newspapers," he said. "When I was involved with boxing, I got a lot of that because I was a matchmaker. But it never bothered me one way or another."

He and his sister, Rita McGinley, a former guidance counselor in Braddock and later the Woodland Hills School District, each owned ten percent of the Steelers. Their father, Barney McGinley, was a good friend and partner of Art Rooney in several sports ventures, including the Steelers. They shared a love for sports and, in tandem, promoted boxing shows in the Pittsburgh area.

They formed Rooney-McGinley Sports Enterprises, a boxing promotion operation, in 1938. Barney McGinley bought his share of the Steelers in 1946 when Bert Bell, who had been an equal partner with Art Rooney, left to become the commissioner of the NFL. Bell had to sell his interest in the Steelers to do that. Rooney bought some of his shares so he would have a majority interest in the club, and McGinley got the rest.

In 2001, the Rooneys owned 80 percent of the team, so each of the five Rooney brothers owned 16 percent of the team. "Originally, Art owned 58 percent of the club, and my dad owned 42 percent," said Jack. "When my brother Bill died, the Rooneys bought his share."

They divvied up the profits accordingly on an annual basis. A handsome check went out to each of the owners. In 2009, the NFL forced the Rooney sons to either abandon their gambling-related businesses or their ownership in the Steelers. The Steelers had been involved in the gambling business since the team originated in 1933. Dan and Art Jr. kept their interest and Tim, Pat and John opted out. The team took on new partners for the first time. The McGinleys remained in the ownership picture.

Jack was married to Art's kid sister, Marie Rooney, and they had a home on Beechwood Boulevard in Squirrel Hill. So Jack was the uncle of the five Rooney boys, and Marie was their aunt. Marie and her sister, Margaret Laughlin, who lived on Marshall Avenue on the North Side, were the only survivors of Art Rooney's eight siblings as my book on Art Rooney went to press in the summer of 2001. Margaret was married to the late Johnny Laughlin, who owned Johnny Laughlin's Shamrock Room, a landmark restaurant on the North Side, not far from the new football stadium. They are all gone now.

It is fascinating to trace some of the connections within the Rooney empire. Art Rooney had some other partners at various times in the early days of the franchise, like Milt Jaffe and then Bert Bell, but they were bought out at different junctures. Milt Jaffe was a professional gambler, so he would have been eventually forced out by the NFL. The McGinleys may have sold some of their shares to the Rooneys through the years, but no one wants to discuss that in any detail.

Jack joined the Steelers' operation in 1941, working in ticket sales and publicity after he graduated from the University of Pittsburgh. Then he did a three-and-a-half year stint as an officer in the U.S. Navy.

Jack McGinley always enjoyed talking to sports writers and broadcasters. The media, in turn, enjoyed Jack McGinley. You had to press Jack to tell stories whereas Art

Old friends gather in press box at Three Rivers Stadium, from left to right, Ed Kiely, Bernie Kabosky, Jack Butler and Jack McGinley Sr.

Jack McGinley, Jr., one of the Steelers' owners and a boxing fan like his father, is flanked by Father Francis Fagini, a good friend of his father, Jack Sr.

offered them up without prodding. There are subjects—such as early gambling room and horse room activity on the North Side involving the Rooneys and bootlegging during Prohibition—that Jack wouldn't touch with a 10-foot shillelagh. You knew not to go any further. The silence was deafening. "There are some topics he won't even talk about to his sons," said one of them, Pittsburgh attorney Jack McGinley Jr., a partner with Eckert Seamans in the U.S. Steel Building, and one of my favorite allies in the sports world. Jack Jr. said his father preferred to look at the world with a more positive outlook. "I've had many happy moments with the team and some great relationships over the years," said the father. "I enjoy being around the guys. I enjoy the business and I understand the business because I've been around it a long time. I'm very comfortable with the way things are."

He sent me a note after one of my interviews with him, and he told me he woke up every day not wanting to hurt anyone. "I am grateful just to wake up." He added that when we were talking about his service in the Navy that he forgot to tell me he had been awarded the purple heart. I still have that hand-written letter in my McGinley files.

"Jack swims every day, religiously."
—Jim Lally

Jack McGinley had a private box—No. 309—at Three Rivers Stadium, right next door to the Pirates box for Steelers games. The McGinley box was always filled to the brim with family and friends. Jack McGinley often stood in the aisleway, leaning against a wall, welcoming those who stopped in to say hello. The McGinleys weren't sure what their arrangement would be in the new football stadium, but they knew security would be tighter, and it wouldn't be as easy for friends to simply stop by for a beer or a glass of wine, or a bite to eat. They were always generously offered to visitors. The McGinleys would miss the casualness of that arrangement. The McGinleys have never stood on formality. Printed invitations were never required to join them.

McGinley usually wore a sport coat and tie, sometimes a button-down navy blue wool sweater. On this particular day he was wearing that sweater under a gray glen plaid sport coat, dark slacks, a white dress shirt with a blue and red tie. He favored a beige trenchcoat and hat, and always seemed dressed for bad weather. There's something very Irish about that. On the other hand, he might have taken his dress cue from Columbo, the TV sleuth.

Jack McGinley was a nice man. He was a pleasant, warm fellow. He always has a well-scrubbed look, with full rosy cheeks, and a welcoming grin or smile. Anyone who missed out on meeting or spending any time with Art Rooney, the late owner of the Pittsburgh Steelers, ought to have said hello to his old friend and partner, Jack McGinley. You'd get a good idea of what you missed, and maybe then some.

He wouldn't forget your name. He was more apt to address you by your baptismal or formal name. He often called me James or Shamus, as in, "James, be well." Or, "James, you take care now." Or, "Shamus, God be with you now."

He had pet phrases the way Art Rooney and his sons had pet phrases. "He has a soft way of saying hello and goodbye, and they have become part of the lexicon of his children as well," said Jack McGinley, Jr. At the end of our telephone conversation one day, sure enough, Jack Jr. said, "James, be well."

Jack Jr. offers the same sentiments to me that his father once expressed.

The McGinleys were ambassadors for Ireland before Dan Rooney received the official appointment from President Barack Obama.

I probably knew Mr. McGinley almost as long as I knew Mr. Rooney, but it wasn't until I interviewed him on several occasions for my book "The Chief" that I came to fully appreciate him. One day, as we were having lunch at his club, the Pittsburgh Athletic Association, or the P.A.A., it struck me like a bolt of lightning.

My God, Jack McGinley was just like Art Rooney. He was Art Rooney. They were so much alike; McGinley could be a ringer for Rooney. Their look, those too-snug button-down sweaters, their modest manner and attire, some of their favorite phrases, their concern, their genuine interest in everyone, their religious devotion, keeping company with priests, their feelings about family, their goodness, the list goes on, are so similar. Their style, or lack of it, was much the same. They were real Pittsburgh guys, to the core. They were proud Irish Catholics—they wore it on their sometimes-frayed sleeves—who walked the talk. McGinley had a soul of his own and attributes that might have been missing from the Rooney repertoire. He was his own man, mind you, and he was a good man.

Dan Rooney recognizes that more than most observers. He knows he had a great uncle in Jack McGinley. "Sure, we're family, but I still say it's an unusual situation," Rooney related several years ago. "There are a number of examples of people who have had problems in family ownership situations in our league. It's no secret that the Maras had problems in New York and the Bidwells had problems in Chicago and St. Louis and the Rams had a situation with Dan Reeves.

"Our relationship with the McGinleys has been super from the beginning. I'm not saying there's never been a difference of opinion, and I can't speak for the old days, but there aren't any problems."

McGinley called me one day in early March 2001 from his winter retreat in Florida because I had left word at his office that I needed to check out something with him. When I asked him when he expected to be back in Pittsburgh, he said, "Holy Week." It caught me off guard, and I had to think a few seconds to know what week he was talking about. Is that a venial sin?

How many people do you know who'd say that? Holy Week!

This is a man who went to Mass every morning and went to the P.A.A. each day, sometimes for lunch, but every day of the week to swim 40 laps in the club swimming pool. That's how he stayed in shape. That's why he always looked so darn clean-cut, so well scrubbed as I said earlier. Sometimes he swam at the same time as Fred Rogers—yes, TV's Mr. Rogers—another famous fellow who favored snug button-down sweaters. For years, McGinley did his swimming at the Downtown YMCA.

One of McGinley's dearest friends, Jim Lally, who looked after Three Rivers Stadium and the labor front for the previous 30 some years, often joined him at the P.A.A. "I can vouch for the fact that Jack swims every day, religiously," allowed Lally.

McGinley did so many things religiously. He was a man of routine. He kept to a schedule. Every Wednesday, for instance, he had lunch with Monsignor Owen Rice, a feisty old Irish-Catholic priest with a presence in Pittsburgh. Anytime you tried to book a date with McGinley, he began by saying, "Wednesday is not good for me." No one was going to bounce Monsignor Rice from McGinley's luncheon schedule.

Monsignor Rice was an outspoken critic and columnist for *The Pittsburgh Catholic* weekly newspaper for many years. Monsignor Rice got on the wrong side of a few bishops in his time. He was pro-labor to the nth degree. He fought ardently for the little people, sometimes annoyingly so. He could be a maverick, but he was never dull. Barry Fitzgerald would play him in a movie. "You got him right on that," said McGinley when I shared that observation.

I shared a glass of dark red wine with Monsignor Rice in the company of the McGinleys after a few Steelers' games at Three Rivers Stadium. The McGinleys, including children and grandchildren, always gathered there for a family dinner after the home games. I was often invited to join them for a glass of wine. I've never quite understood why the McGinleys and the Rooneys always seemed to be in the company of priests. Do they bless the food and wine? Are they good luck charms, like shamrocks? Or are they insurance policies?

I confess, I've always enjoyed talking to priests, ministers and rabbis, just to cover all bases, or in case I need references on Judgment Day. I've always found the clergy interesting and engaging company.

"We go to St. Joseph's in Bloomfield," said McGinley. "We used to go to St. Augustine's, just around the corner from here, but they changed their Mass schedule. We go to the 11:30 a.m. Mass and try to be a daily communicant."

When McGinley got back from his winter's stay in Florida, we made a date to get together again. We met this time, Tuesday, April 24, 2001, at Del's Restaurant in Bloomfield. We were joined by Jim Lally and Father Francis Fagini from St. Augustine's in nearby Lawrenceville. Now McGinley, Lally and Del's are all gone.

Lally told stories about his boyhood in Oakland, where he still lived on Bellefield Avenue, when he met and befriended Babe Ruth and Lou Gehrig and Dizzy Dean and the like while hanging around Forbes Field and the nearby Hotel Schenley, and how he and his friends found ways to get to New York for both of Billy Conn's fights with champion Joe Louis. Lally mentioned how Fritzie Zivic lent him $20 to carry him over during one of those New York stays. All those magic names...

"If you weren't living in that era," pointed out McGinley, "it's hard to envision how big a man Billy Conn was in this city. He was like Michael Jordan."

Lally and I had visited McGinley's office before going to lunch. We both found ourselves once again looking at all the wonderful framed photos he had on the walls there.

McGinley visited his office most days at Wilson-McGinley Beer Distributors on 36th Street in lower Lawrenceville. His original partner was Fritz Wilson, who previously had been in the clothing business. Fritz had gone to Notre Dame and been a classmate of Fred Miller. Fred was from the same Miller family that founded the Miller Brewing Company. That's how Wilson got the franchise for Miller Beer in Western Pennsylvania. Another case of having the right connections. Wilson brought McGinley into the business. Wilson's brother, Father Jerome Wilson, became a vice-president at Notre Dame. He served many years as an aide to Father Hesburgh at South Bend. There is a second generation and third generation of McGinleys and Wilsons working at the Lawrenceville warehouse.

Wilson-McGinley is one of the major beer distributors in western Pennsylvania. They're not on the same level as Frank Fuhrer Wholesale Distributing on the South Side, but it is a thriving business just the same. Wilson-McGinley has a warehouse on the other side of the railroad tracks in Lawrenceville where the row houses say hello to the warehouses, hard by the Allegheny River. It's about five miles upstream from the new stadium and new ballpark on the city's North Side. They were fierce rivals in the beer business, but they both had a passion for Notre Dame football and helped recruit football talent from the Pittsburgh area.

It's a familiar neighborhood for me. My mother, Mary O'Brien, herself a feisty Irish-Catholic, lived nearby on 36th Street, just up the hill at the St. Augustine Plaza, an apartment residence for senior citizens. She lived there for 21 years, from 1977 to 1998. She moved in the same week our younger daughter, Rebecca, was born, that's how I remember the date so well. Then she moved to Mt. Lebanon's Asbury Heights, an assisted-care residence four miles from my home. Jack McGinley often asked me how she was doing, the way Art Rooney always asked me how she was doing.

McGinley's office was a treat to visit, for much the same reason as Art Rooney's office was always so inviting and interesting. There were framed photographs from the past. Jack McGinley is a young man in many of them. He and Marie and the boys are in several. Art and Dan Rooney are in others. There were photos, for instance, showing McGinley presenting the Miller Lite Man of the Year awards to Rocky Bleier, Mel Blount, Lynn Swann, Mike Webster and Jack Lambert.

There were lots of fight photos. Jack's dad, Barney McGinley, co-promoted the famous Ezzard Charles vs. Joe Walcott heavyweight championship fight at Forbes Field in 1951. Buck McTiernan, a boxer from Swissvale in his day, was the referee for that fight, and is shown in several of the photos.

Ezzard Charles works out on speed bag before his fight at Forbes Field with Jersey Joe Walcott for heavyweight title.

In the old days, the big fights eclipsed the buildup. When you talk about "Opposites Attract"—the catchy title for Oscar De LaHoya's star return with Macho Camacho in a supporting role—you remember the real thing. In Louis-Conn I, opposites attacked. There was the ever-stalking Brown Bomber and the nimble-footed, nimble-fisted Pittsburgh Billy. I flew across the country for that one, and my reward was a thirteen-round classic, the cocky 169-pound challenger ahead after twelve. Moving in and out, side-to-side, attacking."

—Budd Schulberg, *Ringside*

WHERE'S ELMO?—It's easy to pick out Primo Carnera in the photo above when the giant of a boxer met members of the Pittsburgh Italian community prior to an exhibition fight to benefit St. Peter's Church on the North Side. See if you can spot Art Rooney in the first row of this 1933 shot. In photo below, Billy Conn is surrounded by family and friends at The Eagles Nest Boxing Club in Millvale in the late '30s.

The trunks that Ezzard Charles wore that night were draped over a chair in a corner of the office. Several hats worn by Billy Conn rested atop the chair. There's boxing memorabilia from Fritzie Zivic, one of the Zivic fighters who grew up in the same Lawrenceville locale. They were all champions.

"Billy and Fritzie were good friends of mine," said McGinley, and he was not boasting.

"There was nobody like Billy Conn. It's hard now to realize what it was like. He was terrific. After the first Louis fight, he didn't fight during the War, except exhibitions. They were charades. I thought Mike Jacobs, a famous promoter, didn't help the situation. He didn't want either of them to fight. So they didn't have any real fights in between their title fights. If Billy had two or three tune-ups before their second fight, I think he would have had a better showing. Who knows?"

During one of my visits, I brought along a buddy of mine, Jack Curley, a spirited Irishman who grew up on Mt. Washington, did a little amateur boxing in his youth and drove a truck all over the East until he retired at age 68. I knew that Curley, at age 71 and still playing competitive basketball with men half his age twice a week, would enjoy Jack McGinley and his gallery of boxing memorabilia. There were letters from Angelo Dundee, who trained Muhammad Ali among many other championship fighters, and was an old friend from my days of covering boxing in Miami and New York.

When I went to Miami in 1969 to be a sports writer with *The Miami News*, I was welcomed and accepted by Angelo and Chris Dundee, who promoted boxing shows on Miami Beach. The Dundees, originally from Philadelphia, had been involved in some boxing promotions in Pittsburgh back when the Rooneys and McGinleys were fixtures in the fight game. If I knew the Rooneys and McGinleys I was all right with the Dundees. It was a door-opener.

When McGinley was wintering in Palm Beach, in a condominium where Kathleen and Art Rooney Jr. also stay, he told me he had spoken to Angelo Dundee, who lived in

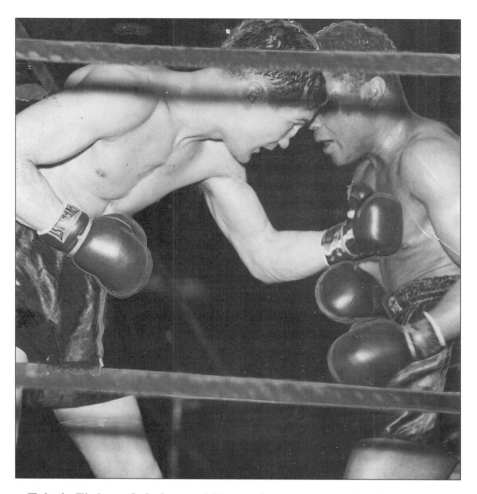

Fritzie Zivic, at left, kayoed Henry Armstrong in the 12th round of their return welterweight title fight on January 17, 1941, in New York. Fritzie had won the championship by decisioning Armstrong in a 15-round bout October 4, 1940,

"*Everything I have in the world, I owe to the sport of boxing and I won't ever forget that.*"
—Oscar De La Hoya

Weston, Florida, not far from the home of the late Dan Marino Sr. "Ange is doing fine," reported McGinley.

In his office that day, McGinley encouraged Jack Curley to pick up the black trunks with white trim once worn by Ezzard Charles and hold them against his own slacks. Curley was reluctant, at first, to touch these treasures, lest they come apart in his hands. He smiled like a lighthouse when he held the trunks to his midsection, and when he doffed one of Conn's ballcaps. Charles came from Cincinnati, but he was managed by Jake Mintz, a Pittsburgh boxing icon who resided in Squirrel Hill.

There were Irish blessings on the wall and in the wall cupboard and boxing items here, there and everywhere in Jack McGinley's office, dinner programs piled high, you name it, and Curley was in a sports fan's heaven. "Ah, this is great!" he said more than once. McGinley got a kick out of Curley and invited him to join us for lunch later at the P.A.A. "I want to do this while your friend can make it, too," said McGinley. That's the kind of guy he is.

I was checking out some of the memorabilia in the office closet and when I looked back, I caught Curley throwing some imaginary jabs at John McGinley to put some punch in one of his boxing stories. McGinley countered with a wide grin. I knew they were getting along well.

There was a team photo of one of Jock Sutherland's football teams at Pitt back in the late '20s, when Art Rooney's brother, Jim, was a running back on the squad. "They were on their way to play Stanford in the (1928) Rose Bowl," said McGinley.

There was a photo of Jack and Marie McGinley having dinner with Walt Kiesling and TV newsman Bill Burns and their wives.

"We used to see them a lot. Bill Burns was maybe my best friend. We loafed together. Our wives were good friends. We had dinner every week. Our families were real close. His wife was from Houtzdale, just six miles from my dad's hometown of Osceola Mills. I was friendly with Bob Prince, too. He was just starting at WJAS.

"We were promoting this one fight at Hickey Park. Bill Burns did the blow-by-blow description and Pie Traynor from the Pirates did the color. That was some combination."

"It's a heartache to go through there."

Jack McGinley grew up in Braddock, where his father owned a neighborhood bar right after World War II. "It was a terrific town," recalled McGinley. "There was really a lot of activity; it was one of the busiest main streets in the area. There was lots of action.

"All those mill towns—Braddock, McKeesport and Homestead—were so alive round the clock. The mills were going 24 hours a day, three eight-hour work shifts. Braddock is a shell of itself now. It's a heartache to go through there.

"I went to Braddock High School. Our church was St. Brendan's, an Irish-Catholic church. Sacred Heart was the Polish church in town. St. Joseph's was the German church for Catholics.

"There were two department stores, and you often had to walk in the streets because the sidewalks were so crowded. People would come from the surrounding towns to shop. I remember three movie theaters, the Times, the Capitol and Paramount. My dad's name was Barney McGinley, and he had a bar called Barney's Place right on Braddock Avenue. He managed the Moose Club before that. There must have been 50 bars on that avenue. Art Rooney's dad owned the General Braddock Brewing Co. right after prohibition ended, from maybe 1933 to 1939. Then he had Dan's Saloon on the North Side.

"My dad was originally from a small town in Clearfield County called Osceola Mills. Then he moved to South Fork, where he ran a hotel, before he came to Braddock. That was in 1920. You know Carl Hughes, the old sports writer who ran Kennywood Park for years? Well, his father was a banker in South Fork.

"Carl Hughes covered boxing and football for *The Pittsburgh Press*, and he took care of everybody. About three or four times a year, I get together for lunch and conversation with Carl and his good friend, Roy McHugh. Now there's a great boxing writer. We get together at Carl's house up on Mt. Washington. Sometimes Bill Henninger, the CEO from Kennywood, joins us.

"I think my father met Art Rooney at a restaurant in downtown Pittsburgh owned by Owney McManus. He was a little guy, about 5-2, but a tough little guy. He was a boxer in his day. He hung out with Patsy Scanlon, who was about 5-5, and had been a good fighter. He fought pro."

Pittsburgh sports writer Pat Livingston provided a story about Owney McManus. "He owned a very popular restaurant in downtown Pittsburgh," recalled Livingston. "He used to run train trips to Steelers' games on the road, and to big fights or other sports events. They were called ham & cabbage specials. He and his buddy were both little guys. They made nearly every road trip with the Steelers in those days. We were playing the Redskins at Washington, and I was talking to their team's owner, George Preston Marshall, before the game. Marshall said, 'Where's the Prez?' That's what he called Art Rooney. I told him that he'd be along soon, that he had probably stopped to speak to someone. Then Rooney shows up on the field with McManus and his buddy at his side. Marshall looked at them and said, 'Here comes Art and his Mick Midgets.' It was funny."

"We didn't know what hit us."

I saw some photos on the wall of McGinley's office from his days in the U.S. Navy and asked to talk about those days. "I was in the Navy for three and a half years, mostly over in North Africa," said McGinley. "I was aboard an LST (landing ship, tanks). We made the landing at Tunisia, Sicily and Salerno and then to England. We got sunk on June 6 when we were returning to England to get another load.

"We got hit around 4 o'clock in the morning. We got hit by Nazi torpedoes (referred to as "tin fish" in one newspaper report). We didn't know what hit us; we couldn't see anything. But it was an E-boat, we realized. We were about 20 miles off the coast of Cherbourg. Many of us were just floating around in the water, for about two and a half hours. We were wearing life-jackets and we had rafts. We got picked up at dawn by a British destroyer.

"We lost half our guys, about 60 guys, when we got hit. I was in getting a cup of coffee when we got hit. Yeah, we lost a lot of guys, James. I was an engineering officer. I had 24 men reporting to me. We lost 16 of them. The torpedoes hit in the back of the crew's quarters. Lots of them were sleeping...

"I was in the battle area for 15 months. I went in at age 19. I was there from May 1942 to November 1945. See these photos here on the wall...we lost these two doctors. We lost this boy. This fellow here was an old gunner's mate. I spoke to him the night before the invasion....

"I wound up a lieutenant. I got to come home for awhile in August, and I finally got a chance to see our son, Jack Jr., who was eight months old at the time. He was the first of our six children. We were living on Perrysville Avenue on the North Side at the time."

During his stay overseas, he ran into his wife's brother, Father Silas (Dan) Rooney, in England. He was serving as a chaplain with the American Forces. In Palermo, he ran into another brother-in-law, John Rooney, who was with the American Invasion Forces in Italy.

* * *

"My dad didn't get involved with the Steelers until 1943," said Jack McGinley Sr. "Art and Bert Bell had the team then. Art had sold his team to a New York guy named Alexis Thompson. Thompson wanted to run a team from New York, so Bell arranged for him to get the Eagles team. Bart brought the Eagles to Pittsburgh and sold them to Art. He and Art had been 50 percent partners before that with the Steelers. The Steelers have operated ever since with franchise papers that were originally awarded to the Eagles.

"My dad was like Art, an extremely bright guy. He worked in the mines as a kid. He led the donkeys out of the mine. When he became a businessman, though, an entrepreneur, he dressed like he was the president of Mellon Bank. He wore a sharp Stetson all the time.

"Art Rooney was a good man. He was a generous man. He was a very religious man. He just did his best and that was pretty good.

"I was doing publicity for the club in 1941 and Bell was the coach when we were in training camp at Hershey, Pennsylvania. Bert was a super guy. We lost the first four games and the team was turned over to Buff Donelli. He was the football coach at Duquesne University at the time. He was very successful at Duquesne. We trained at Moore Field in Brookline. Buff would coach us in the morning and coach Duquesne in the afternoon. It didn't work. He lost the next four games. Then Duquesne had a game with St. Mary's Gallopin' Gaels, and Duquesne was going out there by train. Donelli was expected to be with the Duquesne team. So Art turned the Steelers over to Walt Kiesling. We had three different head coaches that year, and we finished with a 1-9-1 record.

"I remember how we found out Donelli was missing. One of the trainers called and said Buff Donelli hadn't shown up for practice. I called Doc Skender, who was the athletic director at Duquesne. I said, 'Hey, Doc, Buff didn't show up this morning.' He said, 'Jack, he's on the train with our team and they're heading for San Francisco.' So Kiesling finished out the season as coach. We went to Philadelphia and tied the Eagles, 7-7. We won the next game at home against Brooklyn for our only victory of the year.

"We went through several coaches the next four seasons, Kiesling, Greasy Neale, Phil Handler and Jim Leonard, and then Sutherland stepped in.

"We had two rooms at the Fort Pitt Hotel, rooms 241 and 243. That was it. We expanded our offices in 1946 when Sutherland became the coach. There was only Joe Carr, the ticket manager, and me in the office. I'm a young guy, 32, and I have a lot of responsibility. We didn't have any secretaries. All of Sutherland's assistants were part-time coaches. Jock was getting paid $27,500 as the head man. I'd been in the Navy and Jock had been in the Navy. He called me Jock.

"I never knew how much difference a coach could make. Jock Sutherland...what a coach he was. He was a strong disciplinarian. He was extremely bright. He was terrific. He'd have been great for the Steelers if he hadn't gotten sick and died. You know, he lived here at the P.A.A. and he walked to the office downtown each day from here.

"His contract called for him to get 25 percent of the profits in addition to his salary. Fran Fogarty, the business manager, went over the books at the end of the year and figured out what we owed Sutherland. Frank and I were sitting in the office when Sutherland showed up to get his final check for the season. Frank had all the books out for Sutherland to see. Sutherland never took his hat off. He said, 'Did you and Art go over the books? Well, whatever you came up with is fine with me. I don't need to go over the books.' He never questioned anything. 'Just send me the check,' he said. That story goes against his reputation for being a parsimonious guy.

"I was in the office one day, on a Saturday, when we got a telephone call. Art answered the phone. A doctor was calling from Kentucky to tell him that Sutherland had been found in a farm field down there. He said, 'We have a fellow here who works for you people. We found his car along the side of a road. He's not well. His name is Sutherland. We don't have the hospital facilities here to help him.'

"So Art called John Michelosen and he got hold of a fellow named Dave Thompson, who lived in Mt. Lebanon and owned an airplane. Michelosen and Thompson went down and brought Sutherland back here. They took him to the hospital here in Oakland. He had a brain tumor. He died at age 58."

I asked McGinley about his own personal philosophy. "That's petty hard, Jimmy," he said. "My grammar is rather limited. You're pretty limited in what you can do. You do the best you can each day, and you try not to hurt anybody."

Two of the finest fighters ever...

CHARLEY BURLEY

and

SUGAR RAY ROBINSON

Roy McHugh
An overview of boxing history in Pittsburgh

Roy McHugh is the oldest Pittsburgh boxing historian I know of, so I thought it would be a good idea to sit down and talk to him and get his reflections on the fight game. He seemed a bit surprised that I invited him out to lunch, but I'd done that before. This was the first time I'd done it since he went over the century mark.

He was 101 years old. "What's the purpose of this?" he asked. He didn't want to do an interview so we just talked.

"I figured I wouldn't get an opportunity to ask you out for lunch in about ten more years," I said. "I've never had lunch before with a 101-year-old sports writer and newspaper columnist."

I had been invited to his 90th birthday party, and that seemed like only yesterday. Among those in attendance for that event were Ed Kiely, the former Steelers' p.r. man; and Tom "Maniac" McDonough, a Pittsburgh insurance man; and Carl Hughes, a former sportswriter who ran Kennywood Park for many years. Carl and his wife Ann were close friends of McHugh and lived in the same building for many years. Jack McGinley, owner of a major beer distributor in Pittsburgh as well as a minority owner of the Steelers, was with us. They had all passed in the interim. Bob Smizik, the sportswriter, and Doc Giffin, the former *Press* sportswriter who has been Arnold Palmer's right-hand man for many years, and Joe Gordon, who succeeded Kiely as the Steelers' publicist, were there that day. Ann Hughes had died about two months before McHugh and I went to lunch. Now it was just Roy on his own. At 101.

McHugh, Giffin, Smizik, Gordon and myself are the only survivors from that group.

McHugh smiled a small smile. He was about 5-6 or so, the same as his good friend Myron Cope. They were two of the finest sportswriters in Pittsburgh annals, along with

George Kiseda, from Monessen, and Phil Musick, from Garfield. McHugh has always spoken in hushed tones. He's a life-long bachelor, but he managed to slip into his story-telling about two different dates that his fellow sportswriters set up for him many years earlier.

I picked him up at 12:08, and was nervous because I said I'd be there at noon, and he said he'd be in the lobby waiting for me. I took McHugh to a familiar spot so he'd feel comfortable. I took him to Atria's Restaurant & Tavern in Mt. Lebanon, the original outlet by that name, a place I had frequented for 37 years, or since moving back to Pittsburgh from New York in 1979. This was on a Thursday, July 14, 2016.

I attempted to assist McHugh coming and going, when he was coming down or going up steps, but he pulled his elbow out of my grasp both times, faster than Fritzie Zivic might duck a punch. McHugh didn't want anyone helping him to get around. Too proud, I suppose.

I led him to the back room, sort of a mini-boxing museum, moving a few steps ahead of him. We were seated beneath a poster-size hand-colored likeness of Harry Greb, one of the greatest boxers in history. McHugh was able to identify him, upon request, even though his vision was severely limited.

"I'm legally blind, whatever that means," McHugh said. "I can't hear too well. I walk like a drunk. Other than that, I'm fine."

He smiled a small smile once more. We had passed retired sportswriter Bob Smizik in a back booth at Atria's, but McHugh missed him and Smizik didn't say anything as McHugh passed him.

McHugh did manage to identify Fritzie Zivic, in a hand-colored likeness on the wall behind him, and a black and white sketch of Billy Conn by my old friend and fellow collaborator on books about Pittsburgh, the late Marty Wolfson. I was the first child invited to draw with Wolfson when he had an instructional show for young artists on KDKA back in the early '50s. I was a fourth grade student at St. Stephen's Grade School in Hazelwood at the time.

Bruno Sammartino could make more money wrestling than he could playing for the Pittsburgh Steelers or being a professional boxer. Art Rooney and Al Quail tried to get him to turn pro in those sports respectively.

When I returned to Pittsburgh in 1979, Wolfson invited me to edit a coffee table book that turned out to be "PITTSBURGH: The Story of the City of Champions." We broke sales records at Kaufmann's downtown book store for one day and a three day-signing with that book, and McHugh wrote a wonderfully flattering piece about our promotional efforts in one of that week's editions of *The Pittsburgh Press*.

McHugh said my books were "valuable additions to the archives."

There were other great fighters pictured on the walls around us, namely Rocky Marciano, Joe Louis, Gus Lesnevich, Rocky Graziano, Jack Dempsey, Ezzard Charles, Benny Reynolds and Teddy Yarosz, and local fighters such as Joe LaQuatra, Don Alderson, Andy "The Kid" DePaul, who had been the Pennsylvania commissioner of boxing for a long span until his death, Bob Baker, Rich Baker, Don Alderson. Many of the photos were signed to Don Alderson, who was the brother of Wayne Alderson, the late father and father-in-law of Atria's owners Nancy and Pat McDonell.

Nancy and her mother, Nancy Alderson, both fresh from a hair salon and perfectly-coiffed, were having lunch that day in a side room in the front of the restaurant, and I had a chance to say hello. There was also a photo showing Canonsburg High School's WPIAL and PIAA wrestling champions of 1948-52, with two of my friends among the champions, Joe Solomon and Manuel "Buns" Pihakis, who were life-long companions of Canonsburg candy magnate Frank Sarris and his wife Athena.

Setting the scene for a story is something I learned to do from Roy McHugh, and I told him that during our lunch. I visited Henry Aaron in his home in suburban Atlanta when he was playing for the Braves, and I wrote a cover story for *SPORT* magazine. Before I submitted my story to the editor, I had Roy McHugh check it over, the way he always did for Myron Cope through the years.

"Show me you were there," said McHugh. "I want to know you were in his home talking to him." Ever since, I am always careful to make sure I set the scene, as a playwright must do.

Myron Cope comes to mind when I am working on a book. When I was 14, I asked, "Mr. Cope, what do I need to do to be a writer," and he responded, "Kid, you gotta sit down and start writing!"

I remain grateful for those tips from two little guys who were giants in the Pittsburgh sports-writing scene.

I tossed out topics for McHugh to mull on, but he chose to open with a story about Joe Namath and Arnold Palmer that I had never heard before. He took a break from a vodka pasta dish he always ate at Atria's to share this gem. Palmer had already won The Masters and the U.S. Open when he was introduced to Joe Namath.

McHugh wasn't sure Namath had won or lost Super Bowl III, but that hardly mattered now. "Arnold Palmer looked at the long-haired Namath upon meeting him for the first time," said McHugh, "and said, 'I could introduce you to a good barber.' And Namath came back by saying, 'And I could introduce you to a good tailor.' Namath was about 22 years old (actually 25) and Palmer was already one of the greatest golfers in the world, and it didn't matter to Namath." I told McHugh that Namath told a friend of mine, New Orleans Saints' publicist Doug Miller, that Palmer was the reason he always took the time to write his name legibly when someone asked him for an autograph. Palmer told him "if someone cares enough about you to ask for an autograph you ought to write it legibly so the name can be recognized years down the road."

So Namath did pay attention to some advice offered by Palmer, even if he kept his Fu Manchu mustache and long locks. Both have been heavyweights in the world of sports, and two of the best known athletes ever to come out of this region of the country.

Pittsburgh and the surrounding environs produced six Hall of Fame quarterbacks from within a 60-mile radius of Pittsburgh, and it also produced six world champion boxers from within a 50-mile radius of Pittsburgh back in 1934-41.

"It was the Golden Age of Boxing in that time frame, a decade in which six fighters from around Pittsburgh were champions of the world (never more than three at once,

McHugh was careful to point out). This was when there were only eight boxing divisions. Today there are 13.

"They were Teddy Yarosz, Billy Conn, Sammy Angott, Fritzie Zivic, Billy Soose and Jackie Wilson. In the same period, Pittsburgh had some other top-notch fighters: Charley Burley, Al Quail, Harry Bobo and Fritzie Zivic's brothers, to name a few.

"Only Nat Fleischer recognized Tony Marino, a steel-worker from Duquesne, as bantamweight champion in 1936, but Nat Fleischer was the editor of the *Ring Record Book* so his edicts were not open to question."

McHugh had done some research on the early years of boxing in Pittsburgh and was kind enough to share what he had learned.

"In the early years," he said, "you had Frank Klaus, George Chip and Frank Moran. Bunny Buntag, a boxing guy, told me some things about those guys. Buntag and Klaus were from Braddock and Buntag may have worked in his corner.

"Klaus was Pittsburgh's first world champion (middle-weight). Chip, who took the title from him, was born in Scranton but lived in New Castle when he was fighting. Moran was a great white hope. There's an interesting story about his 1914 championship fight with Jack Johnson, a black fighter, in Paris.

"The promoter, an American named Dan McKettrick, asked Moran for an option on his future services. Moran turned him down, which angered McKettrick. Claiming that Moran owed him $1,500, he went to a French law-yer and had the box-office receipts tied up. The day after the fight, World War I broke out, and McKettrick's lawyer was immediately conscripted. I don't know if he ever came back, but McKettick wasn't able to get the money released from the Bank of France. It may be there still. Moran and Johnson never were paid for the fight.

"I don't know who you could talk to about Harry Greb. You remember the sports writer Jack Henry, from the *Pittsburgh Sun-Telegraph?* He was sort of a mascot for Greb."

Jack Henry, a sportswriter at the *Pittsburgh Sun-Telegraph* and later a stock broker in the Union Trust Building, goes over script with Pirates Hall of Famer Pie Traynor, when they teamed up to do a radio sports show in the '50s.

When I was the student sports editor at Pitt in the early '60s, Jack Henry was the color man to Hal Scott's play-by-play call for Pitt football. He was a stock broker and Beano Cook encouraged me to start buying stock with Henry. I have continued to do so with other stockbrokers ever since. I recall Henry, who was one of the greatest story-tellers I ever encountered, talking about carrying a bucket of water into Greb's corner as a young man.

"Billy Conn was a great fighter, but it would be tough to follow Frank Deford who wrote 'The Boxer and the Blonde' for *Sports Illustrated* about Billy and his wife Mary Louise. I helped him on that one, but he made some mistakes with some of the stuff I provided. I had a lot of conversations with Conn, and people who knew him such as Ray Conley, Billy Jr, Timmy, Mary Louise, Joey Diven, Billy Neumont.

"Charley Burley from The Hill was one of the best. I interviewed him in his house in 1984, but Bill Naab beat me to the punch and did a story for *The Press* before I got around to doing it.

"People tried to get Bruno Sammartino to be a boxer and a football player, but he made more money as a wrestler around the world. I had a phone conversation with Sammartino when he told me about the time that Sonny Liston beat him up in a New York gym.

"Ezzard Charles was from Cincinnati, but his co-managers were Jake Mintz, who lived in Squirrel Hill, and Tom Tannas, from New Kensington, so Charles had several big fights around here. His biggest was his fight at Forbes Field (July 18, 1951). Charles was knocked out in the seventh round of a heavyweight title fight when Walcott caught him with a wicked left hook."

A check of *The Boxing Register*, the official record book of the International Boxing Hall of Fame, shows that Charles fought nine other times in Pittsburgh, against such fighters as Charley Burley (twice), Joey Maxim, Archie Moore and Rex Layne. He also fought often in Cleveland and Cincinnati.

McHugh said the post-war years brought about a decline in the caliber of boxers in the region, but listed a few who were pretty fair fighters: Bob Baker, Rusty Payne, Lee Sala, Tommy Yarosz, Charley Affif, Johnny Morris, Art Swiden.

I met Affif and Fritzie Zivic at The State Store on Second Avenue in Hazelwood when my mother was a clerk there in the '50s. Both were wine salesmen. Chuck Cherundolo, who had played center for Penn State and the Steelers, also sold wine and spirits and would come in to promote sales of his products.

Roy McHugh

* * *

There were promoters and managers of fighters that merit mention, according to McHugh. He sent me a type-written letter earlier about the ones he knew best.

"Jack McGinley's father, Barney McGinley, promoted fights with Art Rooney and Jake Mintz. Barney was the grandfather of Jack McGinley Jr., the attorney, and Barney, the judge.

"Some of the early managers were Red Mason, Luke Carney, Ray Foutts, Charley Jones, Jake Mintz and Bunny Buntag. I knew Mintz and Buntag fairly well. The others are just names to me.

"Don Elbaum was a colorful guy. He promoted a lightweight championship fight, Carlos Ortiz vs. Johnny Bizzarro, at the Civic Arena. Archie Litman promoted Ray Robinson's last fight, a loss to Joey Archer at the Arena, and I think Litman also promoted a non-title fight between Hurricane Carter and Emile Griffith at the Arena. Small-time promoters included Ben Anolik, Cowboy DeLuca, Jerry Kiger and that guy (Bill Speney, Sr.) who owned the Palisades dance hall in McKeesport."

McHugh saved one of his best stories for last. "In 1962, I went on a date with Cassius Clay, who was 20 years old and had not yet changed his name to Muhammad Ali. I wrote about it for SPORT magazine. It was only the second story about Clay in a national publication. Cope wrote the first one, for *True.*

"I wrote another Clay piece for *Sport* in 1963, and one for *the Press* Sunday magazine when I went to his camp in the Poconos where he was training for his fight with Larry Holmes. His Pittsburgh connection was his 1962 fight with Charlie Powell. On a night when it was way below zero in Pittsburgh, he drew a big crowd, maybe even a full house, at the brand-new Civic Arena."

More from McHugh's letter to me:

"We had some good amateur fighters. Art Rooney qualified for the 1920 Olympics in Antwerp, Belgium in the lightweight division, but chose to play football at Georgetown instead. The guy (Sammy Mossberg) Rooney beat in the trials won the gold medal. Rooney later beat him again at the P.A.A.

"Jack Zivic won the gold that year in the featherweight division and Pete Zivic was runner-up in the flyweight class to Frankie Genaro, later a world professional champion.

"In the 1940s, Pittsburgh had several national Golden Gloves champions, including Bob Baker, Andy "Kid" DePaul, and if I'm not mistaken, Floyd Morris and Bill Bossio. Cope covered Golden Gloves for the *Post-Gazette*. Leo Sweeney was an outstanding middleweight. The Lawrenceville Boys Club and the Glen-Hazel Boys Club produced a lot of good amateurs.

"Two officials who come to mind were Paul Sullivan and Marion Klingensmith. They were colorful boxing commissioners. Klingensmith had no idea that professional wrestlers weren't legit, and tried to make them observe the rules. At one match, the spectators began throwing things at him. The chairman of the commission finally had to tell him the facts of life. The commissioner's job was always a political plum.

"Havey Boyle doubled as boxing commissioner and sports editor of the *Post-Gazette*. Buck McTiernan and Ernie Sesto were prominent and respected referees in the 1940s and '50s. We had collegiate boxing for a period. Pitt, Carnegie Tech, Duquesne and John Carroll in Cleveland had a boxing league of their own. Leo Houck developed such pros as Billy Soose and Steve Hamas at Penn State. I hope this helps. You should be able to write an interesting book."

McHugh might have been a soft-spoken guy, but for a guy from Iowa and Coe College he sure knew a lot about the fight game in Pittsburgh.

* * *

When the parking lot valet brought my car to us, I asked him to go to the other side of the car and open the door for McHugh, which he did. While he was opening the front door, McHugh started to open the rear door on his own. When he realized his mistake, he reversed his movement, and McHugh took his seat in the shot-gun spot. He was embarrassed.

"See how damn blind I am?" he asked.

When I got him back to his apartment on Grandview Avenue, I forgot and tried to take his arm as he approached the front steps. Again, he pulled his arm away from me as fast as Fritzie Zivic. He wanted no help.

I called him back to the car after I had gotten back in my car. "Roy, I want to thank you for all you taught me," I said. He smiled a thin smile. "I don't know what I taught you," he said. I told him to be careful and to take good care of himself. He replied, "I'm 101 and I hope I don't make it to 102."

Jim O'Brien

Roy McHugh enjoys time with Doc Giffin, his good friend and former colleague on the sports staff at *The Pittsburgh Press*. Giffin succeeded Bob Drum as the golf writer at *The Press*, but left for a position as Arnold Palmer's public relations aide.

Billy Conn
"The Pittsburgh Kid"

"Billy was not meant to be in public life."
—His wife, Mary Louise Conn

Billy Conn can rest assured—in his grave in Calvary Cemetery where Hazelwood and Greenfield and Squirrel Hill share borders—that his family is still fighting for his honor and glory.

Conn, a world champion back in the late '30s and early '40s when it meant something, and helped put Pittsburgh on the international sports map, is best known for nearly winning the heavyweight title from the great Joe Louis. Conn was ahead on the scorecards going into the 13th round, but rather than run and hide for three rounds, Conn chose to go after Dempsey, seeking a knockout. And he succeeded in getting himself knocked out instead. It could have been...

The Conns don't want anyone to forget that their man, William David Conn Jr., was the biggest, toughest and most popular Pittsburgh sports hero of his time. That's all-time, as far as the Conns are concerned.

He was a ruggedly handsome, dark-haired, brutish, hard-hitting hometown hero, bigger in his hometown sports world than the Steelers and Pirates and Pitt teams in those days. He came out of a poor neighborhood in East Liberty to steal the hearts of fight fans and women everywhere with his immense boxing skills, speed, courage and Hollywood looks. Plus, he often said the damnedest things.

He could be funny in his own way.

His dark Irish eyes positively danced during his heyday. They even made a movie about his life, called "The Pittsburgh Kid," and he played himself.

His picture was plastered on the wall of every bar in Pittsburgh back then, and some of them are still on the walls in saloons about town, sharing space with Fritzie Zivic, another hometown favorite.

He was even portrayed on a mural, with Zivic and Harry Greb, on the wall of Pete Coyne's Irish Pub in Oakland, just below the Irish Club. Conn's frequent companion, Joey Diven, heralded in magazines as "The World's Greatest Street Fighter," was a bouncer at the top of the steep wooden stairway. When I had my going-away party at Frankie Gustine's Restaurant in Oakland in 1969, we moved the party to Pete Coyne's Irish Pub in the late hours. I recall Conn and Diven coming in and joining the party, and picking on fellow sportswriters Myron Cope and Roy McHugh, neither one taller than 5-6.

Conn was a hero at the Hibernian Club in my hometown of Hazelwood. He was revered in Ireland, I've been told by Pittsburghers who grew up on the green isle across the Atlantic.

* * *

"America's Guest."

There was a boxing show somewhere every week in the Pittsburgh area when Conn was competing for paydays and world titles. Boxers fought frequently in those days. The purses weren't that big and they had to stay active just to pay the bills. Then, too, the best fighters fought the best fighters, most of time. And then they fought again. And again. But don't tell that to Charley Burley, a terrific fighter from The Hill who had trouble getting good fights because he was a) black and b) because he had a style that could make opponents struggle and look bad. No ballplayer was ever bigger than Billy Conn in the eyes of Pittsburgh sports fans of a certain generation. There was no television. There were no sports talk shows round the clock. Newspapers and radio ruled the day. It was different from what we experience now.

After his boxing days were over, important people everywhere liked to keep company and have their picture taken with Billy Conn. He was a big shot in New York and paid to shake hands with customers at the Stardust Hotel & Casino in Las Vegas. He rubbed shoulders with giants.

He seldom touched his wallet. He was known in his hometown in a derisive manner as "America's Guest." He was known to leave tabs on the table, telling the wait staff to give it to someone else. He was the Big Ben Roethlisberger of his day. He was a close friend and luncheon companion of Art Rooney Sr., a top-notch amateur boxer as a young man.

Joe Louis and Billy Conn became friends and they became, as time passed, two of the most beloved sports figures in this country. Unlike Cassius Clay or Muhammad Ali as he came to be known, they served their time in the military and it cost them both dearly. They were rusty when they returned to the ring. They were routinely seen with U.S. Presidents, showbiz and sports celebrities.

A friend once arranged for Conn to meet President George Bush at a social event. That was George I. "Be sure to address him as Mister President," a friend kept caution- ing Conn beforehand. When it came Conn's turn in the receiving line, he extended his right hand and said, "Hi, George." And President Bush, not missing a beat, replied, "Hi, Billy. How are you?" Before long, Conn was heard to say, "George, I'm going to tell you how to run this country..."

Pittsburghers boasted that Billy Conn was one of their own, indeed, a favorite son. If I want more good inside stories on Billy Conn, I just call his son, Tim, a classmate of mine at Taylor Allderdice High School in the late '50s and book a luncheon date with Tim and his mother, Mary Louise Conn. They are great company and they don't need prodded to tell stories about the head of the family.

Billy Conn was 75 when he died May 29, 1993 after a long stay at the Veterans Affairs Medical Center (still referred to as the VA Hospital), the one in Oakland, over-looking Pitt's Petersen Events Center. In his last months, Billy didn't recognize the best of friends. It was a sad time for old-timers in Pittsburgh who remembered him as a battling young man who once carried their banner so brilliantly. Fritzie Zivic had the same ending at the VA

Hospital. He suffered for years with Alzheimer's disease and died in 1984.

Conn's name still shows up in boxing books and magazines as one of the Top 50 fighters of all time. His family feels that he's too often overlooked or forgotten in Pittsburgh, where his image matters most. It's a popular complaint with the families of many sports personalities of the past. He's in several of my books, so I don't take it personally.

Roy McHugh and Pat Livingston, both former sports editors of *The Pittsburgh Press,* pointed out that Pittsburgh first earned the nickname "City of Champions" during a ten-year span from 1934 to 1944, a decade in which six fighters from around Pittsburgh were champions of the world. McHugh, now over a hundred years old, still loves to talk about boxing and was one of the best at chronicling the sport.

There were never more than three at the same time, but they included Conn, Teddy Yarosz, Sammy Angott, Fritzie Zivic, Billy Soose and Jackie Wilson. In the same decade, Pittsburgh had other top-notch fighters: Charley Burley, Al Quaill, Harry Bobo and Zivic's brothers, Pete, Joe, Eddie and Jack, to name a few. Their father was Croatian and their mother was Slovenian and they were known as "The Fighting Zivics."

I learned from my wife that her mother, nee Barbara Stepetic, a second generation Croatian, had an autographed photo of Ted Yarosz in her home. Yarosz, who was born in Pittsburgh but grew up in Monaca, lost his father at an early age and took up boxing because a job and money were hard to come by during The Depression. His real name was Thaddius Yarosz and his family was second-generation Polish. He was inducted into the Boxing Hall of Fame in 2006. His brother Tommy was a terrific boxer as well.

It was often referred to as "the golden age of boxing" in Pittsburgh. Earlier, there were great boxers from the area such as Harry Greb, a world champion known as "The Pittsburgh Windmill, who grew up in Garfield and was an idol of Conn from the neighboring East Liberty community

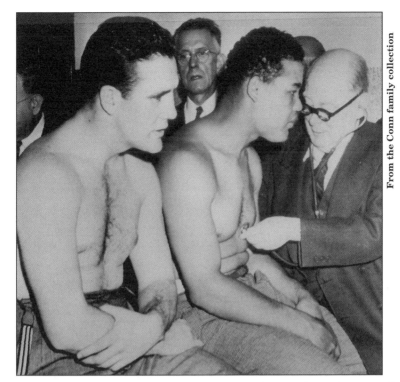

Billy Conn and Joe Louis undergo physicals prior to their famous 1941 fight.

Billy Conn and Joe Louis fought several exhibitions during their four-year stay in the U.S. Army during World War II. Altogether, Louis fought 82 exhibitions before two million soldiers.

in Pittsburgh's East End. Then, too, there were world champions such as George Chip and Frank Klaus.

Spending an evening with members of the Conn family—his wife Mary Louise and sons, Tim and Billy Jr.— at their home in Squirrel Hill was like a scene out of a movie, an opening act in a tragicomedy or, at least, the stuff of sitcoms. We sat around talked about Billy Conn, at least that was the idea.

It was a sit-Conn, for sure, on a Wednesday night, February 10, 1999, a rare winter's day in Pittsburgh when the sun broke through the clouds and warmed the sidewalks of Squirrel Hill, where the Conns had long resided.

At the time, Mary Louise lived, along with her middle son, Billy Jr., namesake of the great boxer, on the second and third floors of an attractive duplex home at the north end of Murray Avenue. She moved there, figuring their former home had become too big for their current needs.

More recently, she took up residence at the Little Sisters of the Poor Home in the Brighton Heights section of the North Side. The name belies the beautiful modern building for seniors. I visited her there in 2016 and had lunch with her and Tim as my guest three times, at California Pizza Kitchen Restaurant at Ross Park Mall, and Atria's Restaurant & Tavern at its McMurray and Mt. Lebanon sites (with Billy Jr. an addition at the latter outlet). I can count upon Mary Louise to get dressed up beautifully for these occasions. She was 92 in 2016 and her eyes still sparkled. The Conns were especially comfortable in the back room at Atria's in Mt. Lebanon because there are lots of boxing photos on the walls, of Billy Conn and Fritzie Zivic, of course, Andy "Kid" DePaul, who used to stop by on occasion. The Conns sat at a table beneath a beautiful colored photo of Harry Greb.

"Let Jim ask the questions."
—Mary Louise Conn

After four frenetic hours in their delightful company in our first meeting at their Squirrel Hill residence, a visitor felt like he had been sparring four rounds with the ghost of Billy Conn, Harry Greb and Fritzie Zivic. You came away with some scars, but also with a smile on your face, because you also came away with some good stories.

These are real people. This is the way you felt when had a spaghetti dinner with Danny Marino's family in their South Oakland home before his senior season at Pitt. Or when you visited Milene and Bill Mazeroski in their home along farm fields in Hempfield Township, just past Greensburg. Talk about hometown heroes...genuine people. You felt comfortable in their company.

The Conns are so passionate about their husband and father, respectively, that they zealously compete for air time. It's not always fair. One starts to tell a tale about Billy Conn, and then one of them butts in and interjects an additional item, or something once said, or an anecdote about Billy or his fabled father-in-law, "Greenfield Jimmy" Smith, or something that had nothing to do with the discussion topic. The boys are swapping stories originally related to them by "Dad" and "Pap," and they remember them well. They're a positive joy. Boom-boom-boom. Get the idea?

The Irish prefer a good argument to a good conversation, or they figure they are one and the same.

"Isn't this supposed to be about Billy Conn?" snapped a perplexed Mary Louise at one point in the free-for-all. "Let Jim ask the questions."

It was like being in a gym where someone is banging into the heavy bag, while two others are working simultaneously on speed bags nearby, skipping rope with one and tattooing the small black bag with the other hand. "Hey, guys, let me talk," begged Mary Louise, exasperated by the rat-tat-a-tat discussion.

"Hold on," Tim retaliates. "I just wanted to tell him..."

"This is about Dad, isn't it?" says Billy Jr. "How about the time...?"

"Can I get back to my story?" cries Mary Louise.

"Yeah, Mom, you can tell it best," yields Tim. "Why don't you...? He's looking for stories..."

"Hold on...," blurts Billy Jr.

It's spirited, combative, festive, a true Irish wake that would have delighted Billy Conn, or his best friend, Art Rooney, the late owner and patriarch of the Pittsburgh Steelers. All that was missing was cigar smoke, or what New York writer Pete Hamill described as "the blue haze" over the ring during the fights.

For the record, Billy Conn wasn't everybody's cup of tea or brand of beer. Conn could be churlish, argumentative, a bit of a bully, though Mary Louise insists he went out of his way to avoid a spat, and would defend him to the death. Some thought he had a huge chip on his shoulders. In that respect, he was a lot like Jack Lambert of the Steelers. Let's just say he was easily annoyed. That's why he fought in the first place.

A lot of fighters have come from challenging neighborhoods. "They're not choir boys," offered my wife Kathie.

His name and remarks were always popping up in the daily sports column of Al Abrams, the sports editor of the *Pittsburgh Post-Gazette* who was more of a man about town and more a celebrity in the city than either Chester L. Smith or Roy McHugh of *The Pittsburgh Press.* Mary Louise once telephoned Abrams to complain about him constantly quoting her husband saying words like "dem" and "dose," instead of "them" and "those" in his column. "To me,"Abrams said in his own defense, "he's a Damon Runyon character, and I want to portray him like that."

She was even more incensed when Abrams reported that Billy Conn "went ga-ga" over singer Phyllis McGuire when she and his sisters were singing at The New Arena Club in downtown Pittsburgh.

"I'll give you ga-ga," she scolded Billy when she next saw him, flashing a fist of her own. *Gaga,* by the way, is from a French word for a foolish old man.

"Billy wasn't meant to be a celebrity."

Mary Louise was in her 80s when we met in her Squirrel Hill home, but she was still a looker, still feisty. "Don't put my age in there! Just say I'm 39," she firmly directed me.

She's fun to be with, a natural. She was wearing form-fitting black slacks and a black jersey top, gold earrings, full makeup and a warm smile. She kept her hair blonde. Her figure and her sense of humor remained intact. On another visit, she wore a light blue sweater and was positively smashing. Mary Louise looked after me like I was a rich uncle, keeping me contented with Diet Cokes, peanuts, cheese curls and, eventually, a share of the pork chop dinner she prepared for herself and the boys. Being Irish didn't hurt in being welcomed into their company. They even offered critical thoughts about a few of Pittsburgh's icons, but that was off the record. Before long, you felt like family, and you were thinking about your own crazy family, and how they once talked with the same pace and fury as the Conns.

"I hope these photos turn out OK," she said more than once. "I'd hate to look good in the photos from my early days, and look like a haggard old woman now. Look after me, Jim. Be kind."

It was funny, informative and, quite often, difficult to comprehend. Taking notes could not have been more difficult if I had been wearing boxing gloves. And Tim handed me a huge scrapbook of newspaper clippings that felt as if someone had shoved a medicine ball into my belly. Mary Louise praised Tim for the job he had done in restoring a scrapbook to a cleaned-up state. It was great to see how much Mary Louise still loved her late husband—he could be a difficult man in and out of the ring—and how her boys were still banging the drum for the old man.

He was a great boxer, a great provider, and he cared deeply about them all, even if he didn't display it much publicly. "He wasn't meant to be a family man," Mary Louise said more than once. "He wasn't meant to be a celebrity. He was somewhat shy, and wanted to be left along. Billy was not meant to be in public life."

They still had a room, a family room, devoted to Billy Conn's career and achievements. There were not as many photos and framed letters from Presidents and political leaders as they were in the last house—which prompted

Sports Illustrated's ace writer Frank Deford to declare it the best collection of boxing photos he'd ever come across. Deford wrote a classic article in *SI* about Billy and Mary Louise Conn called "The Boxer and the Blonde." A copy of the article, which first appeared in June of 1985, was framed on a wall just outside the Conns' cramped kitchen. Deford told me at a writers' fair in Chicago that this story attracted more mail than any other piece in the magazine's rich history.

"I'm as fond of that story as any I've ever done," said Deford for a story written by Gene Collier on the occasion of Conn's death that appeared in the *Pittsburgh Post-Gazette.*

"The thing about that story was the love interest," said Deford. "It was really two love stories. His wife, the whole family really, and his mother. His mother was dying when he was falling in love and trying to win the heavyweight championship of the world while the world was falling apart. You just can't scare up that kind of thing. Against the whole tapestry of history, and of boxing, it was so compelling."

Conn's mother, Maggie McFarland Conn, died in 1941, just after Billy departed Pittsburgh for the Louis fight in New York. On parting, he told his mother, "The next time I see you, I'll be heavyweight champion of the world." To which she said, "The next time I see you will be in paradise."

Talking about his mother once, Billy said, "She was really from the ol' sod. She came over third-class steerage from the old country." His father, William Robert Conn—note they had different middle names—was born in Pittsburgh, and worked 40 years as a steamfitter at Westinghouse Electric Corporation.

There were photos everywhere in the four-bedroom complex, even in the stairway leading up to the third-floor attic retreat of Billy Jr., of some of the greatest boxers ever to grace the ring world, especially Pittsburgh favorites such as Zivic and Greb, but also Sugar Ray Robinson, Joe Louis, Rocky Marciano, Jack Dempsey, James J. Braddock, Max Schmelling, Barney Ross, Sonny Liston, Rocky Graziano and Tony Canzoneri and you name your favorite celebrity.

"My father and Billy both loved Harry Greb," said Mary Louise, as we scanned the photos.

They tested me on identifying individuals in some of the photos. I made a breakthrough with my hosts when I correctly identified a lineup in one photograph, from left to right, Billy Conn, Craig Morton, Bob Mathias, Hank Stram, Keith Morris (a press representative from *Sports Illustrated*), Carl Eller, Billie Jean King and Tony Kubek. Tim said they couldn't remember Keith Morris until I mentioned his name. I had dealt with Morris in my New York days.

The biggest photo in the room shows Conn chin to chin and nose-to-famous nose with comedian Bob Hope. "Here's where I can tell you something that only two other sportswriters in Pittsburgh would know," I boasted.

"In his early days, Bob Hope fought professionally under the name of Packy East in Cleveland."

"Yeah, Roy McHugh told us that," said Tim Conn.

Yeah, I was right on both counts. Myron Cope, a sportscaster who grew up in Squirrel Hill, would also have been able to offer the information about Bob Hope's boxing background.

From one of Bob Hope's comic routine about his days as a boxer:

"Some fighters are carried back to the dressing room. I'm the only one who had to be carried both ways."

"I was called 'Rembrandt' Hope because I spent so much time on the canvas."

* * *

Conn enjoyed the company of Bob Hope, Frank Sinatra, Jimmy Durante and Jayne Mansfield ("she was so big she hurt me when she sat on my lap," he told Mary Louise, as well at John F. Kennedy and Robert Kennedy, George Bush and Ronald Reagan, and they all pop up, along with personally signed correspondence which the Conns kept on display. There was a signed photo to Billy Conn from Stan

Jayne Mansfield

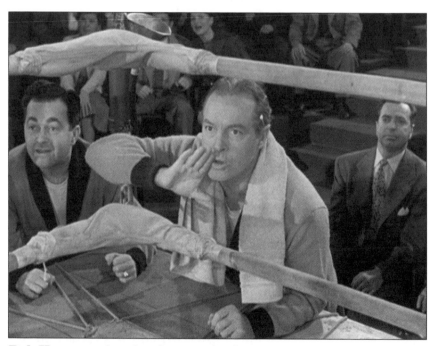

Bob Hope was in a boxing movie. As a young man in Cleveland, he fought under the name of Packy East.

Musial and others showing Billy with Joe DiMaggio and Bob Feller at his side. It's a mini-Hall of Fame and a great backdrop for a discussion about "The Pittsburgh Kid" with his kids and the ever-loyal lady of his life.

Pictures of Mary Louise in bathing suits at the beach with husband Billy in their prime were reminders of that a handsome couple they were.

There were also family photos, including some of youngest son, Michael, a successful Wall Street broker at the time. There were many of daughter, Suzanne Robinson, who had died of breast cancer six years earlier, at age 45. There was still a hole in the heart of the Conn family over Suzanne's difficult illness and passing. She was an attractive woman and Mary Louise proudly pulled framed photos of her off mantles and such to show me. "Don't you think she has Bill's looks?" she asked. There was also a photo gallery of grandchildren and relatives.

There was a signed portrait of Bishop Fulton J. Sheen ("To Billy Conn, God love you. Bishop Fulton J. Sheen").

Bishop Sheen of Catholic University in Washington D.C. had a nationally-popular TV show back in the '50s and '60s called "Life Is Worth Living." Bishop Sheen was a face from my childhood. I remembered those deep-set, dark steely eyes, the winning smile, and his scribblings on the chalkboard to emphasize his lesson points. Talk about TV from another era. He was even better than Billy Graham, the evangelist and not the boxer from New York City, or so we thought at St. Stephen's Grade School.

"Billy just loved Bishop Sheen," said Mary Louise. "He never asked anyone for autographs, but he got one from Bishop Sheen, and we all treasured this."

"If you're going to talk about charisma, Billy Conn had that and more."

Billy Conn Jr. was 54 years old at the time of our visit (Feb. 10, 1999), but he had boyish good looks, brown curls falling on his forehead, a bit of "The Dead End Kids" in his mug and demeanor. He was a dead ringer, I thought, for

Dick McGuire of the New York Knicks organization, and a member of the Basketball Hall of Fame. Billy Jr. does not look that much like his dad, but he carries himself with the same take-your-best-shot surly façade, leading with his chin. His dad liked to loaf and so does Billy Jr. He has worked as a sales rep for a local brewery. "Billy never wanted any of his sons to be named after him," said Mary Louise. "He said it wouldn't be good for him, that it would scar him for life."

I had not taken a seat in the Billy Conn Memorial Room when his namesake started peppering me with lead left jabs, just to feel me out.

"Do you listen to the sports talk shows here," began Billy Jr. "They had a show last week where the callers were encouraged to call in and vote for the greatest athletes in the history of Pittsburgh.

"Of course, Roberto Clemente was mentioned. So was Mario Lemieux, which is fine. Someone said Honus Wagner. But there must be a lot of Penguins' fans who listen to the show. People are mentioning former Penguins you never heard of. Like Dave Burrows. Did you ever hear of him? (A positive nod did not deter Conn from continuing his complaint.) Some of the names were insane. They're trying to come up with a top ten. Rocky Bleier was mentioned. That's OK. Everybody liked him.

"But nobody mentioned Dad. That's nonsense. He's the No. 1 guy. He was 21 when he won the light-heavyweight title. He was the toast of the town. That was in 1939. The Steelers were just starting—Pitt football was bigger than pro football here in those days—and the Pirates weren't drawing that well.

"Boxing was the No. 1 sport in Pittsburgh. If you were a boxer, you were a big star," Billy Conn Jr. said. "New York was No. 1 in boxing. And thanks to Dad, Pittsburgh was No. 2.

"Billy Conn was the No. 1 guy here. He wasn't just a boxer. He was a star. He looked like a matinee idol. Look at that picture...does that look like a boxer? If you're going to talk about charisma, Billy Conn had that and more."

> **"He can run, but he can't hide."**
> **— Joe Louis**

Tim Conn, 56 at that time, was also looking after his dad. A few weeks earlier, the Saturday sports section of the *Pittsburgh Post-Gazette* carried a letter to the editor written by one Tim Conn of Point Breeze. It read:

"The original intention of the Dapper Dan Award was given to the athlete who did the most to publicize the City of Pittsburgh during the year.' This is the inscription that was on the first award given in 1939 to my father, boxer Billy Conn. He was a two-time winner of that award.

"Unless the original intention of the award has changed over the years, I can see no reason that Joe Paterno should be so honored. He has done nothing that I know of to bring attention to Pittsburgh. I am sure there's an athlete whose accomplishments were more in tune with the original purpose of the award."

Billy Conn was close to his mother whom he called Maggie. She was quite ill and dying of cancer just before his first fight with Joe Louis.

As he was departing her home in 1941, Conn said, "Maggie, I gotta go now, but the next time you see me, I'll be the heavyweight champion of the world." Maggie smiled and said, "No, Son, the next time I see you will be in paradise." By coincidence, Louis died in a suburb of Las Vegas called Paradise.

Tim Conn
He keeps the record straight

Tim Conn was a classmate of mine in 1959 and 1960 in our junior and senior years at Taylor Allderdice High School in Squirrel Hill. He was a tall, lanky pitcher for the Dragons baseball team.

He knew all the stories about his dad, the famous fighter Billy Conn, and he had some idea of what life was like for Harry Greb, another great fighter, who lost the sight in his one eye and fought over 100 pro fights with vision in one eye.

Tim had his vision impaired when someone sailed a paper airplane his way one night at dinner in the Conn home in Squirrel Hill and it struck him in the eye. Just silly stuff.

He lives in the Point Breeze section of the city these days, with his wife Veronica. They have two adult children, Ryan and Milena, who both live out of state. Tim is an associate broker in real estate for Berkshire Hathaway (formerly Prudential). He often visits his mother, Mary Louise Conn, at the Little Sisters of the Poor Home on the city's North Side.

"Tim is great with me," says his mother.

He has always been most helpful to me and other authors when it came to sharing stories and photographs of his father, one of the most famous sports figures in Pittsburgh history.

"I was always proud of my father's career," he told me in late August 2016. "He is mainly remembered for his fights with Joe Louis, but people may not know that he beat many great fighters. By the time he was 21, he had beaten 12 current or former world champions. He fought in four different weight divisions, starting out as a welterweight and eventually fighting as a heavyweight. He never fought as an amateur. Almost a third of his fights were against champions or former champions."

Joe Louis
Everyone wanted to shake his hand

From *The New York Post*, May 7, 1971

Actor Horace McMahon, who used to sit behind a desk as top cop in the "Naked City" series on TV, was sitting behind a table at the Rose Restaurant on West 53rd watching folks fuss over Joe Louis.

"He's a lovely man," remarked McMahon. "He must be the most popular fighter who ever lived."

Joe Louis, the fighter of our lifetime, a historic heavyweight champion along with John L. Sullivan and Jack Dempsey, was back in town for the first time since he attended the Joe Frazier-Muhammad Ali title fight early in March.

That had been a remarkable night for Louis. The champion was moved by the thunderous standing ovation which the capacity crowd accorded his introduction. He was also pleased of the response that his most famous foe and long-time friend Billy Conn received that night.

"It's good to be remembered after so many years away," he told his wife, Martha, who was also at his side.

"Yes, it meant a lot to him," she said. "He's so humble, you know."

*   *   *

Louis had been troubled this past year, however, and it was widely reported that he had spent some time in a mental hospital in Denver. The people were glad to see him out and around again, smiling that warm smile of his.

"I'm through with it," he said, referring to his stay in the hospital.

Louis is surprised that people still remember him. That's how humble he is. Art Rooney Sr., one of his big fans, is that way.

"Makes me feel good," he said. "Most of the people in The Garden that night were about 30 years old, and not too many saw me fight."

If they didn't see him fight in person, they have seen the films, and their dads told them about Joe Louis. His name and his presence still mean a lot to many.

People still like to shake his hand, have their picture taken with him, get his autograph. That's how he comes by the kind of jobs that always seem to be there, like the newest one that brought us to the Rose Restaurant. He's been named vice-president of Family Dental-Medical Health Centers, and he's supposed to make appearances five times a month at these centers, like the two he visited in The Bronx earlier in the day.

* * *

"My pleasure," he said, "is if I can do something like this. Then I'm happy. I feel I can repay a lot of people in some small way, who supported me during my boxing career."

Louis, in truth, doesn't owe anyone anything, not even the IRS. He got that cleared up. He supported boxing for a long time. He was that big, and he has survived as a symbol and as a force for good, and also because he happens to be a decent man.

An honest man. This, however, has been his undoing, according to his wife, a practicing attorney, "because we live," she says, "in a dishonest world."

People have always taken advantage of Louis, like the writer yesterday who spewed out all his own personal prejudicial venom about certain fighters, and got acknowledging nods from Louis, who means no one any harm, but doesn't know how to disagree with anyone who approaches him.

The nods somehow became notes and Louis, no doubt, will end up being credited for criticizing the likes of Ali and other current fighters in his column.

Had Ali chosen a life style other than the one he did, Louis believes that he—or Cassius Clay, as Joe continues

148

BROWN BOMBER—Joe Louis was the heavyweight boxing champion for nearly 12 years, from 1937 to 1948. His overall record was 68-3. He defended his title 25 times and won 21 of those by knockout. He stopped Billy Conn in the 9th round of their rematch in 1946. That fight was a big financial success, and Louis made over $600,000 from that fight on June 19, 1946 at Yankee Stadium. Louis lost his last fight, at age 37, to Rocky Marciano on a TKO in the 8th round on October 26, 1951 at Madison Square Garden. This led Marciano to a title fight with champion Ezzard Charles, who was from Cincinnati but fought out of Pittsburgh for Jake Mintz of Squirrel Hill. Marciano won by a unanimous decision in 15 rounds to take the title.

ANNUAL RATING OF BOXERS

25 Cents

FEBRUARY
1941

The RING

BILLY CONN
Light-heavyweight King

HARRY JEFFRA
Featherweight Champion

FRITZIE ZIVIC
Welterweight Champion

LEW JENKINS
Lightweight Title Holder

JOE LOUIS
Heavyweight Champion

STANLEY

OUTSTANDING FIGHTERS OF 1940

to call him—would have been the most popular man in the fight game today.

"He was on his way," allowed Louis, "before that business with the Army. He was a nice kid...but he got lost along the way."

* * *

Louis realizes that others, especially many blacks, praise Ali for his action in refusing military induction.

"I'm just one who thought he was wrong," Louis said, "but millions of people think he was right."

Louis himself entered the military service in 1942, when his duty time was taken up with special appearances and boxing exhibitions with his pal from Pittsburgh, Billy Conn, who also served in the military during the same span. "I couldn't say no," said Joe. "I'm an American."

Louis liked Frazier in the recent fight, but he says if the rematch is held soon he'd switch to Ali. If it's put off for another year, he'll stick with Frazier.

"I'm saying it looking at the fight that night," said Louis. "Clay hit Frazier more often. What Clay couldn't do was follow them up; that's on account of his legs. After the three-and-a-half year layoff, he was just worried about going 15 rounds. Plus, he fooled around too much and it cost him.

"You know, he says stuff about me he don't really mean. Just to be smart. But we're real good friends. But if I think Frazier will beat him, I'll say Frazier."

An honest man to the end. That's Joe Louis.

Norman Mailer on Muhammad Ali

"He is the King of the Hill. He is fascinating – attraction and repulsion must be in the same package. So, he is obsessive. The more we don't want to think about him, the more we are obliged to. There is a reason for it. He is America's Greatest Ego."

152

Gene Tunney on his first fight with Harry Greb:

"When the 12th round ended, I believed it was a good time to take a swallow of orange juice and brandy. I had no sooner done so when the ring started swirling. I had never taken anything during the fight up to that time. Nor did I ever again. I saw two bobbing red opponents rushing at me. I don't know how I ever survived that round."

SQUIRREL HILL MEETING: Billy Conn, Rocky Marciano, restaurant owner Izzy Weinstein and Joe Louis enjoy lunch at popular Weinstein's Restaurant on Murray Avenue near Conn's home in the mid-60s. Weinstein was keeping company with three of the greatest boxers of all time.

"No great fight is unmixed. It is the area of intersection that is crucial, and in the most perfect fights—Louis-Conn I and Ali-Frazier I come immediately to mind—the pyramids of darkness and light, of violent struggle and the virtuoso's finesse, are most intimately joined."
—Ronald Levao

Talking Boxing with Billy Conn
Rooney was a champion, too

"I could hit...I was a champion."
—Art Rooney

"Think about it," boasted Billy Conn, "the best guys in the world are former boxers. You've got Bob Hope, Frank Sinatra and Art Rooney.

"Hope fought under the name of Packy East when he was a kid in Cleveland. He had about 13 pro fights and won all but one of them. Sinatra boxed a little bit out of Hoboken, New Jersey. Sinatra's the highest-class guy in the world. He raised over a million dollars for Joe Louis. No one can put a patch on him...except Art Rooney.

"He's the quarterback on the first-team of the all-nice guy team. There are a lot of bad guys and fools in this world, but a few good guys. A guy like Art Rooney takes up the slack. He's an unassuming real nice guy, the way he treats you, he's just another guy."

Billy Conn, of course, was a former boxer himself. He was the light-heavyweight champion of the world for parts of 1939 and 1940, vacating the title to box in the heavyweight ranks. Twice Conn fought Joe Louis for the title, and twice came up short, though he was ahead on the scoring cards when Louis knocked him out in the 13th round in their first meeting.

Their meetings provided Louis with two of his three biggest purses as a prizefighter until, that is, Sinatra tossed a fund-raising testimonial to him in the late '70s. Conn was talking about Hope, Sinatra, Louis and Rooney in the summer of 1981, when Conn was 64 and Rooney was 80. They were dear friends.

Rooney's life-long love affair with horse racing was more celebrated and chronicled than his romance with boxing, but he was always a big fan of the fight game. He was once both a national and international amateur boxing

154

Photos by Harry Homa

Steelers' owner Art Rooney Sr. shows a framed photo from his Wall of Fame in his office at Three Rivers Stadium showing his buddy Billy Conn landing a punch to the right jaw of Joe Louis in one of their famous fights. Below, sportswriter Jim O'Brien joins the two to listen to their boxing tales in Steelers' dressing room.

champion and qualified for the U.S. Olympic team in the 1920 Games at Antwerp, Belgium.

During his early days as owner of the Steelers, Rooney also promoted pro boxing matches in Pittsburgh with Barney McGinley, a minority owner of the Steelers and the father of Jack McGinley, who would later inherit a piece of the pro football franchise.

Conn and Rooney were reminiscing about boxing's grand old days during lunch at the Allegheny Club at Three Rivers Stadium where diners had an expansive view of the playing field where the Steelers and Pirates played their home games. I was fortunate to be sharing their table.

Conn had offered his highly complimentary remarks about Rooney while the latter was visiting some other friends at a nearby table, pumping hands as usual and inquiring about the health of everybody's wife and family. Rooney rejoined Conn and this writer to continue talking about their boxing ties.

Asked about his boxing skills, Rooney replied without a hint of boasting in his voice, "I could hit. I was a champion."

He began boxing when he was 16, and fought in the national amateur tournaments a few times, and fought in an international tournament in Toronto. He won the light-weight title there. "I beat Arnold Thornberg for an AAU title here at the P.A.A. (Pittsburgh Athletic Association) in an outdoor match around 1917," recalled Rooney. "There was great inner-city competition for amateurs in those days, between teams from the Boston and New York athletic clubs. You could keep real busy."

Rooney turned down a chance to box in the 1920 Olympic Games because he did not want to interrupt his studies at a Catholic school. Friends say Rooney was interested in becoming a priest, not a boxer, at the time.

"I beat Sammy Mossberg to go to the Olympics," Rooney recalled, "and then I didn't go. He won the gold medal at the Olympics and when he came back I beat him again. I boxed for about two or three years; I boxed professional twice. I forgot the first guy I fought, but the second was Sammy Mandell, who later became a champion. We fought in a

Harry Homa

Billy Conn hangs around Steelers' locker room.

preliminary in Chicago to a main event in which Tommy O'Brien fought Pinky Mitchell.

"That's the only time I almost seriously became a fighter. I was supposed to go to Australia and fight Mandell, and stay there and do some fighting. Tommy O'Brien was a champion in Australia at the time. Tommy O'Brien's wife talked me out of going to Australia, and did me the biggest favor of my life."

To which Conn interjected, "That's for sure!"

As Rooney and Conn chatted about their boxing experiences, they tossed around some of the great names of the fight game as casually as other diners at the Allegheny Club were exchanging salt and pepper shakers.

Sammy Mandell and Tommy O'Brien were openers. Others that came into their conversation—and I had to write these names down quickly and check them out later in the *Ring* magazine record book—included Joe Louis, Rocky Marciano and Muhammad Ali. Rooney referred to him as Muhammad Ali and Conn kept calling him Cassius Clay, which gives you additional insight into Rooney and Conn.

Others mentioned were Melio Bettina, Tony Galento, Teddy Yarosz, Harry Greb, Sammy Angott, Frank Klaus, Fritzie Zivic, Tommy Farr, Mickey Walker, Benny Leonard, Jimmy McLarnin, Jersey Joe Walcott, Ezzard Charles, Tommy Loughran, Gene Tunney, Jack Dempsey, Tony Canzoneri, Freddie Miller, Solly Krieger, Oscar Rankins, Charlie Burley, Jackie Wilson, Billy Soose, Joe Frazier, Billy Petrolle and Henry Armstrong.

Jimmy McLarnin was a world champion. He was an Irish-Canadian. He was called "Baby Face" McLarnin and was regarded by many experts as the greatest Irish fighter of all time. I am not sure Rooney and Conn concurred with that opinion.

They spoke of a period when Pittsburgh could have been called "The City of Champions," because the area could boast of having six champions out of the eight weight categories in the pro game. Between September 11, 1934 and November 18, 1941, Conn, Angott, Zivic, Soose, Yarosz and Wilson held world boxing titles, but not all at the same time. Never more than three at the same time. Angott was from Washington, Pa. and Soose was from Farrell and Yarosz was from Monaca.

Conn and Rooney agreed that Greb, who grew up in Garfield, was the greatest fighter in the history of the game. "I never saw him, but I heard plenty about him," said Conn. "He was always in great shape, and he'd fight anybody. Sometimes he'd fight a few times in the same week. He was always willing and ready to go. He must've been something."

Rooney responded with a Greb story on his own. "I saw the first Greb-Tunney fight," recalled Rooney. "Greb beat him twice, though he got robbed once. They fought five times (and, for the record, Tunney won twice, lost once, and there were two no-decisions).

Greb died October 22, 1926, following an operation on his eye. "He's buried here in Calvary Cemetery, near my mother," said Conn. (When he died, Conn was also buried in Calvary Cemetery.)

Greb, who was elected to the Boxing Hall of Fame, was the middleweight champion of the world and the American light-heavyweight champion. He was managed by Red Mason, who once tried to get Rooney to turn pro, and George Engel, who was Rooney's best man when he was married. There is a vintage photo of Greb displayed on the wall behind the bar at Tessaro's Restaurant on Liberty Avenue in Bloomfield, not far from Greb's old neighborhood. It was a prized possession of late owner Kelly Harrington. I talked to Kelly Harrington about that photo on several occasions.

To give further proof of his ties to boxing people, Rooney served as godfather for Timmy Conn, one of Billy's sons, and for Charlie Jones, who managed Sammy Angott, when Jones converted to Catholicism

Rooney once promoted a fight in Pittsburgh between Angott and another local hero, Fritzie Zivic, who often visited him in his Steelers' office.

"I hate to live in the past," said Rooney, "but that's all the guys coming to my office want to talk about every day. I like Sugar Ray Leonard and Roberto Duran, but most of the young guys never saw the kind of fighters I saw."

Rooney recalled a classic fight held in 1936 in Pittsburgh, one of three meetings between Solly Krieger and Oscar Rankins. "It was at Duquesne Gardens," interjected Conn. "It was one of the world's greatest fights. I was there. I fought both of them later."

Rooney was fond of telling a story about the first Conn-Louis fight to his players, as he did later that day with Sam Davis and Gerry Mullins. "Billy, in later years, asked Joe Louis why he didn't let him win that fight," related Rooney. "Billy said it would have been good for both of them if he'd taken the title away from Louis. He told Joe they could have fought for the title again in a return match in six months, for really big money, and Louis could have reclaimed his title at that time. Joe told him, `Billy, I gave you the title for 13 rounds, and you didn't know what to do with it. What would you have done with it for six months?' "

Later, Rooney said he brought Conn into the Steelers' clubhouse a year earlier and none of the players recognized his name. "But I asked the black guys if they'd heard about Joe Louis, and they all sure knew him!"

It was a two-way street, however. This writer was present when Jack Lambert, the Steelers' All-Pro linebacker and the UPI's Defensive Player of the Year in the AFC, was confronted by Conn and Rooney in the hallway at Three Rivers Stadium one afternoon.

Rooney said, "Jack, you know my friend, Billy Conn," and Lambert nodded. Then Rooney turned to Conn, and said, "You know Jack here, don't you, Billy?" And Conn nodded and said, quite seriously, "Sure, Jack Ham, right?" The sour look on Lambert's face should've tipped off Conn to his mistake.

"I have an excuse," Conn conceded later on. "I took too many punches to the head. But what's the big deal?"

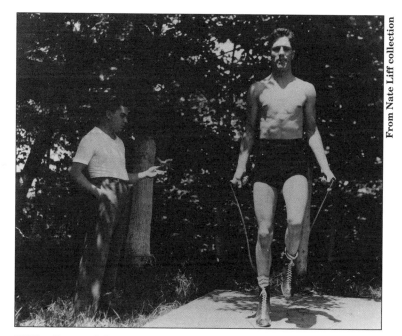

Billy Conn skips rope in training at Eagle's Nest boxing camp near Millvale that was owned by boxing trainer Nate Liff, at left.

"The Pittsburgh Kid" takes a tumble in one of his early fights at Duquesne Garden.

To which Mary Regan, Rooney's long-time secretary and Gal Friday, offered, "Billy, how'd you like somebody to mistake you for Fritzie Zivic?"

Louis and Conn did fight again, and for big money. In fact, it was a record gate at the time. A crowd of 45,266 showed up at Yankee Stadium, and the gate was $1,925,505. Louis got $625,916.44 and Conn received $325,958.22. Conn was KO'd at 2:19 of the eighth round the second time around.

Even so, Conn remained popular in New York, more so than in Pittsburgh, at least to hear Conn. "Here, I'm a bum!" bellowed Conn. He told a story to make that point.

"Budd Schulberg, who's a wonderful guy, wanted me to be in a movie based on his book, 'On The Waterfront,' but I told him I made one stink-bomb movie about myself —'The Pittsburgh Kid'—and I didn't want to make another.

"So I went to see the movie when it was playing in Pittsburgh. Marlon Brando is this fighter who raises pigeons, and he's sitting in a taxi talking to his older brother, who was played by Rod Steiger. Steiger tells him, 'If you behaved yourself, you'd have been another Billy Conn.' And this guy tells his girlfriend in front of me in the theater, 'Isn't he a big enough bum as it is now?' Even I had to laugh at that one."

Conn couldn't stop with one story. "Do you know who the toughest, guttiest guy is of all time in the fight game?"

Even Rooney didn't respond to that one.

"It was Battling Ski," Conn came back. "He had to be the gamest guy to ever come along. He was black and he defended his title against Mike McTigue on St. Patrick's Day in Dublin, Ireland. He had as much chance as a snow-ball in hell of winning that fight."

Sure enough, a check of *The Ring Encyclopedia and Record Book* revealed that Battling Siki, born Louis Phal in French West Africa, lost his title in a 20-round fight to McTigue on March 17, 1923 in Dublin.

Then Conn talked about Cuddy D'Marco, who came from the western Pennsylvania community of Charleroi. "They called him 'The Shiek,' and he was the handsomest, best-dressed guy," recalled Conn. "He once beat 161 guys in a row. Hell, you can't beat 161 girls in a row!"

Rooney chortled over Conn's tales, and told a few of his own. "There used to be a romance aspect to boxing," said Rooney. "You had some great managers, and they were real characters in their own right. There was Billy Gibson, Red Mason, George Engel—I could listen to him all day—Mike Jacobs, Jimmy Johnson and Johnny Ray."

Rooney recalled the time Conn came home on a three-day pass from the Army to attend his son's christening. Art was there as the godfather for Timmy Conn. Billy's father-in-law, a storied gentleman named "Greenfield Jimmy" Smith, was still smarting over his daughter's decision to marry Conn.

"I could tell there was going to be trouble," recalled Rooney, "just by the look in their eyes. They both had a short fuse. Before you knew it, they were tossing punches at one another in the kitchen. Billy broke his right hand hitting his father-in-law. But the father-in-law got in some good licks, too. You should have seen the wall in the kitchen. It looked like somebody had tossed a bucket of red paint on it."

Conn kept laughing as Rooney told the twice-told tale. "When I was 23," recalled Conn, "a guy wanted to lay an 8-to-5 bet I'd never be 27." Art said, "I agree."

That was good for another laugh. "The Pittsburgh Kid" and "The Chief" were having a good time.

Art Rooney was asked by sports columnist Phil Musick to answer a list of questions, including naming his favorite Pittsburgh athlete: It was former light-heavyweight boxing champion Billy Conn. "He was as much a part of Pittsburgh as the steel mills."

City of Champions

P ugilists from Pittsburgh and Western Pennsylvania claimed six of the eight world boxing titles during a seven-year span, never more than three at the same time, when Pittsburgh was first called "The City of Champions." During a 23-month stretch from July 13, 1939 till May 7, 1941, Western Pennsylvania claimed five world titles. Today there are 13 different weight divisions and three different boxing organizations overseeing the fight activity.

TEDDY YAROSZ

Born in Pittsburgh but from Monaca, he was the middleweight champion in 1934 and 1935. He was trained by Ray Arcel. He won the title by beating Vince Dundee on September 11, 1934 in Pittsburgh. He lost the belt to Babe Risko on September 19, 1935. He was inducted into the International Boxing Hall of Fame in the Class of 2006. He died at age 63 on March 29, 1974 in Rochester, Pennsylvania.

BILLY CONN

artwork by Marty Wolfson

Out of East Liberty, Conn won the light-heavyweight title over Melio Bettina at New York's Madison Square Garden on July 13, 1939. He was trained by Johnny Ray. Billy, known as "The Pittsburgh Kid," defended his title a few times and surrendered it to move up to heavyweight ranks to fight Joe Louis. In what is regarded as one of the greatest fights of all time, Conn led on the scorecards going into the 13th round and he went after Louis, seeking to knock him out, and got knocked out instead. He had only 14 KOs to his credit. "I couldn't knock anyone out and I tried to knock out Joe Louis," he said afterward. He was inducted into the International Boxing Hall of Fame in 1990. He is forever known for nearly upsetting Joe Louis. He died on May 29, 1993 at age 75 from Alzheimer's disease at the VA Hospital in Oakland—just like Fritzie Zivic. Friends who visited him at the VA said he was a mere shadow of himself, having dropped a lot of weight during his illness.

Boxing Weight Divisions

The World Boxing Council and the World Boxing Organization agreed on January 1, 2015 to the following weight divisions:

Mini featherweight	105 pounds
Light flyweight	108 pounds
Flyweight	112 pounds
Bantamweight	118 pounds
Featherweight	126 pounds
Lightweight	132 pounds
Light welterweight	141 pounds
Welterweight	152 pounds
Middleweight	160 pounds
Super middleweight	168 pounds
Light Heavyweight	175 pounds
Cruiser	200 pounds
Heavyweight	200 plus pounds

Box Rec

Heavyweight Primo Carnera and flyweight Rocky Genaro.

SAMMY ANGOTT

From Washington, Pennsylvania, he won the lightweight title on a decision in a 15-round bout with Davey Day on May 3, 1940, and then decisioned Lew Jenkins in 1941 to solidify his title. His birth name was Salvatore P. Angott. He fought Sugar Ray Robinson, Beau Jack, Fritzie Zivic, Henry

Armstrong and suffered only one knockout—to Beau Jack. His career record was 94-29-8 with 23 knockouts to his credit. He was inducted into the Boxing Hall of Fame in 1998. Along the way, he defeated reigning featherweight king Willie Pep in a 10-round non-title bout. He was nicknamed "The Clutch" because he liked to grab and hold his opponents. Angott lost a bout to Sugar Ray Robinson at Duquesne Garden on March 4, 1946. He died at age 65 on October 22, 1980.

FRITZIE ZIVIC

From the Lawrenceville section of Pittsburgh, his birth name was Ferdinand Henry John Zivcich. His dad came from Croatia and his mother from Slovenia, and Zivic was called "The Croatian Comet." He was the champion of the welterweight division from October 4, 1940 till July 29, 1941. On October 4, 1940, he battered Henry "Hammerin' Hank" Armstrong at Madison

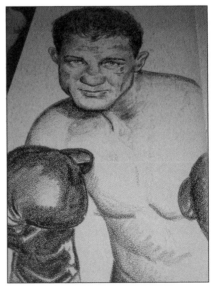

Artwork by Marty Wolfson

Square Garden to win the title. He lost it in a 15-round decision to Red Cochran on July 29, 1941 in Newark, New Jersey. He was inducted into the International Boxing Hall of Fame in 1993. He became a boilermaker, a worker on a Pittsburgh city work crew and a wine salesman in later years. He died after a long bout with Alzheimer's disease at the VA Hospital in Oakland on May 16, 1984.

JACKIE WILSON

Not the one who sang "Lonely Teardrops" and "Your Love Keeps Lifting Me Higher" and appeared at the Holiday House in Monroeville in the mid-60s. This one was born in Westminster, South Carolina but came to Pittsburgh and lived in the city's Homewood section. He fought Richie Lemos for the National Boxing Association title at the Olympic Auditorium in Los Angeles and won by decision. He won the title on November 18, 1941. And he beat Lemos is a rematch at the same site. He lost to Willie Pep in Pittsburgh. Wilson died at age 57 on December 2, 1966.

BILLY SOOSE

From Farrell, Pennsylvania, Soose beat two future middleweight champions in 1940, Ken Overlin and Tony Zale. Then he beat Overlin for the middleweight title on May 9, 1941. He never defended his title, retiring after losing a bout to Jimmy Bivins in 1942. He had been on the boxing team at Penn State before turning pro in 1938. Early in his career, he lost to Charley Burley in Pittsburgh. His career record was 34-13-6. He was inducted into the World Boxing Hall of Fame.

From Gerald Smith collection

167

Pat Livingston
He saw Fritzie Zivic and Billy Conn
up close as a kid in Oakland

Pat Livingston loved sports. It's no wonder. He grew up in Oakland within walking distance of Pitt Stadium, Forbes Field and Duquesne Garden and not that far from Motor Square Garden and The Armory in East Liberty. He even found his way to Hickey Park in Millvale where outdoor boxing shows were held in the summer.

Sports events took place at all those venerable venues and Livingston found a way to get in for free, most of the time, and observe sports at its best in the late '30s and '40s. He worked as a vendor in some of those places during his student days at Central Catholic High School.

"The first radio boxing match I ever heard was the Dempsey-Tunney fight in Chicago," allowed Livingston. "We never had a radio before that." That fight took place at Soldier Field in Chicago on September 25, 1927, and was famous for "the long count" that saved Tunney after he had been knocked down by Dempsey. It cost Dempsey the fight.

Livingston matriculated to St. Francis of Loretto College and then law school at Duquesne University. He earned a law degree but didn't practice law like his brother Tom, a well-known attorney in the city. He served a stint in the U.S. Navy, as a deep-sea diver who defused bombs in the ocean floors. That may have accounted for his nervousness as an adult.

He was good friends with Art Rooney Sr. and his family and served as a scout and publicist for the Pittsburgh Steelers for a short stint in the mid-40s, until he got into an argument with Jock Sutherland, the dour coach who had previously won national championships at Pitt.

It was Sutherland who suggested Livingston scout college talent for the Steelers, something that was seldom done in the National Football League at the time. "What do I know about scouting?" Livingston asked Sutherland.

168

"You know a good football player when you see one," said Sutherland, an observation that remains true to this day, but is seldom employed. It's too simple.

Livingston joined *The Pittsburgh Press* as a sportswriter in 1959, and covered the Steelers most of his career. He became the sports editor in 1972, succeeding Roy McHugh in that post. He was inducted into the writers' wing of the Pro Football Hall of Fame in 1980. I was there in Canton, Ohio to witness the event.

I joined *The Press* as a sportswriter in 1979, coming back home after nine years in New York and a year before that in Miami. I sat in many press boxes next to Livingston. He was one of the regulars at Dante's when I frequented that bar-restaurant in Brentwood when I was 20 and 21, back in 1962 and 1963. Myron Cope would be there, too, mixing with Steelers stars such as Bobby Layne, Ernie Stautner and Myron Pottios.

Cope, who was 5-6, challenged Layne to a fight there one night, and Pottios pulled Cope away and planted him on the sidewalk outside.

Livingston was as combative as Cope in his heyday. He once got into a brief scuffle with Bears' coach George Halas, who had been a boxer as well as a football player in his youth. Bears' players pulled Livingston away from Halas in the Bears' locker room.

"Pat was a good writer," Cope said when Livingston died at age 82 on August 16, 2003. "He was especially good when he was angry about something."

Cope and Livingston also liked to hang out at The Living Room, a nightspot in Upper St. Clair owned by numbers kingpin Tony Grosso, and at The Jamestown on Banksville Road in Dormont, owned and operated by Jim Breen. They'd get into arguments about sports wherever they traveled. Both were feisty little guys who liked to smoke and drink and argue.

When I was alongside Livingston in the press box, I'd always ask him what he was going to write about the game so that we didn't write the same story. He'd reply, "Something general." That was real helpful. So I started

169

feeding him locker room quotes and topics to steer him into something and away from what I planned to write.

I liked Pat Livingston. I visited him a few times when he was a patient at St. Clair Hospital when he was in his mid-70s. On the way out on one occasion, I stopped and told a nurse, "I don't think Mr. Livingston's color looks good. He's turning yellow."

She reported that to Livingston's doctor and he discovered that Livingston was bleeding internally. He was air-flighted to Allegheny General Hospital where Dr. George J. McGovern, Sr., a highly-respected heart surgeon and cardiac care director, operated on him and saved his life.

I visited Pat when he was a patient at Mercy Hospital when he was 82. I felt like I was at bedside with my father. I held his hand and tried to reassure him. He died a month later at Mercy Hospital from complications from surgery.

When he was 73, Livingston shared stories with me about his experiences with boxing. I found the notes on a yellow legal pad when I was going through my files in June of 2016 when I was working on this book. I always say that good things fall out of the sky on me when I am working on a book. I also found a poem he had written about Billy Conn, something sports columnists did in his day. Grantland Rice, the dean of sportswriters in Pat's youth, and Chester L. Smith, the sports editor of *The Press* when Pat joined the paper, also wrote poetry on occasion and had a fictional character named Joe Punt offer his thoughts on the sports scene on Mondays.

Ed Kiely, who followed Livingston as the Steelers' publicist, praised him for his work ethic. And his mind. "He had a memory that lasted forever," claimed Kiely.

During one of my visits to Pat when he was in the hospital, I took advantage of having him being captive and interviewed him about boxing. The following is what he had to say that day:

170

"CITY OF CHAMPIONS"

Pittsburgh first got its name as the City of Champions because of boxing. This was a great fight town and we had a half dozen world champions within a two-year period in the late '30s and early '40s.

Every time you turned around there was a fight somewhere in this city or region. I lived on the edge of The Hill, so I knew about Charley Burley. He was a great fighter. I saw him in the amateurs. He and Leo Sweeney were both great amateur fighters. Leo never made it as a pro, and nobody wanted to fight Burley. He beat Archie Moore and Fritzie Zivic. To the day he died, Charley Burley was really a good guy. He was a buddy of mine for many years. I always thought Burley had the wrong manager, a guy named Chappy Goldstein who owned a restaurant in the Lower Hill.

I remember how Billy Conn got into a fight with his father-in-law, "Greenfield Jimmy" Smith, on the day Billy's son, Timmy, was baptized.

When I was a student at Central in 1933, a fellow named Mike Gallagher had the concessions at The Garden. He hired me during my freshman year. There were five boys in our family, Gary, John, Henry and Tommy and me, and we all worked as vendors at one time or another, whatever they gave me to sell. I loved to get peanuts. They were a big seller. You know, Cope was a vendor at Forbes Field when he was a kid.

The Garden was like an upholstered car barn. Bob Drum used that line once in a story in our paper. That remark got John Harris, who ran the building, very angry. Harris founded the Ice Capades at The Garden to fill the time between periods of a hockey game. His brother's name was Harry and he's the only guy I know of who emptied the food from his refrigerator to make room for beer. I know, because I often delivered beer to his place.

171

They blew the basketball franchise. John Harris got mad at Walter Brown, who owned the Boston Celtics. Brown had promised him a coach to direct the Pittsburgh Ironmen, but didn't come through on the deal. Press Maravich, the father of Pete Maravich, played for the Ironmen during their one year in the league.

We lived on Adelaide Street, right across the street from Herron Hill Reservoir and Park. We had picnics at that park on Sunday. It was four square blocks on top of The Hill.

That was great. The Garden was a long narrow place and you were so close to the fighters. It was a great atmosphere. Everybody said that if that place ever caught on fire we'd be doomed. But it had a lot of doors so maybe we were safe. They were doing boxing at Motor Square Garden and Hickey Park, but the best matches were at Duquesne Garden.

The best fight I ever saw there was between Oscar Rankins and Solly Krieger. It was on March 18, 1937 and Rankins, from Los Angeles, won the fight. They had fought before at Duquesne Garden and at Madison Square Garden. In May of 1937, Billy Conn beat Rankins at Duquesne Garden.

I saw Conn get murdered by Rankins in the first round, but Conn came back to win. I saw Conn fight Zivic and I thought Zivic won, but Conn got the decision.

When Rankins and Krieger, both middleweights, fought they knocked each other out, but both were saved by the bell.

The first time I ever went to Florida, we got a late plane and arrived there late at night. We went to a bar called the Bonfire. It was a late-night place. Somehow the name Solly Krieger came up. The bartender mentioned him. I said, 'Does he come in here?' And the bartender said, 'He's in here now.' I saw him and went over to him. I told him I was Pat Livingston and that his fight with Rankins was the greatest fight I ever saw. He took me to the back room so I could tell his friends. I wrote a column about this chance meeting. Cope read the column and said it was a great column.

It was a super fight. I remember that Rankins was knocked down just before the bell ended the round. They came out from his corner and grabbed him by the hair—he had red hair—and dragged him back to the corner. They never stopped punching. Both won championships later. That's when they had one weight class and one champion for each weight class.

The first time I saw Billy Conn fight he was up against Ralph Chong in a preliminary fight at Duquesne Garden (on Oct. 22, 1936). I saw all his preliminary fights. After he beat Fritzie Zivic, he quit fighting in Pittsburgh. He became a big money fighter in New York. Conn later beat Krieger at Duquesne Garden and again at Madison Square Garden. After he beat Krieger a second time he fought Melio Bettina (On July 13, 1939) at Madison Square Garden and won the light-heavyweight crown.

Fritzie Zivic was the dirtiest fighter I ever knew.

I saw Ezzard Charles fight here a few times. He was a damn good fighter. You had to be a good fighter to be a fighter in those days. He was from Cincinnati, but he was managed by Jake Mintz of Squirrel Hill and Tom Tannas from New Kensington. That's why he fought here and in Cleveland so much.

Art Rooney Sr. and Barney McGinley Sr. promoted all the fights here in those days. Al Abrams was the sports editor of the *Post-Gazette*. Dick McCann, the p.r. man for the Washington Redskins, once described Abrams as "the sportswriter in Pittsburgh who always looked like Paris had just fallen."

When I was in the Navy, I drew an assignment to do public relations for the Navy out of Radio City Music Hall. This was right after the War, in June of 1946. I'd go to Toots Shor's every day. Bert Lahr, Jackie Gleason and Frank Sinatra came in regularly.

The best boxing writer in Pittsburgh was Regis Welsh. I was there one night in the office when Welsh went after Beano Cook with a pair of scissors.

There were so many boxers in Pittsburgh. Eddie Zivic was one of four Zivic brothers from Lawrenceville who fought. Billy Soose, a Penn State guy from Farrell, and Sammy Angott of Washington, Pa. Harry Bobo of Pittsburgh was pretty good. He married Bea Williams, one of the prettiest black girls I ever saw. The other one was Lena Horne. She lived near us on The Hill. Bob Baker from The Hill was a good heavyweight, but he had bad hands. Jackie Wilson, who moved from Uniontown to Homewood, was a world champion. Al Quail was a good fighter at the beginning, but he got murdered when he had his first big fight. They always had a good team in the Golden Gloves from your hometown of Hazelwood.

The Pirates were the most important team in town, followed by boxing and then college football. Pro football hadn't caught on yet like it would later on. The Steelers were down at the bottom. The Steelers started to attract attention when they got Jock Sutherland to coach the team.

They had Sutherland and they sold out every game he coached. I think they led the NFL in attendance one year. They sold out Forbes Field with John Michelosen as coach the following two years.

During my four years at Central Catholic, I went to Duquesne Garden often. They had skating there, a marathon dance. It was on my way to school and I'd check in on the six-day bike race. My god, they'd be at it. I walked to Pitt Stadium, I walked to Forbes Field. I walked to Schenley Oval to see horse races every Wednesday. We used to jump off a cliff into a pile of horseshit that was covered by hay. It was a lot of fun. Nobody ever died from it.

I always liked it. My dad didn't have time to take us around. I was the oldest of five boys so I led us around town. I was a boxing fan and that's when I knew the fighters. I didn't just know the old fighters. I met Muhammad Ali and Larry Holmes and I liked both of those guys. Ali was a wonderful guy.

Press sports editor Pat Livingston presents Bob Prince Award to sportswriter Jim O'Brien at Thompson Club Sports Dinner.

Sports columnists often wrote poems to capture the essence of sports. Here is one that Pat Livingston wrote about Billy Conn when the Pittsburgh boxer beat Melio Bettina on July 13, 1939 for the light-heavyweight crown. Keep in mind that Livingston was Irish and proud of it.

The Crown

Tonight ten thousand people watched the
    crowning of a king
A ruler, not of war-torn lands
But of a canvassed ring
A monarch on the throne tonight holds
    undisputed sway
Of a sovereignty, a boxing class, he didn't
    hold today
The fiery glare of dago red replaced by Kelly
    green
To greet all coming challengers no better
    color's seen
He's sitting on the throne tonight a monarch
    to the core
and on his head the jeweled crown which
    once Bettina wore
For Billy Conn is ruler now
Forever may he reign
And may he have the power so he can stand
    the strain
of beating off the challengers who pound his
    castle door
In hopes of shaking loose the crown which
    once Bettina wore
And then we say salute the king, a ruler
    strong and brave

Again we say salute the flags which o'er his
    castle wave
And may the crown rest lightly on his brow
    forever more
And may Billy Conn be worthy of the crown
    Bettina wore
Listed among the ranks of the great
With the speed and the grace of a fawn
Was a noted young fighter known far and
    wide
Who answers the name, Billy Conn
He'll fight till he stops
And he'll slug till he drops
For fighting lays claim to his soul
And I won't be surprised, if, while in the
    casket he lies,
He's fighting to get out of the hole

Billy Conn, left, battles Melio Bettina for boxing's light-
heavyweight crown.

25 Cents
30 cents in Canada

P.D.C.

The

RING

MARCH
1950

INTERNATIONAL
RECOGNITION
1950

EZZARD CHARLES

Stanley
Weston

A keen memory of
Ezzard Charles

Ruth Black keeps a memory alive of when she first met Ezzard Charles, once the heavyweight boxing champion of the world.

Ruth is a friend of mine at Westminster Presbyterian Church in Upper St. Clair and she was telling me about this framed photograph of Ezzard Charles she had recently seen at a Cracker Barrel Restaurant in Washington, Pennsylvania.

"He's as handsome in that picture as I remember him," she told me following a service one Sunday in August of 2016.

She was Ruth Kirchner and 19 years old when she first took a job at a Pittsburgh law firm back in 1952. She came from Chattanooga, Tennessee. "I was just a little ol' Southern girl with quite the accent," she recalled.

The firm was I. Ecker Law Firm, and Mr. Ecker's two sons, Jim and Ronnie, were young lawyers. Jim Ecker would later become one of the most famous defense lawyers in the city. "If Jim Ecker is representing you," people would say, "you're guilty as all hell, but you'll get off easy."

Jim Ecker, a silver-haired, dapper little man would just smile when I'd repeat that to him. I knew him because he was a big sports fan, and he liked to talk to the media.

"We were in the Bakewell Building at the corner of Grant Street and Diamond Street (now Forbes Avenue)," recalled Ruth Black. "One of our clients was Jake Mintz, who managed Ezzard Charles and some other fighters.

"Mintz was a man who liked to talk. He just talked, talked, talked and waved his hands and some people thought he was dumb. But he was smart and shrewd. He'd be in our offices a lot. I was the secretary there."

Al Abrams, the sports editor of the *Pittsburgh Post-Gazette*, called in often, to speak to Jake Mintz, and get a boxing note for his column. "After I answered his call one day," said Ms. Black, "he asked my boss, 'Do you have a little colored girl working for you?' Abrams would come to our office now and then later on he realized his error.

"I'll never forget Ezzard Charles. He came in one day wearing a white silk dress shirt and pleated pants," she said. "I remember he was fussy about how he tied his shoes, his dress shoes and his boxing shoes. The laces had to be flat and they were crossed in a pattern; it's hard to describe how he did it. But they had to be just so. He had quite the physique, but I shouldn't say that. He was an impeccable dresser, a handsome man. He'd comb his hair just so. He was always pleasant, quick with the smile. I didn't realize he fought in Pittsburgh. I knew he was from Cincinnati, but his manager, Jake Mintz, lived in Squirrel Hill."

A bio sketch of Ezzard Charles appears just ahead of Billy Conn in *The Boxing Register*. He was the heavyweight champion from 1949 to 1951. He fought 12 times in Pittsburgh, and his final appearance was his most famous. He lost his title, getting knocked out by a left hook in the seventh round by Jersey Joe Walcott at Forbes Field on July 18, 1951. It was called The Fight of the Year by *The Ring* magazine. That was the year before Ruth Kirchner came to work at the Ecker Law Firm, that's why she wasn't aware that he fought in Pittsburgh.

Jim O'Brien

Ruth Black recalls Ezzard Charles

Teddy Yarosz
A hero in steel-making community

Teddy Yarosz of Monaca, Pennsylvania was a classic case of why young men turned to boxing to make a living during the Great Depression. It was difficult to get a job in those days during the '30s and '40s—my own father went seven years without a permanent job, but managed to bring home money from doing odd jobs in the neighborhood—and the Yarosz family needed someone to bring home the bacon.

His father died at an early age, leaving six youngsters with their mother at their home in Beaver County, and Teddy made the money in boxing to pay for the family's bills. He was referred to, in one report, as "the youthful boxing idol of the steel district."

He was a Polish-American. My late mother-in-law, who was of Croatian descent, rooted, naturally, for Fritzie Zivic, known as "The Croatian Comet," and Teddy Yarosz. She gave me a picture of Teddy Yarosz, a handsome fellow, that he signed for her when she was Barbara Stepetic of Duquesne, and not Barbara Churchman, my wife Kathie's mother in the White Oak section of McKeesport. That picture appears with this story. His signature is still legible, unlike the signatures of most professional athletes these days.

Yarosz beat Vince Dundee of Baltimore on September 11, 1934, to win the middleweight title, and lost it a year later, on September 19, 1935 to Eddie "Babe" Risko, another Polish-American, from Syracuse.

Yarosz was the most famous and beloved athlete from Monaca until the Davis brothers, Mickey and Brad, came along in the '70s and starred in basketball at Duquesne University and the University of Maryland, respectively, and then in the National Basketball Association.

They are all in the Beaver County Sports Hall of Fame, and Yarosz was inducted into the International Boxing Hall of Fame in the Class of 1996.

Even those brothers weren't as popular as Teddy and his two brothers, Tommy and Eddie, who were also noteworthy boxers. It was just a different time. The other brother, Johnny, the only one who wasn't a boxer, died in a bomber crash during World War II.

In 1929, Ray Foutts, a tavern-owner from East Liverpool, Ohio, happened to be in the Grand Junction Arena when Teddy Yarosz, a middleweight from Monaca, won his first pro fight in an exciting four-rounder. Foutts liked the way Yarosz avoided being hit and bought his contract for $150. Five years later, Yarosz won the middleweight boxing title.

He had 59 fights before losing one.

He was successful against many of the top boxers in Pittsburgh, such as Jimmy Belmont, Joe Randall, Jack "Buck" McTiernan, and beat a number of top-rated fighters, including Vince Dundee, and then took the title from Dundee.

The crowd at Forbes Field to see Yarosz defeat Dundee was 25,000, which was the largest crowd to see a fight there until Ezzard Charles and "Jersey Joe" Walcott drew 28,000 for their heavyweight championship match on June 5, 1952. The Charles-Walcott bout was promoted by McGinley-Rooney of Steelers fame.

Yarosz suffered a knee injury in a fight in New Jersey with Risko on New Year's Day, 1935, and was never the same after that, sometimes dragging his leg during a bout. He went to the Mayo Clinic in Minnesota but surgery was not successful in correcting the injury. It cost him the title in a return title match with Risko.

During his career, Yarosz moved up in weight class, and fought light-heavyweight Billy Conn. He lost two controversial decisions to Conn in Conn's hometown of Pittsburgh before soundly beating Conn in July of 1938. Those fights took place at Forbes Field, Duquesne Garden and again at Forbes Field.

Late in his career, Yarosz scored a decision over heavily-favored Archie Moore in a bout in St. Louis. He boxed as a professional for 13 years and had a fine record of 106-21-2. As Conn liked to say, "show me a boxer without a loss in his record and I'll show you a problem."

Yarosz lost a 10-round decision to former heavyweight champion Ezzard Charles in 1941 and retired after one more fight. Yarosz could proudly boast that during his boxing career he defeated ten fighters who at one time were world champions.

TEDDY YAROSZ
A handsome hero

Is it Duquesne Gardens or Duquesne Garden?

Actually, either way is correct. The main sports arena in Pittsburgh during the first half of the 20th century was originally built as a trolley barn in 1890. There are signs and game programs with Duquesne Garden on the cover and, by the mid-50s most sports fans were referring to it as Duquesne Gardens. When it was razed in 1956 the marquee over the entrance read simply THE GARDENS.

Nearby, in Shadyside, you have Motor Square Garden and in New York you have the most famous sports arena in the world, Madison Square Garden. So why Duquesne Gardens? Why the s?

Duquesne Garden came into being as a sports arena in 1896, after the Schenley Park Casino was leveled by a fire. The Casino was one of the first places in North America where pro hockey games were contested.

Duquesne Garden was the home for several pro hockey teams that played in minor leagues, the Pittsburgh Pirates, the Pittsburgh Shamrocks, the Pittsburgh Yellow Jackets, the Pittsburgh Hornets. I went to some Hornets' games there as a young teen. They were one of the best teams in the American Hockey League. The cop at the side-door nicknamed "Doughbelly" was from my hometown of Hazelwood and he let me in for free. He once gave me a broken hockey stick signed by Bobby Sollinger, one of the Hornets' best players. That was in the days of defenseman Frank Mather and goalie Gil Mayer (No. 1 and 0).

The place seated just over 6,000. It was reputed to have the largest ice surface in North America. The ice rink was 50 feet longer than today's NHL surfaces. The Ice Capades were started there to entertain hockey fans between periods. John H. Harris, whose father John P. Harris had the first movie theatre in the country, owned the hockey teams, as well as the Pittsburgh Ironmen. He was married for ten years to ice skating star Donna Atwood, one of the top attractions of the Ice Capades.

The Ironmen were charter members of the Basketball Association of America, a predecessor of the National Basketball Association, and lasted one season (1946-47). Press Maravich, the father of Pistol Pete Maravich, was a member of the Ironmen.

Golden Gloves boxing tournaments and pro bouts were held there. Fritzie Zivic, Billy Conn, Charley Burley and Solly Krieger fought there often. Duquesne University played its basketball and hockey games there. The Dukes were in four-team boxing and hockey leagues with Pitt, Carnegie Tech and John Carroll University of Cleveland. Circuses were held there and public skating as well. It was located at 110 North Craig Street. That strip now has an honorary sign— Billy Conn Blvd.—on the side of the street where St. Paul's Cathedral stands tall.

The Garden was razed in 1956 to build apartment buildings on the site. They are still there, within a block of Central Catholic High School, Oakland Catholic High School, WQED Studios and Rodef Shalom Temple.

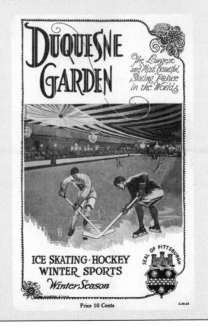

185

Lee Sala
One of many great athletes
from mill town of Donora

This was during The Great Depression when jobs and money were hard to come by, especially in a mill town along the Monongahela River such as Donora.

There were five siblings and two cousins living in Lee Sala's home in the Mon Valley. His dad was a bricklayer but he didn't work regularly and was challenged to make enough money to pay the mortgage and put food on the table.

Lee Sala spent two years in the U.S. Navy and served on the Battleship Iowa, mostly in the South Pacific, during World War II. He had two uncles who were boxers in the '20s, Bruno and Libro Sala. Lee's older brother Tony was an All-American football player at Villanova University and a collegiate boxing champion for four years. Lee followed in their footsteps.

When he was honorably discharged from the Navy he came home and started boxing to make money. He had a 47-bout winning streak and posted a career (1946-1953) record of 78-7-0. His manager, Braddock's Bunny Buntag, a well-known figure in the fight game in Western Pennsylvania, put up $50,000 to help underwrite title bouts for Sala with Sugar Ray Robinson and Jake Lamotta, but those bouts never came about.

Sala spent most of his career as a Top Ten fighter in the middleweight ranks. He had trouble getting bouts with some of the best boxers because "he hit too hard." He had 48 knockouts in 85 bouts to his credit. Think about that... Billy Conn had 14 knockouts in 76 bouts in his career.

Sala lost a fight to middleweight contender Carl "Bobo" Olson later in his career and retired soon after. He married a beauty queen, Adeline Mordello, and moved to Tampa, Florida. They had two children. He became a whiskey salesman and then the sheriff of Hillsborough County. He refereed some boxing matches now and then.

He is often overlooked when people name the great athletes from Donora that included Stan "The Man" Musial, "Deacon Dan" Towler, Ken Griffey Sr. and Ken Griffey Jr. (Baseball Hall of Fame in 2016 on first ballot), Arnold Galiffa and his nephew Bernie Galiffa, Bimbo Cecconi, Roscoe Ross and Rudy Andabaker. Sala died at age 86 on December 3, 2013.

"Lee Sala was a big deal for us kids in Donora," recalls Cecconi, who played and coached football at Pitt and Indiana State University, and was later a teacher and administrator at Steel Valley High School. "We knew all about him, and we'd get excited when we saw him in the neighborhood. He came from a real good family. His father was a brick-layer just like my father-in-law, and those guys had a reputation for having a great work ethic. Lee Sala deserves to be mentioned when they talk about the great ones from Donora."

**Donora dandy Lee Sala
stands over fallen opponents.**

From Nate Liff Collection

Mary Louise Conn
The Boxer and The Blonde
were a great 1-2 combination

I had four dates with Mary Louise Conn in 2016 and she got dolled up for every one of them. And somehow I knew she would. She wore nice sweaters, with beautiful necklaces—one was black and silver—sharp black slacks, a white blazer on one occasion, and open-toed shoes that shined. She was a knockout every time and she was 92!

She was generous with her eye make-up, bright red lipstick and she was doing a great job of fighting off the natural effects of aging.

When I took her picture, she said, "Jim, you're going to show these pictures next to the ones of me in a bathing suit when I was young. You're going to show me as an old hag next to a bathing beauty. Please look after me, Jim."

I'll try but she said some things that might be shocking to some, but show how honest and genuine she remains to this day. Her husband was that way, too, but he was so straight forward at times that he was difficult to deal with.

"Billy was not meant for public life," she has told me more than once.

Billy was Billy Conn, of course, once the toast of the town in Pittsburgh where he was bigger and better than the Pirates or the Steelers during the '40s.

Billy always struck me as a bit of a brute, a guy with an enormous chip on his broad shoulders. He was easily bothered, annoyed by most of the remarks he heard a hundred thousand times. Mary Louise looked the part and played the part well of a movie actress, someone such as Esther Williams. She had gone to a private all-girls high school (Mount Mercy Academy in Oakland) and an all-girls cloistered college in Philadelphia, Rosemont College. Her father, "Greenfield" Jimmy Smith, a former combative and trash-talking ballplayer for the New York Giants baseball team, disapproved of her dating Billy Conn or any athlete for that matter. He was a trash talker before the phrase came into vogue. He got thrown out of a World Series game.

Smith instructed the mother superior at the college to keep Billy Conn away from his daughter. He didn't mind her dating the more proper students from St. Joseph's and Villanova University.

Conn first caught sight of Mary Louise when she was 16 and they eloped when she was 18. When he first met her, he said, "I'm going to marry you some day." And she responded, "You're crazy."

They were right on both counts.

Frank Deford, maybe the best writer of sports the past 40 years in America, wrote a story about the Conns for *Sports Illustrated* in July of 1985. It was called "The Boxer and The Blonde." I had a chance to talk to Deford when he appeared at a writers conference in Chicago six or seven years ago. He told me that *SI* got more mail about that piece than any other story in the magazine's history.

He said he still hears from the Conns on occasion, a letter with an up-to-date photo of Mary Louise Conn. "She's still a knockout at the age of 92," said Deford more recently. "She was really gorgeous."

Tim told me that his mother gets post cards on a regular basis from Art Rooney, Jr., the second oldest son of Steelers' founder Art Rooney Sr. Art Sr. had been a champion amateur boxer and 2-0 as a pro and later a boxing promoter with Barney McGinley Sr. Art and Billy Conn were frequent luncheon companions. Art always picked up the tab, leading one Steelers' executive to critically call Conn "America's Guest."

I visited Mary Louise on the first of our four meetings at The Little Sisters of the Poor Home in the Brighton Heights section of Pittsburgh's North Side in the winter of 2016. The name is misleading. I remembered The Little Sisters of the Poor holding baskets in their laps and accepting alms for the poor. This is no modest manse.

Well, their residence for seniors is something that caught me off guard. It's a beautiful building, quite new, with a great support staff. Mrs. Conn looked quite comfortable in her well-polished room. There are pictures on the wall of her and her husband in their heyday. There were more pictures on the walls in her second-story residence in a home in Squirrel Hill when I had visited her about ten years earlier. I was familiar with several of the photos.

"You and Billy came from different backgrounds," I said to her when she was sitting in a chair in her room. "He dropped out of Sacred Heart and dropped out of Washington Trade School and two other trade schools. You went to private schools. What did you have in common? What was it that bonded you?"

Mary Louise looked to the door of her room to see if anybody was nearby, and said, "Sex!" She said it like Eartha Kitt might say it. She flashed her blue eyes to accent her comment.

I think she was looking to see if any of the Little Sisters of the Poor were within earshot.

"You're not going to use that, are you?" she asked. "Don't get me kicked out of here."

I think if she says a rosary or two, she'll be forgiven.

I didn't see that line in Frank Deford's article, great as it was.

She shared two stories about her life with Billy Conn that aren't in any of the books that have been written about her husband, famous for his near-victory over Joe Louis for the heavyweight boxing crown in 1941.

Billy and Mary Louise liked to go out at night in a Pittsburgh that no longer exists. One night, they went to the Hollywood Social Club that was located upstairs of a movie theatre in the Shadyside community of the city.

As sometimes happened, a fellow who had too much to drink spotted Conn coming through the door, and confronted him right after someone slipped a drink in Billy's hand.

"You're not so tough," the guy growled. "I could beat you."

Billy was with Mary Louise and he didn't want to create a scene, so he tried some diplomacy, which was not his strong suit.

Billy and Mary Louise Conn cut quite the figures on the beach at Atlantic City.

"Look, pal, leave me alone, OK," countered Conn. "You're a tough guy and I'm terrified. When you go home tonight, get out your record book and put my name in there and mark it as a 'W' in your favor."

"Oh, you're a real wise guy," said the challenger. "You think you're a big deal, but not in my book."

With that, Conn tossed an overhand right—"my bread and butter punch," he always said—and floored the guy, right there in the middle of the Hollywood Social Club. One punch and the guy was out cold.

Conn moved his drink from his left hand to his right hand and held it over the flattened body, and poured the drink slowly onto the guy's forehead. "You should have quit when you were ahead," Conn said. "You're like I was with Joe Louis, too dumb to know better!"

There was another incident that comes to the mind of Mary Louise Conn, mostly because it was something she learned about on Mother's Day, and it wasn't the kind of gift she was hoping to get to celebrate the occasion.

Billy had been out the night before with his buddy Jack Cargo, who owned a candy business in Pittsburgh, but was better known for being a loud and curt customer at saloons and night-spots throughout the city. He was a reputed gambler and a good-time guy, much more outgoing than Billy Conn. Cargo and Jimmy Fallon once owned a night club called Jack & Jimmy's New Arena in downtown Pittsburgh. It was on Grant Street and it was a big hit. Conn didn't have any money in the venture. His job was the usual, sit around and sip a drink, smoke a cigarette and offer handshakes and boxing stories to the clientele. He was paid to hang around. Fritzie Zivic drew paydays for similar duty as a greeter at saloons around town.

One Saturday night, Cargo and Conn visited the Gas Light, another popular night spot in Shadyside. They got into a fight and tore the place up. A story about it was in the next day's newspaper. When Mary Louise came across the story, she said to Billy, "Thanks, Hon, for the nice Mother's Day gift."

Mary Louise Conn and her husband Billy, the light-heavyweight champion of the world (1939-41) were a handsome couple.

From the Conn Family Collection

I took Mary Louise and her dutiful son, Tim, to lunch at California Pizza Kitchen at Ross Park Mall. Another time I joined them for lunch, with Billy Conn Jr. in their company on this afternoon at Atria's Tavern & Restaurant in Mt. Lebanon. They were seated at a table beneath a hand-colored portrait of the great boxer, Harry Greb, who was a world champion from Garfield.

There were photos on the surrounding walls of her husband, of Fritzie Zivic, and other boxers of national and local renown. It set the tone for a follow-up conversation.

Somewhere in between those meetings, I had her and Tim as the guest stars at a luncheon series I have hosted for two years at South Hills restaurants called The Good Guys Luncheon. Bill Hillgrove and Dick Groat were guests at one of the luncheons. Hillgrove began by saying, "Jim calls this the Good Guys Luncheon because Old Farts was already taken." Mary Louise and Tim were a big hit at Atria's Restaurant & Tavern in McMurray, a suburb about 15 miles south of downtown Pittsburgh.

They brought along some photos of her and Billy when they were young, a handsome and often-photographed couple. "I was Miss Jersey Shore and Miss Atlantic City, not to boast," she told the roomful of 62 men in a most understated manner.

One of the Good Guys was Eddie Johnston, the former general manager and coach of the Pittsburgh Penguins, best known in Pittsburgh for drafting Mario Lemieux, and in Boston for being the last goalie to play every game in an NHL season and be the backstop for two Stanley Cup teams of the Bruins.

Johnston had boxed for $10 a show as a young man in Montreal. He was Irish and a big fan of Billy Conn. "It was during the Depression and that was a lot of money at the time," he says now. "I often fought in the local prison and there were a lot of guys from my neighborhood in there and so I had my own rooting section."

Like all the men in the room, Johnston enjoyed the stories offered by Mary Louise and Tim Conn. Pictures of her were passed around the room. "I can still see that picture of her in the white bathing suit," said Pat Santelli about three months later. Pat took notes of some of the stories she told.

Near the end of the nearly two-hour session, Mary Louise looked out at the roomful of men and said, "You're a nice-looking group of guys. Call me."

* * *

I paid another visit to Mary Louise Conn at Little Sisters of the Poor on Benton Avenue on the North Side's Brighton Heights section.

This was on Tuesday, August 6, 2016, and she was sitting in her wheelchair under a portico at the entrance to the senior care facility, waiting for me. It was hot out, with temperatures in the high '80s.

She said her sons, Billy Jr. and Tim, had just left. They said they were sorry they missed me, but they had to leave. I had told Tim I'd be over at 1:30 p.m. and it was 1:47 p.m. and I had no idea I was on the clock. I was delayed by construction work on the highways.

Mary Louis Conn told me it was a shame because Tim knew all the stuff about his dad, going back to his earliest days as a boxer. She said Billy Jr. was not as interested and was shy. I was happy, in all honesty, to have Mary Louise to myself. She wore blue slacks, blue matching shoes, a black top, but no make-up this time. She still didn't look her age.

She told me she had never seen her late husband, Billy Conn, in a boxing match. "I didn't like boxing and I wasn't into boxing," she said, "and I wouldn't have wanted to see him get hit, or shed some blood. I couldn't take that.

"Billy boxed to make a living and he was good at it. He wasn't good at school. His dad, also Billy, but we called him Westinghouse, because he worked as a steam fitter for 40 years at Westinghouse in East Pittsburgh, took Billy to work with him one day and that was enough to convince Billy he didn't want to work like that to make a living.

"Billy never really had a job, but boxing was a tough way to make a living. He didn't fight as an amateur. He said if he was going to get hit he wanted to get paid. His manager, Billy Ray, agreed with him. He fought in Pittsburgh for the most part until he was good enough to fight the best guys and then he fought mostly in New York. He could get a better payday there, and he loved New York. And New York loved him. He often stayed there, especially if he got cut up. He didn't want me to see him until he healed up.

"The boxing world was alien to me. I'd gone to a private high school, Mount Mercy in Oakland, and to a private girls' college, Rosemont, on the Main Line in Philadelphia. I thought I was somewhat sophisticated, but I got snapped up by a boxer of all people. My pap, 'Greenfield Jimmy' Smith played for a World Series championship team with the New York Giants baseball team, but he didn't want me marrying any athlete. My pap loved Harry Greb, and he liked boxing. He liked to play golf. But he didn't want me getting involved with a boxer, even one that liked to play golf.

"But Billy was so handsome and he looked after me. He loved me and I loved him. We were different, but that didn't get in the way of our relationship.

"I told you he wasn't made for public life, but he was made for me. Joe Louis liked me, too. And I got along well with Joe's first wife. Her name was Beulah. Joe would say, 'How to do?' when he saw me."

The name Al Abrams came up in the conversation. He was the sports editor of the *Pittsburgh Post-Gazette* in the '30s through the '60s, and Billy Conn was often mentioned in the notes section of his six-times-a-week column, on the far left of the front page of the sports section.

"I didn't care for him," said Mary Louise. "I told him I didn't like the way he portrayed Billy. He said it was more colorful to do it his way. He'd have Billy using all kinds of bad grammar. He once wrote that Billy was going ga-ga over Phyllis McGuire, who was singing with her sisters at the New Arena Club downtown. I told Billy I'd ga-ga him when he got home."

Abrams started the Dapper Dan Club in 1936. This group was one of the sponsors and helped promote a heavyweight championship fight at Forbes Field in 1951 between Ezzard Charles and Jersey Joe Walcott. The Dapper Dan Sports Awards Dinner also had an up-and-coming heavyweight boxer named Cassius Clay make his first Pittsburgh appearance in 1961. He met the Pirates' Willie Stargell at that event at the Hilton Hotel.

"I met Muhammad Ali and he was real friendly," said Mary Louise Conn. "He told Tim, 'Your dad was the best.' Jimmy Cannon, the writer, loved Billy. They were often together. Joey Diven was Billy's best friend. They looked after each other and made sure no one gave them a bad time. Billy also loved Chicago. He had a chance to meet Bob Hope. He had been a boxer early in his life, and he did a fund-raiser for Joe Louis to help him out. I have so many good memories, and I'm doing my best to hold onto them."

Tom McGuire

Eddie Johnston, Mary Louise Conn, author Jim O'Brien and Tim Conn were big hits at Good Guys Luncheon program at Atria's Restaurant & Tavern in McMurray.

Seeing 'Brown Bomber'
Once-in-a-lifetime thrill

Steve "Froggy" Morris, the proprietor of "Froggy's," a popular watering hole near Market Square in downtown Pittsburgh during the '80s and '90s, was a big boxing fan. He had a framed copy of the following article on the wall to the left of his backbar on the first floor of "Froggy's," and pictures and paintings of Pittsburgh sports personalities all over the place. After 25 years in the business, Morris closed the place in 2003.

You're a Joe Louis fan. So when you're visiting Las Vegas in April of 1981, and you see an article in the *Sun* that a "Salute to Joe Louis" will be held there the next night at the Frontier Hotel you want to see him in the flesh—just one more time.

You were in Las Vegas to talk to the sports information directors of the University of Las Vegas and the Mountain West Conference in your role as editor of *Street & Smith's Basketball Yearbook.* You also had gone to a fight gym and were fortunate to find Sugar Ray Leonard there, talking to folks and other writers at ring side during a sparring session.

You had heard Joe Louis wasn't doing that well, his health wasn't good, that he was relying on a pacemaker. Who knows? You might never get the opportunity again. At least those were the thoughts that ran through your mind.

But you didn't know if you would go or not. There's always something else to do in Las Vegas. Lots of competition for your attention.

Some other boxing greats were scheduled to appear, and several of them had a great deal of appeal. Like Sugar Ray Robinson, Rocky Graziano and Tony Zale. You'd like to meet and mix with those greats of the fight game. Anyone would. That's why I always liked to attend all-star games for basketball, baseball and hockey, while many sportswriters hated those assignments.

The Las Vegas Chapter of the National Veterans Boxing Association was putting on the benefit show, and some of the oldtimers were going to don boxing gloves again and shadow box in the ring. For fun. For their old fans.

What sealed the deal about going was bumping into Gene Kilroy, a frizzy-haired former business manager of Muhammad Ali, who had always been helpful when you were on the boxing beat during Ali's second championship reign. Kilroy came from Philadelphia, had a special affection for Irish sportswriters, and wanted to show you his new town. He was then the executive assistant to the chairman of the board at The Dunes Hotel & Casino.

So you make a date with Kilroy to see Joe Louis and the other fight game greats. Kilroy has some trepidations about the old-timers' boxing show. "I hate to see those guys get up there and box now," complained Kilroy. "Who'd want to see Jesse Owens run the 100-yard dash when he was an old man? I hope Muhammad Ali never does this. That's why I hate to see him boxing anymore."

We went to the Frontier Hotel on a Saturday night, April 4, and, as advertised, there was Joe Louis at ringside. He was sitting in a wheelchair, smiling for all those who approached, like Larry Holmes, the reigning heavyweight boxing champion who was scheduled to defend his heavyweight title the following Saturday.

Louis' face was puffy, and tired-looking, more so than when you'd seen him up close eight and ten years earlier, when he was brought to press conferences to help promote some of those Ali and Joe Frazier and George Foreman fights at places such as New York, Miami Beach, Houston and Las Vegas. He still had the glad hand for everybody, but it was a limp hand. The strength was gone. And his heart needed help from a pacemaker.

Jimmy Cannon once wrote of him: "Joe Louis was a credit to his race—the human race."

It was still special to see him, the way it was always special to see a Jack Dempsey, greeting customers at his Broadway restaurant, or Joe DiMaggio, Red Grange, Bronko Nagurski, Maurice Richard, Jean Beliveau, George Mikan, Bob Cousy, Sugar Ray Robinson and Rocky Graziano. They were all greats when you were a kid, reading profiles and reminiscences about them in sports magazines, so they were larger-than-life. Sugar Ray Robinson's last fight was at the Civic Arena in Pittsburgh, a defeat at the hands of No. 1 ranked contender Joey Archer on November 10, 1965, when you were home on leave from the military service and were in attendance.

It's the same sort of thinking that prompted you to visit the boyhood home of Babe Ruth and the cemetery grave site of Edgar Allen Poe when you were in Baltimore for a Yankees-Orioles ballgame.

At least, Louis was in Las Vegas, as promised.

Sugar Ray Robinson was a no-show. Rocky Graziano backed out at the last moment because he wanted paid to appear. I recall that Rick Barry didn't attend an ABA reunion once in Indianapolis for the same reason. Rick requested money to make the event and his demand was rejected.

Being a Pittsburgher, you mentioned Billy Conn to Louis, and that elicited a purr of a laugh. "He was just out here to see me," said Louis, straining to talk. "He's always been a friend."

That was it. I couldn't press the conversation because Louis was there for everyone to see and share. To shoot with Polaroids. It wouldn't have been fair to anyone if I overstayed my welcome.

Louis left early, telling Joey Curtis, who put the program together, that he was too tired to stay on, that he was going home. He wasn't there by the time that Billy Graham, an old favorite on the Friday Night Fights on TV, sparred playfully with Art "The Golden Boy: Aragon."

Afterward, there was a private party for the participants and fight folks and media types. It looked like a casting party for "Guys and Dolls," the Damon Runyon-inspired Broadway production. Graham was telling George Abrams how great he was, and George Abrams was telling Graham how great he was. That's the way most of the conversations went.

Also there were Joey Maxim, Joey Giambra and Lou Nova. Tony Zale was there, a real champion from Chicago. Zale had fought Billy Conn once in New York, too, and talked about Billy and some of the other famous fighters from the Pittsburgh area, such as Fritzie Zivic, Sammy Angott, Billy Soose, Frank Klaus and Teddy Yarosz.

You won't forget those reflections. You thought about what long-time fight fans, guys you know, would have given to be there, too. Zale was wearing a hearing aid and you had to repeat some of the questions, but it was worth the effort.

Conn had been to Las Vegas a few days earlier, as Louis had said. Conn had gone there to visit Milt Jaffe, the former Pittsburgher who once managed him along with Johnny Ray. Jaffe was in bad health, too. Steelers' owner Art Rooney had recently visited Jaffe, a former business associate, on his return from the NFL Owners' Meeting in Hawaii. You went to cream-colored stucco church on Maui on St. Patrick's Day with Wellington Mara, the owner of the New York Giants, Jim Murray, the general manager of the Philadelphia Eagles, and Rooney and their wives. That, too, was a memorable experience.

When Joe Louis died of a heart attack on April 12, 1981, only 14 hours after watching from ringside as Larry Holmes successfully defended his World Boxing Council title against Trevor Berbick at Caesars Palace, people mourned throughout the world.

Everyone loved Joe Louis. Conn received phone calls from everywhere, to eulogize his good friend and former foe in two celebrated title fights. He was glad he had seen him near the end.

Rooney was a fan of Joe Louis, too, and boxing in general. He'd been an Olympic-worthy fighter himself as a young man. "He was really a nice guy," Rooney related to me when I visited him in his office. "When you're in the limelight like that, and the champ as long (1937-1949) as he was, usually somebody has it in for you. I never heard anybody put the zing on him. Never an unkind word about him."

You called Kilroy, who had looked in on Louis from time to time, and cared about his well-being, to see how he was taking it. He had gone out to dinner with Louis and some fight folks after the Holmes-Berbick match. They ate in the coffee shop at Caesars Palace. This was on the eve of Joe's death.

"Joe was alert, he joked and laughed," recalled Kilroy. "He couldn't comprehend some things, and he didn't talk that well. But he seemed to be enjoying himself. People stopped by the table and asked him how he was doing, while he was trying to eat. He was used to that. But he'd put down his knife or his fork and reach out his hand. He was truly a man of greatness."

From the Conn Family photo collection

GOOD SOLDIERS—Billy Conn and Joe Louis both put on boxing exhibitions for the troops in 1942 during their stints in the U.S. Army during World War II.

Cy Obremski
No one could touch his Golden Gloves team at Glen-Hazel Boys Club

I came to Kansas City on February 14, 1965, riding on a bus from Louisville to get there. I was in the Army and I was wearing my dress greens. I had drawn a rather cozy and safe assignment after ten weeks of basic training at Fort Knox, Kentucky. There's a lot of heavy metal at Fort Knox—gold bars and tanks.

I can still see this sergeant major standing on the company street at Fort Knox reading out our next assignment posts. He hesitated when he came to my name. I was not one of his favorites. "O'Brien, James," he shouted. "What the hell kind of an assignment is this? 603 Hardesty Avenue, Kansas City, Missouri!"

I had originally been assigned to be a stenographer at Fort Benjamin Harrison, Indiana, but Beano Cook wrote to Robert McNamara, the Secretary of Defense, saying that would be a waste of my time and work skills. Next thing I knew a General Robert A. O'Brien, who was in charge of military deployment, was changing my orders and sending me instead as an editor at the U.S. Army Home Town News Center at, yes, 603 Hardesty Avenue.

I was excited about going to Kansas City. I knew the song "Kansas City" by Wilbert Harrison, I saw towns like Kansas City and Wichita in so many western movies as a kid, and I knew they had major league sports teams.

What I did not know, at first, was that 603 Hardesty Avenue, an abandoned department store warehouse, was located only a few blocks from Municipal Stadium on Brooklyn Avenue in Kansas City. I could walk there, which was a good thing, because I didn't have a car. I had my own room, a large cubicle, with no door. It was Spartan to say the least. I was responsible for leading a team of servicemen and a civilian secretarial staff in sending stories about the activities of men and women in the Army to their hometown newspapers.

Thanks once again to Beano Cook, I had connections with the A's of the American League in baseball and the Chiefs in the American Football League. I would work in the press boxes for both teams on my own time.

I also knew that a young writer named Ernest Hemingway had been a reporter for the *Kansas City Star.* His typewriter was on display in the lobby of that newspaper, as I would later discover. That added to my enchantment with Kansas City.

The first night in town I saw a neon sign outside of a stage theatre in downtown Kansas City that read "God's Little Acre." I had read the book by Erskine Caldwell and I had seen the movie starring Robert Ryan, Aldo Ray, Tina Louise, Fay Spain and Buddy Hackett. Future TV stars such as Michael Landon, Vic Morrow and Jack Lord were also in the cast of that movie.

I went to see the stage show my first night in Kansas City and reported later to the Home Town News Center. I recall seeing signs posted on telegraph poles about the Golden Gloves Boxing Tournament coming up at the Municipal Auditorium later that month.

It made me think about Cy Obremski and the Glen-Hazel Boys Club. I had covered that team for my hometown newspaper and they dominated the boxing tournament for over 12 years at that time.

The next day I received a letter from my mother telling me that Cy Obremski had died on February 12, 1965. He was 50 at the time. He worked in the Jones & Laughlin Steel Mill on the South Side and died in a nearby hospital after having a heart attack.

Once, when I was wearing that same dress green uniform in downtown Kansas City, I saw former President Harry Truman getting out of a limousine in front of the Muehlbach Hotel. I didn't know at the time that he came to town to celebrate his birthday each year. I went over to him and extended a hand and shook his hand. I thought about how that hand had signed the papers to allow the U.S. to drop the atomic bombs on Hiroshima and Nagasaki in early

August of 1945—the only times that nuclear weapons have been used in war.

During the short time that I went to the Glen-Hazel Boys Club at the community center high above Glenwood and Hazelwood, Cy Obremski looked after me and made sure he never over-matched me. He always pitted me against kids of similar size and similar skill sets.

President Harry S. Truman

Tina Louise

Wilbert Harrison

Lenny Dawson

"I never could give anybody hell. I told the truth and they thought it was hell."
—President Harry S. Truman

Sonny Liston
Memories of watching the baleful bear working out for fight in Pittsburgh

I can still see Sonny Liston's foreboding, baleful so-dark black face. Like it was yesterday. He was slamming his gloved fists into a heavy bag hanging on a chain from the ceiling of a dimly-lit gym in the East Liberty section of Pittsburgh. This was in November of 1968 and he was training for a fight the following week with Roger Rischer at the Civic Arena in The Lower Hill.

His eyes were large and they were focused on a large target. It was difficult to take your eyes off his eyes. "He was born with dead man's eyes," *Vanity Fair* contributing editor Nick Tosches wrote of Sonny Liston.

Liston was in Pittsburgh for ten days. It was said he visited several Pittsburgh bars at night and enjoyed his stay immensely. That was Sonny's lifestyle. He was a big man, 6-5, and always looked annoyed. No one wanted to mess with Sonny Liston He had underworld connections. He had done time in the Missouri State Prison for armed robbery.

Liston had been an enforcer for mobsters, a guy who was sent to break your arm or leg if you forgot to pay a gambling debt, a bouncer at late-night drinking establishments. The way he crushed some of his opponents in his early days in the ring, Liston looked unbeatable.

His name was in the newspapers again, because Monday, May 25, 2015, marked the 50th anniversary of his infamous fight with Cassius Clay in Lewiston, Maine. Clay would later change his name to Muhammad Ali and become one of the most controversial yet popular boxers of all time. He became much more than a former boxer.

Clay had won an earlier decision over Liston for the world heavyweight championship in Miami Beach and this was a rematch. Liston hit the floor in the first round and stayed there, rolling over on his back. There's a famous photo of Clay standing over him waving his right gloved hand, challenging him to get up.

Few could figure out what happened. It was called a "phantom punch." It brought shame to the game of boxing. It was an embarrassment for Lewiston, Maine, which was hoping this fight would put it on the map. It did, but for the wrong reasons.

I spent a weekend in May of 2015 at the Sports Card & Memorabilia Show at Sewall Center on the Robert Morris University campus, and a young woman sold me a ticket for a closed-circuit showing of that Clay-Liston fight at the Syria Mosque that was once part of the University of Pittsburgh landscape. Remember when major fights were shown by closed-circuit at movie theatres? Now they are on pay-tv.

The ticket, which appears here, originally sold for $7.50. It cost me $10.00. "Someone here told me you were associated with Ali," said the young woman. I told her I covered his title fight with Joe Frazier from a ringside seat at Madison Square Garden, and some of his other fights when I worked for *The New York Post* in the '70s.

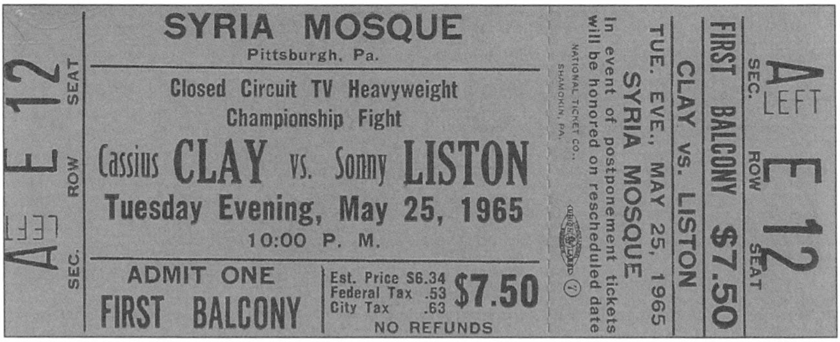

SYRIA MOSQUE
Pittsburgh, Pa.

Closed Circuit TV Heavyweight
Championship Fight

Cassius **CLAY** vs. Sonny **LISTON**

Tuesday Evening, May 25, 1965
10:00 P. M.

ADMIT ONE

FIRST BALCONY

Est. Price $6.34
Federal Tax .53 **$7.50**
City Tax .63
NO REFUNDS

SEAT A 12
ROW E
SEC. A 12
LEFT
In event of postponement tickets will be honored on rescheduled date
NATIONAL TICKET CO.
SHAMOKIN, PA.
TUE. EVE., MAY 25, 1965
CLAY vs. LISTON
SYRIA MOSQUE
FIRST BALCONY $7.50
SEC. A
ROW E
SEAT 12
LEFT

Ticket for closed-circuit telecast of Clay-Liston fight here in Pittsburgh at Syria Mosque.

Seeing stories about this fight as the anniversary neared reminded me of another Liston fight, the one with Roger Rischer in Pittsburgh.

Rischer was a longshoreman from San Francisco and a journeyman fighter. Liston was making a comeback from his shameful performance in Lewiston. He had won nine

Sonny Liston works out on speed bag.

Motor Square Garden still stands in East Liberty. It was the scene of many great fights in Pittsburgh.

straight fights, seven by KO and two by TKO, most of them lasting about three rounds. He was one of the strongest punchers in the sport.

This match-up at the Civic Arena was for the benefit of former boxing promoter Ben Anolik, who was Pennsylvania's first heart transplant patient. Liston donated his purse to Anolik's cause and Rischer pocketed about $10,000.

They say boxing is a violent game, but this exceeded that reputation when all three of the featured figures were dead just over a year after the fight. Anolik died a few weeks later of a failing heart. Rischer was shot in the head in a street fight in San Francisco. He was 37. His nickname had been "Roger the Dodger," but he obviously failed to dodge some bullets in a street brawl.

Liston was found dead in his home in Las Vegas, the victim of an overdose of heroin. He was 38. Liston was known to dread needles and there was suspicion that someone else administered the shot that killed him. Like the fight in Lewiston, the circumstances of his passing were suspicious.

At the time of their fight, Robert Lipsyte of *The New York Times* referred to Liston as "a bum," and to Rischer as "a bum's bum."

They were both stiffs by the time they met in Pittsburgh. Still, there was a fascination in just looking for the first time into Sonny Liston's face, the one that had scared so many with "that baleful glare," that week before his fight here. Once the dark destroyer, he still seemed more than Rischer could handle alone.

Liston trained only a few blocks from our apartment, the Pennley Park Apartments at Penn and Negley that were fairly new when Kathie Churchman and I were married in August of 1967. We'd been there 15 months when Liston came to town.

Some of my neighbors at the Pennley Park Apartments included Pirates Roberto Clemente, Maury Wills, Alvin O'Neal McBean and Juan Pizzaro. I'd see them coming and going routinely and I still scold myself for not getting closer to Clemente.

My favorite in the building was Moe Becker, one of the famed "Iron Dukes" of Duquesne University (1940-41) basketball, and then the coach at Braddock High School. He'd see us in a mini-market and demonstrate his latest strategy, using my wife Kathie to set picks.

It was easy enough for me to walk from our apartment to the nearby second-floor gym. I watched Liston's workouts each day for a week. The gym was right out of Hollywood, like the ones developed from Budd Schulberg's book "The Harder They Fall." Everyone in the gym who wasn't boxing looked like the movie actor Edward G. Robinson or the old boxer "Two Ton" Tony Galento.

There were always so many interesting characters in the ring world. It was my favorite sport to cover and now I can't name you one heavyweight boxer, unless the Ukrainian Klitschko Brothers are still boxing.

It all comes back now. Liston working on a speed bag that had cement blocks jumping up and down on the platform above, and you wondered whether the whole thing would collapse on his head. His sweat splotching the wooden floor as he flailed away at the heavy bag, shaking Dick Sadler, the man who was holding the heavy bag as Liston banged away at it.

Sadler, who also trained George Foreman and other top-notch fighters in his day, was standing behind the bag, leaning into it to offer resistance to Liston's slam-bang attack. Sadler's face was alongside the bag, where Liston's right hand would strike, again and again, and on-lookers winced whenever Sonny's smashing right flashed past Sadler's face. Yes, I learned, he had knocked Sadler down doing that once before.

Sonny Liston had the biggest fists of any heavyweight fighter in history. They measured 15½ inches around and he had to have custom made boxing gloves. His left jab "pushed through you," according to one trainer for an opposing fighter, and he had a great right hook. He crushed many of his opponents, and most experts thought he'd crush Clay. "He was the most unconquerable of heavyweight boxers," noted Nick Tosches, the New York-based author of "The Devil and Sonny Liston."

Clay carried on like a madman before the fight, and some thought Liston became wary of him because he couldn't believe some of his antics, and what he was saying about him before their fights. But Clay or Ali was afraid before most big fights, in a manner similar to the Steelers' Terry Bradshaw on the eve of four Super Bowls. Members of the Steelers' support staff just about had to hold Bradshaw's hands to comfort him before a big game.

Sonny skipped rope, so gently for such a big brute, to the loud sounds of "Night Train," as the 45 rpm spun on a little plastic machine nearby. He was something to watch when he skipped rope, one of the best in the boxing business, they said. Clay could make that rope sing, too. You'd learn later that Liston always skipped rope to "Night Train," the tune to which he and his wife, Geraldine, often danced to at night. It was Geraldine who discovered him in their bedroom in Las Vegas after he died.

There was no drug apparatus to be found in the bedroom. Just the mark on Sonny's body. The medical examiner performed an autopsy and said there was heroin in his blood.

Thanks to the Internet, you can now watch a great short documentary called "Sonny Liston's Greatest Hits," in which he displays his great skill at jumping rope, and flooring the likes of Cleveland Williams (several times), Zora Folley, Floyd Patterson and Eddie Machen, all to the James Brown version of "Night Train." You should watch that while you are reading this chapter. You might want to start skipping rope if not taking up boxing.

One of those days at the gym in East Liberty, Sonny showed up, unbelievably enough, wearing red trunks and a soiled-looking well-wrinkled yellow mustard-colored T-shirt that said: "Poland Springs Resort Hotel" front and back. It was like Davey Crockett wearing a T-shirt that had an image of The Alamo across the chest.

Why, one wondered, would the man want to wear something that reminded anyone of Lewiston, Maine, and

212

that dreadful showing against Cassius Clay, since known as Muhammad Ali? Lewiston was the smallest town ever to host a heavyweight title match since Jack Dempsey defended his title in Shelby, Montana. Most of the populace of Lewiston were French-speaking and poor mill workers.

That one round knockout and that phantom punch?

The town never recovered. The resort hotel was turned into a home for wayward girls. The T-shirt was wrinkled. It's unlikely it had ever been laundered. It wasn't sanitized, for sure, or martinized.

"You just reaches into the bag," said Sadler, when I asked him about Liston's choice of T-shirt, "and whatever you comes up with, that's what you wears!"

I figured one of Sadler's skills as boxing trainer was not doing laundry too often. That Poland Springs Resort T-shirt looked like it had been a long time since it had a bout with soap or detergent or Mr. Clean.

Rischer put up a good front that week, but he sagged to the apron after Sonny slammed a lazy left hook into his ribs and knocked him out in the third round of that fight on November 12, 1968. Before the fight, Rischer had told me, "I fear no man who walks this earth."

After the fight, I told Liston what Rischer had said.

"Man, when he got up on that ring," said Sonny, smiling at his own humor, "he wasn't on this earth no more."

Liston was not known as a good interview, but that remark was the sort of line more associated with Cassius "The Lip" Clay or Muhammad Ali.

I later had one of the four best seats in the house for the Ali-Frazier fight. During the week before the fight, the greatest sports event I ever covered, Frazier was working a hand exerciser and Ali his jaw, citing all his previous conquests, and pounding the table for emphasis at a press conference at Toots Shor's Restaurant in Manhattan.

When Ali got to talking about Liston, the man he stopped suspiciously twice, Frazier jumped up and shouted, "Forget Sonny Liston! You're going back in time twenty years! Quit talking about all your victories! You ain't fighting Sonny Liston! Sonny Liston is all over!"

Sonny Liston was sent to a Missouri prison for armed robbery as a young man. It was there a priest encouraged him to box and he won the prison heavyweight title and then turned pro.

He had several altercations with police after that. He broke the knee of one policeman. That same policeman, a black man, held a gun to Liston's head and pushed Liston into an alleyway and told him the police weren't going to put up his nonsense anymore. He was told that "no fuckin' nigger like you is going to abuse us anymore." He was told to get out of town and he obliged.

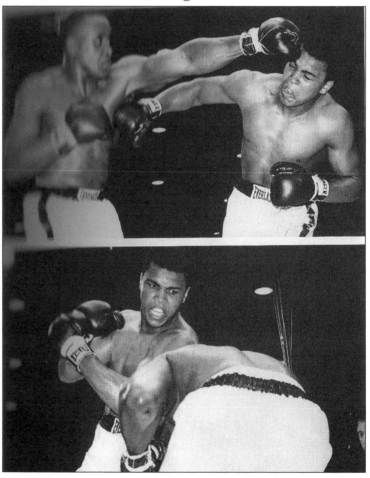

Cassius Clay, later to be called Muhammad Ali, boxes Sonny Liston in Lewiston, Maine.

The death of Rocky Marciano

My wife Kathie and I had moved to Miami in the winter of 1969 where I was going to be covering the Miami Dolphins in their final year in the American Football League, as well as boxing and basketball for *The Miami News.*

We were there, on September 1, when the headline of the Miami newspapers reported in WORLD WAR BREAKS OUT type on their front page that the great boxing champion Rocky Marciano had died in an airplane crash in Iowa.

This was the day when Rocky was to return to his home and family in Miami to celebrate his 46th birthday. This was big news.

Even today, people who knew Marciano will tell you he died because he was so cheap. He was notorious for being tight with his money. He had hired an amateur pilot to take him in a small single engine Cessna 172H airplane from Chicago to Des Moines, Iowa. The pilot had no experience at night flying or flying in bad weather and his plane was low on fuel. It was dark and it was raining hard.

The plane crashed just two miles from the Newton, Iowa airport where Glenn Belz, a 37-year-old pilot, was attempting to land it. He had bypassed an earlier opportunity to land at a larger airport in Des Moines because he might have lost his pilot's license over the mistakes he had made and his failure to heed warnings from the traffic controller at the airport tower.

Marciano was on his way to deliver a speech for the son of a boxer friend Louis Fratto, and then was going to fly home to celebrate his birthday and his wife's birthday. They had adopted a son named Rocco Kevin, who was 17-months-old and just starting to walk. Rocky wanted to see that.

Frankie Farrell, 21-year-old friend of Marciano, was also on the plane. He and Belz were thrown 30 feet from the plane, and the plane's engine landed on Belz's chest. Rocky Marciano was pinned in the wreckage and a piece of shrapnel had pierced his head.

Iowa had been the scene of two other airplane crashes that gained national attention. On January 18, 1960, the Minneapolis Lakers team was on a charter flight on a DC-3 that went down in a cornfield in Iowa. No one was killed. I have heard the tale of that incident told by "Hot Rod" Hundley and Bob "Slick" Leonard, two members of that team, during the years I was covering pro basketball. They have turned it into a funny story. They have to laugh or they'd cry.

That was not the case when three Rock 'n Roll icons were killed in a plane crash near Clear Lake, Iowa on February 3, 1959. Richie Valens, Buddy Holly and The Big Bopper lost their lives in that crash. Waylon Jennings had to get off that plane just before take-off because there was too much weight on the plane.

"Only a man who knows what it is like to be defeated can reach down to the bottom of his soul and come up with the extra ounce of power it takes to win when the match is even."
—**Muhammad Ali**

Don Elbaum
Promotes a dream world

"Boxing is a sickness and I love it."

DON ELBAUM
Boxing's
Don Quixote

Old-timers who frequented the 5th Street Gym loved to swap stories about the golden days of boxing. Oh yes, those were the days my friend, we thought they'd never end...

"They're like veterans talking about Omaha Beach," Dr. Ferdie Pacheco, the fighters' physician, observed one fine day.

On and on they'd go, wonderfully, filling the close air with tall tales about Dempsey, Louis, Marciano and Conn. They talked mostly of white fighters because they themselves were white. It's as simple as that.

They got a kick in June of the summer of 1969 when Don Elbaum blew in and told them about this kid of his who could have been another Billy Conn.

"He was even better looking than Conn," Elbaum was saying. "He was beautiful."

Elbaum was beautiful, too. Also, almost unbelievable. As a character, not as a story-teller. Cincinnati-born but working out of Erie, Pennsylvania and more often his two-ton suitcase, Elbaum might have been boxing's last hope. He did his best to keep the game alive in Pittsburgh and thereabouts, rivertowns like McKeesport and Weirton.

He was, indeed, the sport's Man of LaMancha. His quest seemed like an impossible dream. Elbaum promoted fight shows and managed fighters (who signed contracts with his father). It's illegal, but the boxing commissioners looked the other way. Without the likes of Elbaum, there's no cash anyway in the commissioners' coffers.

Elbaum lived on Will Street in Erie, Pennsylvania and in his world where there's a Will there's a Way. He would do whatever it took to put a boxing show on somewhere.

Somewhere on the horizon, perhaps in some nether land, Elbaum saw a fortune to be made in the fight game. It was his life's work. He searched for his Billy Conn. He'd have been satisfied with another Jerry Quarry.

Elbaum, 33 at the time, was an indefatigable fight promoter. He had booked 16 shows over a 20-week span when he showed up at the 5th Street Gym. A few weeks earlier, when a fighter failed to show in McKeesport, Pennsylvania, my wife's hometown, he couldn't come up with any bodies in a nearby graveyard, Elbaum went into the ring himself.

He exchanged knockdowns with his opponent – which either says a lot for Elbaum or a lot more about the caliber of boxers he dredges up – and lost a four-round decision. The story made newspapers everywhere the next day.

Elbaum, who looked a lot like Buddy Hackett when he squeezed his eyes shut as he smiled and told this story, was happy he was still able to tell it.

"He's amazin', absolutely amazin'," said Chris Dundee, the Miami Beach promoter. "I don't know how he does it. This guy is a throw-back to the old-time carpetbagger days. You never heard of the fighters or some of the towns this guy puts on shows in."

Elbaum was still talking about this kid who could've been another Billy Conn.

His name was Jack Rodgers, and he was making a living as a model in Uniontown, Pennsylvania, where modeling opportunities are obviously limited, as were, unfortunately, his boxing skills. He also sold shoes at a local shop when pressed for cash.

"I tried to talk Playboy magazine into making him the first male Playmate-of-the-Month. I could see that centerfold," cried Elbaum, closing his eyes in ecstasy. "Jack Rodgers lying there, across three pages in a fig leaf."

I had seen Rodgers back in Pittsburgh and he was, indeed, a handsome light-heavyweight the same as Conn. That is, until he tossed a punch. "I brought him along perfectly," exalted Elbaum. "I dug up the deepest graves to get him the right opponents. I just about had Dick Tiger set for $75,000 and a title fight, when it happened."

Rodgers, whose record was 25-1, losing only to Joey Giardello in Philadelphia (he wuz robbed, of course), was in a warm-up against a workhorse in McKeesport, a local brawler named Mert Brownfield.

"Mert was in shape," sighed Elbaum. Rodgers was crying to the referee about a low blow that night when Brownfield belted him on the chin. Jack Rodgers, the title shot, the $75,000, and Elbaum's dream, all crashed, ingloriously, to the canvas.

"I knew Jack couldn't beat me," said Brownfield.

Elbaum had this other Irish heavyweight, Jimmy McClain, undefeated and coming along good. A real crowd-pleaser. "I put him in with Brownfield, who was on a comeback then and had lost six straight," said Elbaum. "So what's he do? He knocks out McClain."

Which brought Elbaum to Miami Beach with, of all people, Mert Brownfield.

After Brownfield lowered the boom on Rodgers, Elbaum, never a sore loser, signed him up. Brownfield was set to go against Rufus Brassell in a scheduled 10-round headliner at Miami Beach Auditorium.

In Brownfield's previous fight on the Beach, in December of 1968, he got off the floor to stop Tony Ventura. ("I needed Ventura knocked out," cried Chris Dundee, "like I need another hole in my head!")

Mert was in shape, according to Elbaum and Dundee nods his head in approval, watching Brownfield flail away in front of a tall mirror. Two weeks earlier, Brownfield scored an eight-round TKO over Art "Curly" Miller and less than an hour later he was at work, shoveling coal into a hungry open hearth furnace at U.S. Steel's National Tube Works in McKeesport.

"They were short on help," explained Mert.

Asked about Elbaum's reaction to his KO'ing his dream, Brownfield said, "I know he didn't like it. I spoiled it for him. He cursed me cause I messed up his money."

Brassell was being boosted on the Beach as a comer. "He looks like Clay," said Elbaum. He couldn't help himself. That's just the way he talked.

Brassell beat Brownfield. So much for Mert's comeback and Elbaum's latest dream.

* * *

I found scraps of paper from a notebook in which I had scribbled notes from an interview with Elbaum back in 1969. It was in a file folder marked Pittsburgh Boxing.

Elbaum told me he had an uncle named Danny Greenstein, from New Bedford, Massachusetts, who had been an outstanding amateur boxer in his day. "He won 50 straight," said Elbaum. "Al Weil tried to sign him. My uncle was my idol."

Al Weil was regarded as one of the greatest, if crooked, fight managers of this time and guided Rocky Marciano to the heavyweight title.

Elbaum visited his uncle one summer and heard people talking about how tough he was. He heard a kid coming out of a movie saying John Wayne couldn't beat Danny Greenstein. "That did it," said Elbaum, "I was hooked on my uncle and on boxing.

"There is no sport like boxing. Once you're in it, you can't get it out of your system. Boxing is a sickness and I love it."

Elbaum's earliest promotion was a Wild West show in Western Pennsylvania. He moved from that into boxing shows. He would do anything to make it work.

He once posed as a doctor at a pre-fight physical in a small town in Virginia. He had a stethoscope draped on his chest and he said a few "hmms" and pronounced two fighters fit to box. No one suspected anything.

He promoted Sugar Ray Robinson's last pro fight. It was against Joey Archer at the Civic Arena in Pittsburgh on November 10, 1965.

Elbaum brought some old boxing trunks to the pre-fight press conference and said they were the trunks Robinson wore in his first pro fight 25 years earlier. No one was more excited about that than Sugar Ray Robinson.

It turned out Elbaum was lying. Sugar Ray was keenly disappointed. He didn't know about Elbaum's Conn game.

He was more disappointed when he lost his last fight—the 210th pro bout of his glorious career. Archer won a 10-round decision. Robinson is regarded as the best boxer ever. Archer floored him during that fight and Robinson struggled all evening. I was home on leave from the Army and wrote about the fight in *Pittsburgh Weekly Sports*.

Elbaum got in trouble for failing to report $570,000 in income from 1983 through 1985 and did some time in Allenwood Prison in Western Pennsylvania. "I was something of a celebrity in there, being a boxing promoter and telling the guys stories about boxing," he said proudly. "I shouldn't have gone to prison. I never got in any trouble and I had good character."

George Foreman floored Rufus Brassell three times in the first round in Foreman's hometown of Houston on March 31, 1970. The fight lasted 2 minutes and 42 seconds. Brassell had beaten McKeesport's Mert Brownfield a year earlier on Miami Beach.

We're never going
to be an ambassador to Ireland

H ere's a tough question for the day: What do Art Rooney Sr., Jim O'Brien and Billy Conn have in common?

Well, for one thing, we are never going to be confused with the Holy Trinity.

But the answer is that we all blew our chances to become America's ambassador to Ireland. In each case it's because of something we said. That's often the source of difficulty for anyone who's Irish.

Billy Conn, of course, was the most famous fighter ever to come out of Pittsburgh, born and bred in the city's East End.

He fought Joe Louis for the heavyweight boxing title twice. In their first fight, back on July 18, 1941, there were 54,486 fans on hand at the Polo Grounds in New York, and that included an estimated 6,000 Conn supporters who traveled from Pittsburgh to New York to root for their favorite fighter.

Conn had campaigned as a light heavyweight fighter and had won the title in that division. But he surrendered the title to move up and fight Louis. Louis had been on top for four years. He was 27 and Conn was 24. Conn weighed in at 169 pounds and Louis at 199 pounds, but those weights were not the ones that appeared in that day's late editions of the afternoon newspapers. They didn't want the boxing fans to know how much bigger Louis was than Conn.

Conn was so popular in Pittsburgh in those days, by the way, that a Pirates' game at Forbes Field was inter-rupted the evening of their first fight as they broadcast the fight over the public address system and play resumed after the fight was concluded. Imagine that.

Conn was a clever boxer, savvy and quick on his feet. Conn was beating Louis going into the unlucky 13th round. He was advised to stay away from Louis, who packed a lethal punch, and tie up the heavier fighter through the

15th round. But Conn's huge ego got the best of him. He was determined to knock out the great Joe Louis. That would impress his buddies back in East Liberty.

Conn went after Louis in that 13th round, pressing him with a flurry of punches. Louis knocked out Conn with a right to the jaw. Afterward, when Conn was questioned about his strategy, he responded, "What's the sense of being Irish if you can't be stupid?"

That didn't boost his popularity in Ireland or with the Irish in New York or even Pittsburgh, for that matter.

Years later, Conn told Louis, "You should have let me win that fight. We'd have made so much money with a rematch."

And Louis told Conn, "I let you have the title for 12 rounds and you didn't know what to do with it."

Conn and Louis met again, after they both had been in the military service, and it was no contest this time. Conn looked out of condition. Louis knocked out Conn in the 8th round on July 19, 1946.

Before their second fight, when reporters prodded Louis beforehand about how he could handle the swifter Conn, and he responded with one of the most remarkable lines of all time: "He can run but he can't hide."

Conn and Louis were both popular pugilists and became "America's Guests" when their fighting days were over. Both worked as greeters in Las Vegas hotels. Both were often paid to attend big fights to lend their presence to the event. I had an opportunity to talk to both of them on different occasions when there was a big fight in Las Vegas.

Promoters paid to get Conn to come to Ireland in the summer of 1972 to help boost the gate for a fight between Muhammad Ali and an opponent named Alvin Lewis that was held in Dublin. That fight took place on July 19, 1972. Conn was the toast of the town in Dublin, treated like a king wherever he went.

As he was about to return home to America, he was interviewed at the airport in Dublin. "So what did you think of the homeland?" one Irish newspaperman asked Conn.

Without thinking twice, which was his nature, Conn came back with this: "I'm just glad my mother didn't miss the boat."

And that's how Conn blew any chance he might have had of becoming America's ambassador to Ireland.

Art Rooney Sr. had been a top-notch boxer in his heyday, even qualifying for the Olympic Games in Antwerp, Belgium. He declined to go. Sammy Mossberg went instead and won the gold medal. Upon his return to America, Mossberg fought Art Rooney in Pittsburgh and Rooney beat him again.

Art Rooney and Barney McGinley promoted fights in Pittsburgh. Their biggest promotion was the fight at Forbes Field in which Archie Moore won the heavyweight championship against Ezzard Charles. That was on a 10-round decision on May 20, 1946.

Rooney was quite proud of his Irish heritage, mind you, but Tunch Ilkin, the former Steelers' standout tackle who remains on the scene as an analyst to Bill Hillgrove's play-by-play call of the Steelers' games on radio here, recalls how Mr. Rooney often greeted him.

Ilkin was born in Turkey. In fact, his beautiful mother once held the crown of Miss Turkey. Ilkin grew up in Chicago, but often boasted that he was born in Turkey. So whenever Mr. Rooney spotted Ilkin, his favorite player of the 70s, according to his son, Art Rooney Jr., he would always say:

"Tunch, my boy, how are the Turks doing? Are they still killing each other like the Irish?" I can still get a chuckle out of Ilkin when I remind him of that exchange.

That's how Art Rooney blew his chances of ever being named an ambassador to Ireland.

Then there's my story. As Billy Conn said, "What's the sense of being Irish if you can't be stupid?"

I was offered two positions by Dan Rooney through his right-hand man Joe Gordon, the team's publicist during their first four Super Bowl triumphs, and into the '80s.

It was in the mid-80s that Gordon offered me the job as editor of a weekly newspaper the Steelers planned to

Joe Louis is the winner by a knockout in the 13th round of first fight with Billy Conn before 54,487 fans at the Polo Grounds in New York on June 18,1941. That is Conn, at far right, being tended to by famed trainer Whitey Bimstein. Joe Louis and Billy Conn sign contracts for their first fight in New York with famed promoter Mike Jacobs looking over their shoulders. See how everyone is mugging for the camera? Boxing people are notorious for knowing how to get their faces in the picture.

publish called *Steelers Digest*. I was offered $35,000 and told I could continue to write books about Pittsburgh sports and do free-lance writing on my own.

I accepted the job and kept it about as long as Conn had the heavyweight championship crown in his hands, and then turned it down. I just didn't want to go back on the road with the Steelers, or any sports team for that matter.

I recommended two beat writers for the assignment, both working on Westmoreland County newspapers at the time. One was Bob Labriola and the other was Vic Ketchman. Labriola took the job and still has it. Ketchman, by coincidence, ended up editing a similar weekly for the Jacksonville Jaguars. When that paper folded, Ketchman became the keeper of the Jaguars' website. He has since taken his talents to Green Bay.

Gordon didn't think either of them would be interested since they were writing for daily newspapers, but I thought they would jump at the chance. It was a better job than the one they had, that's why. Gordon later came back with another offer. He said that Dan Rooney wanted me to serve on the board for the American-Ireland Fund. Rooney and Tony O'Reilly, the former Irish rugby hero who ran the Heinz Co. on the North Side, were the movers and shakers behind the American-Ireland Fund.

The organization raised money for peace-keeping efforts in Ireland.

I never felt the same way about Ireland as the Rooneys or the McGinleys. My grandparents on both sides were born in America. Then, too, we lived on a street in Hazelwood where most of the residents were of Italian heritage. I'm not into genealogy. I know there's no money or royalty in the bloodlines and I fear what research might turn up in the way of knaves and thieves.

As a kid, it never made much sense to me to pound my chest and proclaim that I was Irish. All it would get me was to have some Italian kids pounding on my chest in response. So I kept a low profile on St. Patrick's Day. Columbus Day was a bigger deal in my neighborhood.

So when Gordon asked me to be on the board for the American-Ireland fund I declined. Worse yet, like Conn I was a bit of a smart-ass. I said, "I'm not from Ireland. I'm from Hazelwood."

There went my chances of ever being America's ambassador to Ireland. I realize now that was a big mistake on my part. I don't think Dan Rooney has ever forgiven me for that retort. He always looks like he's wearing shoes a size too small when he sees me coming. Either that or he has a bad case of hemorrhoids. I'd be willing to tote his suitcases if I could accompany him to Ireland these days.

I remember that whenever I visited the Steelers' offices and was wearing a suit or a nice sports coat. Art Rooney would see me coming and holler out, "Hey, Dan, come out here and see this dude from Hazelwood!" I might have been living in Upper St. Clair at the time, but to Mr. Rooney, I was from Hazelwood. To him, that was a better address.

I'm happy for Dan Rooney. He wanted to be the ambassador to Ireland. He knew the job was open. He campaigned for it when he campaigned for Barack Obama for President. Remember when the Steelers won the Super Bowl against the Arizona Cardinals and Rooney was interviewed immediately after the game and thanked Obama for his contribution? That confused a lot of former Steelers and Steelers' fans. "I was wondering what Barack Obama had to do with us winning the Super Bowl," said former Steelers' star Mel Blount. "But Dan doesn't do anything without a good reason. He knew what he was doing."

Dan Rooney had to love being named the American ambassador to Ireland. And I was happy for him. I am sure that his dad and Billy Conn would second the motion.

I even voted for Dan to be inducted into the American-Irish Hall of Fame in Chicago.

"I never got into training to be any All-Irish boxing champ or to win a belt. At the start, I just got into it to learn how to defend myself when I got into situations."
—Conor McGregor

Art Rooney and Billy Conn in their heyday.

Monaca's Teddy Yarosz is floored in first round by Jake LaMotta, a left to the jaw, but Yarosz was up with no count to continue and lost a close decision in a 10-rounder on December 3, 1948. LaMotta was portrayed by Robert DeNiro in the movie "Raging Bull."

Emile Griffith
New York boxer killed Friday Night Fights feature on TV at Civic Arena in Pittsburgh

Emile Griffith was a great fighter. He won the welterweight and middleweight boxing titles and fought professionally for 20 years, but he was best known for killing Benny "Kid" Paret in a savage bout at New York's Madison Square Garden.

That happened on March 24, 1962 and it was mentioned in the first paragraph of Griffith's death notice in *The New York Times* on Wednesday, July 24, 2013. He died the previous day at age 75 in Hempstead, N.Y. from kidney failure and complications of dementia. He didn't know where he was; it's the way many boxers end up.

Bill Buckner was a wonderful baseball player with the Boston Red Sox but when he dies the first paragraph of his obituary will include how he misplayed a ground ball in extra innings of Game 6 of the 1986 World Series and it gave the New York Mets the opening to win the game.

The Mets then won the deciding game to win the second World Series in the team history, and Buckner was blamed for the disappointing setback. Buckner had 2,700 hits in a 20-year career, almost 500 more hits than the great Joe DiMaggio, but Buckner is best known for blowing that fielding play at first base for the Boston Red Sox.

Griffith's worst moment as a boxer defined his career.

Griffith was born in the Virgin Islands, but grew up in New York. He worked in a New York factory that made women's hats—he was a milliner—and he was rumored to be gay.

He trained in Gil Clancy's gym on West 28th Street in the Fashion District of lower Manhattan, not far from Madison Square Garden.

Paret had taunted Griffith before their fight, calling him a *maricon*—Spanish for homosexual, queer or faggot—and an angered Griffith just kept punching Paret in the head in the 12th round of a scheduled 15-round fight and left him senseless. Paret died ten days later in a New York City hospital. Referee Ruby Goldstein, one of the best in the business, was hotly criticized for not stopping the fight earlier. That was in the first paragraph of Goldstein's death notice. Goldstein was a veteran official who understood the situation too well. He didn't think Griffith was a finisher—that was also his reputation—and he feared that Latin fight fans would riot if he stopped the fight in favor of Griffith. It was said, in an essay on boxing by Joyce Carol Oates, "Benny Paret, trapped in the ropes as referee Ruby Goldstein stood frozen, unable to interfere..." It was a story about the violence of boxing, the evil side of boxing, the primal and savage side that shames us to watch it and support it.

It's that way in sports and in life. Everyone eventually pays for their sins.

Reading the story about Griffith's passing was personal for me. I knew all the names and places. I had met Emile Griffith and interviewed him on several occasions. I had been in Gil Clancy's gym in the Chelsea section of Lower Manhattan, and I had been in Griffith's dressing cubicle, about the size of a confessional box, with the ambience of one of those wooden shacks I saw upon visiting Tijuana, Mexico while in San Diego with the New York Mets. I interviewed George Foreman, a heavyweight champion, in that same gym.

I found photographs in my files showing me interviewing Griffith and Foreman in Gil Clancy's gym.

I covered many of Clancy's fighters. I had played tennis with Clancy at a public park in Hempstead. Clancy died in an assisted-care residence in Lynbrook New York at age 88 in 2011. Angelo Dundee had managed Griffith and would later be the cornerman and trainer for Cassius Clay who became Muhammad Ali when he converted to being a Muslim.

He was in Joe Frazier's corner, as a second to Yancey Durham. Arthur Mercante was the referee of that fight. He, too, liked to play tennis and we played in a park near his

Lethal combinations—In the 12th round Griffith pounded the suddenly defenseless Paret into a coma.

Referee
Ruby Goldstein

home in Westbury. I took my lead in that respect from reading the autobiography—*The Tumult and the Shouting*—of Grantland Rice, the most respected sports writer in the nation who played golf and cards with the likes of Bobby Jones, Babe Ruth, Ty Cobb and Jack Dempsey and got to know them and got better inside stories because they trusted him. He also knew what not to write because it would not help you in the long run.

Mercante was the most respected boxing referee for a half-century and worked 140 championship fights, for the likes of Ali, Frazier, Floyd Patterson, Sugar Ray Robinson, Sugar Ray Leonard and Mike Tyson. Mercante was born in Brockton, Massachusetts, the hometown of undefeated heavyweight champion Rocky Marciano. Mercante died at age 90 in 2010. I covered the Ali fight with Joe Frazier for the heavyweight title on March 8, 1971 at Madison Square Garden. It was billed as "The Fight of the Century" and "The Fight." I had one of the four best seats in the house, sitting at ringside with some of the greatest sports writers of that era. I was honored by the company I was keeping. My wife Kathie was in the 31st row, not a bad seat in the sold-out Garden. She was back there somewhere with Diana Ross of The Supremes. It was a star-studded show. It was the biggest sports event I ever covered.

* * *

None of the Pittsburgh dailies mentioned that Emile Griffith was also given credit for killing TV's Friday Night Boxing series. It happened in Pittsburgh, at the Civic Arena. The Civic Arena is gone and now Griffith is gone. The Friday Night Fights have made a comeback, but it's not the same.

My friend Tommy Nee, a former assistant football coach for Rich Lackner at Carnegie Mellon University, said he watched Friday Night Fights on TV with his father, and before that listened to the fights on the radio. "That's how I became a boxing fan," he told me.

The Civic Arena had been the sight of some great boxing shows. I saw Sugar Ray Robinson fight at the Civic

Arena in 1965 and lose a decision to top-ranked Joey Archer in Robinson's last pro fight. I saw Floyd Patterson knock out Bill McMurray there. I saw Sonny Liston TKO Roger Rischer there.

Griffith went up against Rubin "Hurricane" Carter, a fierce fighter from New Jersey, at the Civic Arena on December 20, 1963. The TV series was sponsored by Gillette, the razor blade company. There were four shopping days left to Christmas and a razor and razor blades were one of the most popular gifts for men during the holiday season. Carter was a walking advertisement for razor blades because he shaved his head bald. Marvin Hagler, another fine boxer, would later follow his lead in that regard.

Griffith got knocked down twice in the first round, getting up both times at the nine count—ten and you're out—but Buck McTiernan, a first-rate referee from Swissvale, stopped the fight after the second knockdown.

The Gillette people were not happy. All the ads they planned on running between the rounds would never get seen. They lost the national audience after one round. Archie "Tex" Litman, who owned a beer distributing company in Braddock, and was a boxing promoter in Pittsburgh, once told me that fight prompted Gillette to drop its sponsorship of "Friday Night Fights." The series would come back years later with different sponsors.

I was midway through my senior year at Pitt and I was editing a weekly tabloid called *Pittsburgh Weekly Sports* that Beano Cook and I started that year, and I was able to get a ringside seat for that abbreviated bout.

* * *

Emile Griffith's death brought back so many good memories of my days in New York.

People often ask me what sport was my favorite to write about and are often surprised when I say boxing.

It was the best because there were so many characters and so many good stories—most boxers had to work for a living and they had better experiences to talk about—and sportswriters enjoyed great access to boxers.

Boxers and the people associated with them wanted sportswriters to pay attention to them. They were the most aggressive and approachable people in sports. The press agents came after you with story ideas and invitations to sit down and talk to the fighters. You were permitted to go behind the scenes. It was an interesting and fascinating world. I wish I had carried a camera with me all the time, but little digital cameras weren't available then.

Boxing had a strong appeal to great writers such as Ernest Hemingway, Norman Mailer, Budd Schulberg, E.J. Liebling and William Saroyan, to name a few. It was a macho sport, a dangerous game. Most of those writers went into the ring for supposedly "easy" sparring sessions with some great champions, but got nicked just the same. I never felt inclined to follow their lead in that regard.

My wife Kathie and I lived on New York's Long Island for nine years, two in a small apartment in East Rockaway where you could catch a train that took you into Penn Station, directly below Madison Square Garden, about an hour's ride, and seven more years in Baldwin. We lived our first month there with friends from my Pitt days in Lynbrook, where Arthur Mercante lived.

We fondly remember going to parties hosted by the owner of a dress factory in Manhattan, Irwin Goldberg was his name, I believe, where former fight champion and TV regular Rocky Graziano (Somebody Up There Likes Me was the name of his book, and it became a movie starring Paul Newman). Rocky was a funny man and often appeared on The Johnny Carson Show and with Martha Raye.

Kathie recalls seeing Muhammad Ali while she was waiting for me at a boxing arena in Manhattan before one of his fights. We met Don King, the outspoken boxing promoter, in Manhattan. It was the best of times.

"I was with Arnheim & Neely Realty and I got on an elevator in the Grant Building and Muhammad Ali and two big guys were already in there. I remember Ali's shoulders were as wide as the elevator. I was told he was buying a home for a friend in Mt. Lebanon."
—**Bob McClurg, Mars, Pennsylvania**

* * *

Kathie and I were married on August 12, 1967 in my hometown of Hazelwood. We had our wedding reception at the Croatian Club in Duquesne. Our 50th anniversary is coming up.

We moved to Miami two years later where I covered the Miami Dolphins in their last season in the old American Football League, and where I covered boxing shows on Miami Beach. They were promoted by Chris Dundee, the older brother of Angelo Dundee, who trained many champions at the Fifth Street Gym including Ali and Luis Rodriguez.

Griffith and Rodriguez fought several times, each winning and losing titles in those bouts. Two years after Griffith was floored by Hurricane Carter in a non-title bout at the Civic Arena he retained his title by beating Rodriguez in Las Vegas.

I had met and interviewed Rodriguez on many occasions during my year in Miami. He was a fun guy and, like so many boxing people, great company. He had an easy smile, a great grin.

* * *

When we moved to New York we chose to live on Long Island for several reasons.

Our apartment in East Rockaway and our home in Baldwin were both about five miles from Hempstead.

The only 24-hour Western Union office on Long Island was located in Hempstead. I went there many late nights to file my copy for *The New York Post*. That's the way stories were dispatched to newspapers in those days. Milton Gross, the star sports columnist at *The Post*, had told me to move somewhere close to Hempstead.

He lived in Rockville Centre, right next to Baldwin, and about five miles from Hempstead. Both of our daughters,

Sarah and Rebecca, were born in Rockville Centre at Mercy Hospital.

His daughter, Jane Gross, was a sportswriter at *Newsday* and later *The New York Times,* and one of the first female sportswriters to cover all sports, and one of the first to enter that sanctity of dressing rooms where male athletes were often nude or half-covered up. That was in 1975. Robin Herman was the first to represent *The New York Times* in a similar manner. "Let them wear towels," said Robin Herman. I covered several sports with Miss Gross and Miss Herman. I recall that the Rangers' great hockey player Phil Esposito started wearing a bathrobe in the locker room. I was once permitted to enter the women's dressing room of the New York Sets, but the women, including Virginia Wade and Pam Teegarden, were still in uniform.

Some guys thought they were amusing the crowd if they remained uncovered when the female sportswriters were allowed in after games to participate in interviews.

Milton's son, Michael, was the author of many outstanding books. He is regarded as one of America's most provocative writers and the author of three *New York Times* best-sellers.

I respected Milton Gross. He took great pride in being a newspaperman, a real reporter and not just a feature columnist. I recall an incident that showed his true colors. We both attended the weigh-in that preceded the Ali-Frazier "Fight of the Century." It took place at mid-day. *The New York Post* was an afternoon paper with several editions in the same day.

I sat down immediately after the weigh-in in the office of John Condon, the boxing publicist at the Garden and typed a story about what occurred at the weigh-in. It was for the late edition, the one commuters could pick up after work. As I finished a few paragraphs, Gross grabbed the copy, and called our office and dictated the copy to someone there who retyped it. Today, of course, I could transmit the story on my computer or I-Pad directly to the office and no one would have to re-type it. Gross did not regard calling the office with my story beneath his station on the staff. He wanted to help me and he wanted to make sure the story was in the late edition.

He also developed a formula for writing a column that I have often used. And he often told me, "If it don't write easy it don't read easy."

I am told I am easy to read. He used to tell me it was better in the old days, when teams often traveled on trains, and it was easier to get to know the athletes and to get their stories. It's always been better in the old days.

* * *

There was a small sports arena in Hempstead called Island Garden and that's where the New York Nets played their home games. This was 1970 and the Nets were coached by former St. John's University coach Lou Carnesecca. He would return to St. John's after two years with the Nets in the American Basketball Association.

His star forward was Rick Barry, who had jumped from the NBA, where he was a scoring champion, to the ABA. Carnesecca could have had Julius Erving—the great Dr. J—but didn't want to take a player out of college early. So Dr. J left UMass after his junior year and signed with the ABA's Virginia Squires instead.

Erving and Al Skinner both grew up in Roosevelt, a community that bordered Hempstead, and would be team-mates when the Nets acquired Erving in a trade with the Squires.

Erving would lead the Nets to two ABA titles in the early 70s when they moved into the brand new Nassau Coliseum which was located in Uniondale, right next to Hempstead. The New York Islanders, an expansion team in the National Hockey League, would play at the Nassau Coliseum as well. Now the Nets and the Islanders are in Brooklyn.

I covered both the Nets and the Islanders—they won just 12 games in their first season (1972) in the NHL and were often referred to as "the hapless Islanders."

237

Bill Torrey, who had worked in Pittsburgh as a front-office executive with the Pittsburgh Hornets of the American Hockey League, was the general manager of the Islanders. I witnessed him putting together a team that would win four Stanley Cup championships from 1980 to 1983.

The Coliseum was located near Garden City and Roosevelt Air Field where Charles Lindbergh took off in an airplane—The Spirit of St. Louis—and flew to Paris on May 21, 1927. It was the first solo non-stop aircraft flight across the Atlantic Ocean and made Lindbergh a national hero.

Lucky Lindy was the biggest hero in that neck of the woods until Joe Namath of the Jets, Dr. J of the Nets and then Bryan Trottier and Mike Bossy of the Islanders came along.

Hempstead was the home of Hofstra University and the New York Jets were headquartered on its campus in a building that would become known as Weeb Ewbank Hall, named for the coach of the Jets when they upset the heavily-favored Baltimore Colts to win Super Bowl III in 1969.

"The Miracle Mets" won their first World Series that same year, so I came to New York in the wake of the city winning two major sports titles. I covered the Knicks when they won their first NBA title in team history in the spring of 1970. It was, indeed, the best of times.

Paul Zimmerman covered the Jets for our newspaper. He would later become more famous as Dr. Z, the pro football writer and expert for *Sports Illustrated*.

Joe Namath did not care for Paul Zimmerman. So on Zimmerman's day off each week I was dispatched to go to Hempstead to interview Joe Namath. He was from Beaver Falls and we knew some of the same sports people back home in Western Pennsylvania, so I was OK in Namath's blazing eyes.

I had no need to be critical of Namath or the Jets on my once-a-week involvement, so we got along fine. Namath was one of the most celebrated sports figures in the country at the time, so it was a real star assignment for me.

All these things about our days living on Long Island, and covering all the sports in New York where there are two teams in every pro sport, and where the biggest of boxing and soccer events were often staged, were sparked by the week's news out of New York. Emile Griffith's death brought back all those wonderful memories and images.

Sportswriter Jim O'Brien is flanked by fight trainer Gil Clancy, left, and fight champion Emile Griffith in New York City gym.

Jim O'Brien joins Emile Griffith outside his dressing cubicle in fight gym in Manhattan in early '70s.

Madison Square Garden

At the weigh-in before the 1962 fight was the second at which Paret (left) had taunted Griffith about his sexuality. He obviously went too far.

"I remember very well that I could not sleep the night that Benny Kid Paret was knocked into a coma by Emile Griffith in a welterweight championship bout in March of 1962. I had watched that fight on television and when Paret was carried from the ring, unconscious, and, for all intents and purposes, lifeless, I felt myself quivering on the inside."
—**Gerald Early**

Teddy Brenner
Say it isn't so, Joe

Teddy Brenner went from being a shirt salesman to booking fights at arenas around New York such as Eastern Parkway and eventually managed to get the top job at Madison Square Garden. Brenner was a dapper gentleman with a sense of humor as sharp as his nose.

It was always a pleasure to visit him and Harry Markson, who was the director of boxing there, and John Condon, who was the boxing publicist as well as the public address announcer at Knicks' home games. They were the best in the business. Condon always had story ideas and hooked you up with people to interview.

Barney Nagler, a boxing historian and writer, was usually there. He was a crusty old cuss, with eyeglasses down on his nose, who knew more about boxing than any of the writers on the beat, and often reminded them of that. He looked at you over those eyeglasses when he wanted your full attention. So you'd learn something.

Nagler wrote a book with Brenner called "Only The Ring Was Square." In it, Brenner talks about being in Sonny Liston's locker room before the "phantom punch" first-round knockout by Muhammad Ali in Lewiston, Maine in 1965. Joe Louis was in there, too.

"Joe, I don't feel so good," said Liston to Louis.

"What do you mean...you don't feel so good?" came back Louis. "You gonna win."

Liston looked down, according to Brenner, and took Joe's hand, "Just ain't right, Joe."

TEDDY BRENNER
MSG Boxing Matchmaker

Floyd Patterson
Sitting alone with a mirror behind him in the 5th Street Gym on the Beach

From New York Post *January 14, 1971*

Floyd Patterson insisted his incentive for fighting, at age 35, did not die with Sonny Liston last week.

It has been suggested that Patterson's return after a two-year layoff was spurred by his need to fight Liston once more and defeat the man who took his title away.

The comeback began in September of 1971 with a knockout of Charlie "Devil" Greene.

Liston became champion by flattening Floyd in the first round in 1962, and he did it again in 1963.

"I don't want revenge," said Patterson. "Why must someone assume they know how I feel? These things aggravate me.

"Yes, I wanted to fight Sonny Liston again, but only the Sonny Liston that defeated me. The Sonny Liston of 1970 had nothing.

"He became an old man overnight. He was so slow; there was no movement. It was pitiful. His arms were like sandbags.

"I had several offers to fight him in recent years, but I ducked them. I didn't want to fight him the way he was. I hoped he'd come into the ring one night and be his old self, the Sonny Liston of old, and then we could fight again, but I knew he never could.

"When he died, they said he was 38, but he was much older. I'm sorry he died, leaving the kind of thoughts he did. I didn't like the things that were written about him when he died.

FLOYD PATTERSON
Two-time
heavyweight
champion

Blood samples and tissues taken from the body of Liston continue to be studied to determine the cause of his death. Natural death has been ruled out, but there are still some questions to be answered.

Patterson seemed to think his own life had been under a microscope ever since he became a boxer 21 years earlier. "Am I complex?" he said. "How do you define complex?"

I skipped that question. I could define complex, but I could not define Floyd Patterson. I didn't know him that well. This was the first time I had ever been with him, chin to chin, just talking in the locker room of the 5th Street Gym. I had talked to a lot of champion and ex-champion boxers in that same space, but never before had I faced Floyd Patterson.

I had read a wonderful profile of him by Gay Talese in *Esquire*, and would recommend that you check it out on the Internet if you want to know more about Floyd Patterson. When I read the story I wrote after talking to him for a half hour I was pleased with what he had to share.

I had not planned on being in Miami for Super Bowl week when Patterson was scheduled to fight Levi Forte, a fixture as a bellman and shoe shine man at the famous Fontainebleau Hotel, and someone who had been in the ring as long as Patterson.

I was there because Burt Schultz, the ABA publicist, thought we needed to take his new fur coat to warmer climes. There were no flights available to Bermuda, so we settled for Miami. Since I was there, I thought it a good idea to visit Floyd Patterson and do a one-on-one interview. Muhammad Ali began training that same day for his fight with Joe Frazier on March 8, 1971.

"I want one more chance at the championship, just one," said Patterson. "Then I can say my greed has come to an end. Sonny Liston no longer holds that championship.

"Maybe I'm a masochist...not really. But the more people tell me to retire the more determined I become to prove them wrong."

Patterson reminds you that he is the "only one ever to win back a championship." And confessing to being in a rare placative mood, he went on to disclose some other thoughts and stories about Sonny Liston.

My timing in visiting the 5th Street Gym was propitious.

"I went to his hotel room in Lewiston after he got knocked out in the first round by Clay. I tried to console him. I had two experiences like that and I knew how he felt.

"I was there. I saw the punch—some say there was no punch—but there was. That punch wouldn't even have fazed him in 1960 or 1962—his strong years—but he had become an old man overnight.

"I was told he trained very hard for that fight, but when you get older you can't train too hard, or it takes too much out of you.

"I had told him time would heal all wounds. I told him of my own embarrassment and how it, too, had passed.

"You know that cold look of his, that stone-faced glare. Well, that was the first time I ever saw softness in his face. It was a look of appreciation, of acceptance.

"I never knew Liston personally, but I saw him with kids, and I read about him with kids, always having them over to his house, and I would've liked to have gotten to know him better.

"I thought he had a hell of a lot of good in him. But boxing needed a villain and he filled the bill.

"Liston was heavyweight champion of the world, and that is enough to say about the man."

With that, Patterson may have been writing his own epitaph.

"One thing I admired about Liston is he got knocked down twice by Clay but he didn't disappear or wear a beard or disguise himself like I did. He continued to be seen and make appearances.

"I would have disappeared for a while. I have carried a false beard and mustache with me ever since I lost the title to (Ingemar) Johannson.

"I didn't carry it just to duck people. I carried it because when a fighter is beaten, he is ashamed of himself. I didn't want people to see me in shame.

"Maybe Liston didn't give a damn. I do."

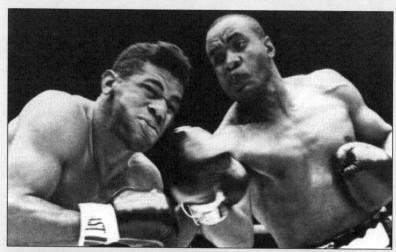

Sonny Liston lands a crushing overhand right to chin of Floyd Patterson.

Floyd Patterson, in an interview with the writer Gay Talese for *Esquire:*

"You have no idea how it is in the first round. You're out there with all those people around you, and those cameras, and the whole world looking in, and all that movement, that excitement, and 'The Star Spangled Banner,' and the whole nation hoping you'll win, including the President. And do you know what all this does? It blinds you, just blinds you. And then the bell rings, and you go at Liston and he's coming at you, and you're not even aware that there's a referee in the ring with you.

"Then you can't remember much of the rest, because you don't want to...All you recall is, all of a sudden you're getting up and the referee is saying, 'You all right?' and you say, 'Of course, I'm all right,' and he says, 'What's your name?' and you say, 'Patterson.'

"And then, suddenly, with all this screaming around you, you're down again, and you know you have to get up, but you're extremely groggy, and the referee is pushing you back, and your trainer is in there with a towel, and people are all standing up, and your eyes focus directly at no one person—you're sort of floating.

"It's not a bad feeling when you're knocked out. It's a good feeling, actually. It's not painful, just a sharp grogginess. You don't see angels or stars; you're on a pleasant cloud."

Bob Foster
Death of outstanding boxer
brings back memories of Detroit night

Downtown Detroit was dimly lit as it neared midnight. I was standing on a corner in front of The Hotel Pontiac with two of the finest fight chroniclers in the country, Roy McHugh of Pittsburgh and Jimmy Cannon of New York.

There was no one else to be seen in the surrounding streets of The Motor City. "This town," I observed, "makes Pittsburgh look alive at night!"

To which Cannon came back with "This town makes Pompeii look alive at night."

I was no match for Cannon when it came to great lines. He was one of the best in the business and McHugh, while not as well-known on the national scene, was quite the wordsmith himself.

McHugh just smiled a thin smile in appreciation of Cannon's comment.

I was smiling, too, happy just to be keeping the kind of company I was keeping that night, November 17, 1970. I was 28 at the time and I had the boxing beat for *The New York Post*, then one of the largest circulation afternoon newspapers in the country.

It had been my good fortune to come by the boxing beat that year, my second year in New York after moving there following one year at *The Miami News* where I covered the Dolphins in their final year in the American Football League. Vic Ziegel, a talented sportswriter on our staff, had decided he wanted to become an editor and had given up the boxing beat in favor of a chair on the night desk at *The Post*.

I was in Detroit to cover a championship fight between Joe Frazier and Bob Foster, a light-heavyweight champion moving up for bigger paydays and more recognition. It was held at Cobo Hall in Joe Louis's hometown of Detroit.

BOB FOSTER

Bob Foster, above, moved up in weight class to fight the likes of Muhammad Ali, below, as well as Joe Frazier, and lost to both heavyweight fighters. No fighter moving up in weight class has ever won a heavyweight title fight.

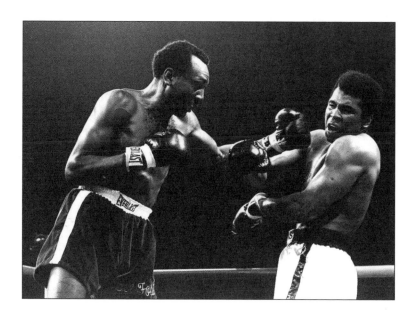

Two of the greatest fighters in history called Detroit their hometown. Joe was born (Mary 13, 1914) in Alabama as Joseph Louis Barrow, but boxed out of Detroit, and Sugar Ray Robinson was born in Georgia as Walker Smith Jr. (May 3, 1921) but grew up in Detroit.

For the record, no light-heavyweight going back to Pittsburgh's Billy Conn fighting Louis twice for his heavyweight title in the '40s, has ever beaten the heavier boxer in such a match-up.

Frazier knocked out Foster in 49 seconds of the second round. It was not a fair fight. Frazier outweighed his foe by 25 pounds. You can still see that fight on the Internet.

That fight came to mind in late November of 2015 when Foster died at the age of 77 in Albuquerque, New Mexico with his wife Rose and his family at his side.

Foster was a fine fighter. He's in the Boxing Hall of Fame. He was a skinny-looking 6-foot-3 boxer with a hammer for a right hand. His career record was 56-8-1, including 46 knockouts. Frazier hurt him at the outset of the second round with a left hook to the side of his lowered head and put him away with another left hook to his head.

I remember several things about that assignment in Detroit, starting with standing on the street corner with Cannon and McHugh.

When Frazier unleashed one of his punches to Foster's face, blood shot out of Foster's nose and splattered across a Western Union teletype machine at ringside. The woman who was operating the machine, sending out information about the fight on the wire, as was done in those days when there were no personal computers in front of the reporters at ringside, was startled by the sight of blood flying through the air in her direction. She passed out, her face landing on her teletype machine.

I was sitting in the second row at ringside. I can still find myself in the background of the fight action in a film version of the fight that is on the Internet of the computer I am using to write this story. I had a black mustache in those days, and could have been mistaken for Pancho Villa.

Dave Brady, a white-haired writer for *The Washington Post*, and a man I admired in the business not only because he could write so well but also because he was so kind to young writers, was sitting directly in front of me.

His typewriter went haywire, the black ribbon unraveling, and he could no longer use it. He wrote for a morning newspaper and had to write while the fight was going on in order to meet a demanding deadline. A writer for an afternoon newspaper like *The Post* has a chance to consider what he witnessed, and has more time to compose a piece that includes some post-fight comments by the combatants.

Typewriters that sportswriters carried in those days were compact and made a lot of noise that disturbed passengers on late-night flights when one was traveling with baseball, football, hockey or basketball teams who often left immediately after a game to get home at some reasonable hour. They went clickety-clack, clickety-clack. That is no longer a problem because there is no noise with the modern communication devices.

I exchanged typewriters with Dave Brady. I fixed the tape on his typewriter while he resumed typing his story on mine. Brady was even kinder to me in the years that followed that fight night.

Few of us can recall where we were on most nights of our life. Those in Pittsburgh and Western Pennsylvania of my age, 73, and some a decade or so younger, can remember where they were on October 13, 1960 when Maz hit the home run to slay the mighty Yankees in the World Series, or where they were on November 22, 1963, when JFK was killed in Dallas. Those two events were bookends for my student days at the University of Pittsburgh. I was on the campus in Oakland when I learned of both events.

I find newspaper clippings in my files at home and see the dateline and recall where I was on certain dates. I could not tell you where I was on most dates, so the clippings come in handy. I keep my calendars so I can refer to them to learn where I was a year ago or five years ago.

People are often surprised when they ask me what sport I most enjoyed writing about and I say boxing.

251

Muhammad Ali is still one of the most intriguing and fascinating sports figures I was fortunate to interview and spend time with. I had opportunities to talk to Joe Louis, and to Billy Conn, Sonny Liston, Sugar Ray Robinson, Jack Dempsey and Sugar Ray Leonard. Fighters often had interesting backgrounds and they liked to share their stories.

Boxing holds little interest among sports fans these days. Wladimir Klitschko of the Ukraine lost his heavyweight boxing title in late November 2015 in Germany to a British fighter named Tyson Fury. I knew Mike Tyson but I have never heard of Tyson Fury, and I didn't know that Klitschko, a 6-6 giant of a man, had held the title for the past 9½ years. Who knew?

When Conn fought Louis at New York's Polo Grounds on June 18, 1941, the fight was broadcast on national radio. The Pirates' game with the New York Giants that night was halted by the umpires in the seventh inning and the fight broadcast put on the PA system, the only time this ever happened in major league baseball history. The baseball game was resumed when the fight was over.

Intrepid reporter Jim O'Brien takes notes at ringside at weigh-in of Joe Frazier before his first fight with Muhammad Ali. Madison Square Garden publicist John Condon his holding the mike, and Frazier's trainer Eddie Futch is in the fashionable black hat at right.

Conn was winning on the scorecards when Louis kayoed him at 2:13 of the 13th round of a scheduled 15-round title fight. Louis weighed 199½ and Conn 174 for that match.

There wasn't a bigger sports figure than Conn.

Ali on Frazier
Knocks Joe as white man's fighter

"I'm the first talking fighter."

From *New York Post* January 8, 1971

S
even years ago, Sonny Liston sneaked up behind Muhammad Ali, who was then called Cassius Clay, and slapped his face. Hard.

"You talk too much for a child your age!" snapped Sonny.

Liston is gone now, baffling everyone once again who asks how and why, and Ali is among us again, still talking too much.

To the delight of some, the annoyance of others, he talks, talks, talks. He had a talent at the box office to polarize the public. There is no middle of the road reaction to Ali.

Looking to his March 8 (1971) title fight with Joe Frazier at Madison Square Garden, Ali says, "Many want me whupped because I'm arrogant.

"Many want me whupped because of my stand on the military draft, and many people have always been against me because I'm black.

"Many people want me to win because of the way I talk. Many want me to win because of the way I look at the draft, and many people like my view about blackness.

"If I lose, there'll be some people crying. If I win, there'll be a lot of people crying. It's the biggest fight because he looks unbeatable...and I am unbeatable."

Harry Markson, director of boxing at the Garden, has seen them all, but none like Ali. "Ain't he something?" asked Markson of the writers around him. "There's never been anyone like him."

Already, the Garden is getting swamped with ticket orders as THE FIGHT, and requests for closed-circuit TV outlets around the world are piling up.

"I'm the first talking fighter," Ali proclaims, proud of his contribution.

As far as Ali is concerned, Frazier is "a flat-footed, slow, awkward fighter," who's cashing in on Ali's magnetism and drawing power.

"Joe Frazier has never did no shuffle," Ali points out. "He's never predicted on rounds. Joe Frazier doesn't answer questions. And he doesn't even look like a champion.

"This fight," Ali goes on, "will be watched in Red China, in Arabia, in Thailand and...even in Italy."

He smiled at the delayed addition, looking to his trainer, Angelo Dundee, Italian through and through, when he said it.

"Even Egypt and Israel both want it," said Ali. "On this, they agree."

Frazier's trainer, Yank Durham, says he'll stop Ali in seven, changing the prediction from an earlier sixth-round forecast. Durham explains his change. "Now I'm serious."

"Forget it," shouts Ali. "I predict the world will be shocked. More shocked than they were at the Sonny Liston fight."

Since Liston died in Las Vegas just a few days earlier, newsmen had been telephoning Ali to get his personal reaction to it, but Ali was not available.

"His phone's not cooperating," said Dundee, who had been trying to reach Ali as well, to find out when he was coming to the 5th Street Gym to train. He heard Frazier was going to the Poconos to train.

"I hope," said Dundee, "he freezes his butt off up in those mountains."

Author Dick Schaap on Ali:

"He was the most significant, the most charismatic, the most charming person I've ever met. He was the most quotable human being on earth."

 Angelo Dundee, the trainer for Muhammad Ali, sent me a note identifying the man between Ali and me in the accompanying photo as Hugh McIlvanney, whom I have since learned was the premier boxing writer in the United Kingdom. McIlvanney wrote the following before the Joe Frazier-Ali fight in New York on March 8, 1971:

"For more than a decade now, whether calling himself Cassius Clay or Muhammad Ali, the man has sought the whole world as an audience. If anything is consistent in him, it can only be the hunger for universal attention, his constantly articulated fantasy that when he puts himself at risk, when he lays his invincibility on the line, the world holds its breath. On Monday night Muhammad Ali will go as close as any athlete ever could to making that fantasy a fact. His fight with Joe Frazier at Madison Square Garden in New York will be filmed, photographed, described in the spoken and written word, analyzed and argued over as no sports event ever has been before or is ever likely to be again.

Hugh McIlvanney of United Kingdom on Frazier and Philadelphia:

"If Nemesis there must be, Joe Frazier is classically equipped for the part. He is, as they say around the gyms here, 'all fighter.' Since moving north as a boy from Beaufort, South Carolina, he has lived in Philadelphia, which also happens to be the hometown of Angelo Dundee, Ali's trainer. 'Philadelphia,' Dundee has said, 'is not a town. It's a jungle. They don't have gyms there. They have zoos. They don't have sparring sessions. They have wars.' Frazier is true to that background."

After the fight:

"Joe Frazier, a thoroughly pleasant and admirable man, is also a champion fit to share a ring with any who have held the world heavyweight title. 'I have fought anybody y'all put in front of me and God knows I beat them,' he said afterwards. 'What more can I do?' Now I've got to live a little, man. I've been working for ten long years."

THE
FIGHT

FOR THE LIGHTWEIGHT CHAMPIONSHIP OF THE WORLD — NO TV

MADISON SQ. GARDEN | MON. SEPT. 13TH

31st ST. TO 33rd STREET ON 7th AVE.

AT 8:30 P.M.

MAIN EVENT — 15 ROUNDS

ISMAEL LAGUNA

KEN BUCHANAN

Scotland - Lightweight Champion Of The World

vs.

ISMAEL LAGUNA

Panama - Twice Former Lightweight Champion Of The World

SEMI FINAL — 10 ROUNDS

KEN BUCHANAN

ROBERTO "ROCKY" DURAN vs. BENNY "BANG BANG" HUERTAS

SENSATIONAL UNBEATEN PANAMANIAN K.O. ARTIST. SCORED 21 KAYOES IN 24 FIGHTS

SLAM BANG PUERTO RICAN PUNCHER

— SPECIAL 6 ROUND ATTRACTION —

"IRISH" WALTER SEELEY vs. JOSE FERNANDEZ

SAYVILLE, L. I. - UNBEATEN FEATHERWEIGHT CONTENDER

DOMINICAN REPUBLIC - NEW YORK GOLDEN GLOVE CHAMPION

Prices: Ringside & Loge $30 - 1st Promenade $20 - 2nd Promenade $15, $10 - Mezzanine $5.00

COLLECTOR'S ITEM FROM BOXING ILLUSTRATED $1.00

THE FIGHT OF THE
CENTURY
JOE FRAZIER VS. MUHAMMAD ALI

WORLD HEAVYWEIGHT CHAMPIONSHIP
MADISON SQUARE GARDEN / MAR. 8, 1971

EXCLUSIVE FEATURES

records, statistics, biographies and predictions of Muhammad Ali and Joe Frazier

winner picked by 50 former champions / Floyd Patterson / Jose Torres / Gene Fullmer

35p

Senator John Heinz stops by to say hello to Billy Conn and Joe Louis at dinner at downtown Hyatt to honor Conn. Chick Cercone, a former boxer from McKees Rocks, at right, manages to get into photo. This dinner was sponsored by another former boxer, Joe LaQuatra.

Heavyweight champion Rocky Marciano knocked out Jersey Joe Walcott in the first round of Walcott's final pro fight, on May 15, 1953, in Chicago.

Jack Lambert and Billy Conn enjoy lunch at Allegheny Club at Three Rivers Stadium. Conn mistook Lambert for Jack Ham. "How'd you like someone to mistake you for Fritzie Zivic?" asked Mary Regan, personal secretary for Steelers' owner Art Rooney Sr.

Dan Marino Sr. and his wife, Veronica, were good friends of Angelo Dundee, at right, when they lived in Weston, Florida. "I went to a lot of functions where their son, Danny, was the feature attraction," said Dundee. "Our family's name was originally Mirena, so maybe the Marinos are distant cousins of Chris and me." They look like they're related.

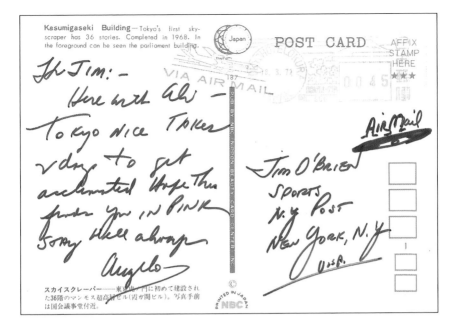

Here's a postcard Angelo Dundee sent from Japan to New York Post sportswriter Jim O'Brien. Dundee was traveling with Muhammad Ali at the time.

Photos by Jim O'Brien

Mayor Tom Murphy presided over honorary naming of Craig Street at Fifth Avenue as Billy Conn Boulevard on 57th anniversary of Conn's famous title fight in New York with heavyweight champion Joe Louis on June 18, 1941. Among those in attendance that day, June 18, 1998, were, left to right, Freddie Manns, Tim Conn, Jack McGinley Sr. and Art Swiden. Below, McGinley shows trunks worn by Ezzard Charles when he was defeated by Jersey Joe Walcott in heavyweight title fight at Forbes Field on July 18, 1951. He was KOd in the seventh round, leveled by a left hook.

Myron Cope and Olympic wrestling champion Kurt Angle pose before a hand-colored photo of Harry Greb in the back room of Atria's Restaurant & Tavern in Mt. Lebanon, where Cope and Angle were residing at the time. Actor Tom Atkins of Peters Township poses in same spot when he was playing the part of Art Rooney Sr. in a one-man show called "The Chief" at the O'Reilly Theater.

Photos by Jim O'Brien

Former Steelers defensive backs Judge Dwayne Woodruff and J.T. Thomas were both influenced as young men by Muhammad Ali. Woodruff is a graduate of the University of Louisville in Ali's hometown. Thomas said Ali "was the first rapper" and "someone who helped us young blacks in the South find our identity."

Ray "Boom Boom" Mancini of Youngstown won the lightweight boxing championship in 1981. He is seen here with Steelers' head coach Chuck Noll at a Dapper Dan Sports Award Dinner at the former Hilton Hotel.

Photos by Jim O'Brien

The late Kelly Harrington of Tessaro's Restaurant in Bloomfield was a big sports fan and loved to show off the framed photo behind him at his bar of the great Harry Greb of Garfield, one of the finest fighters in boxing history. Bruno Sammartino, a former world's wrestling champion, is flanked by Art Rooney II, the president of the Pittsburgh Steelers, and Kevin Colbert, the club's general manager, at Dapper Dan Dinner.

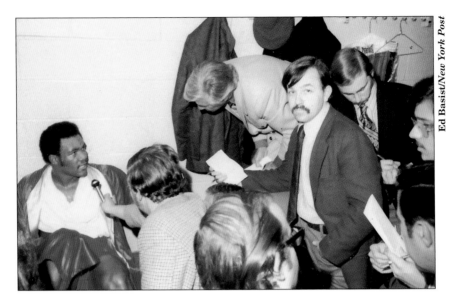

George Foreman, former heavyweight boxing champion, talks to media, including left to right at top, Dick Young of New York Daily News, Jim O'Brien and Greg Gallo of New York Post. Below, O'Brien is seen between Ali's red-tasseled boots at ringside of Frazier-Ali "Fight of the Century."

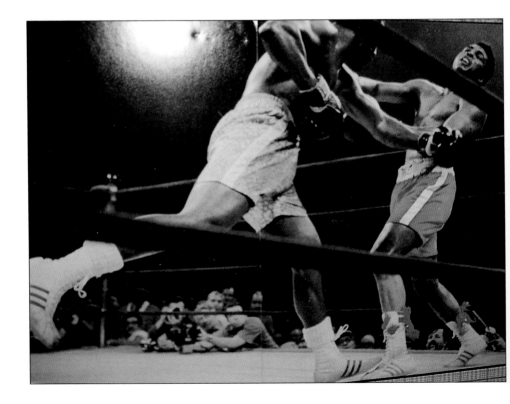

Author Jim O'Brien kept Christmas card sent to him by Chris and Angelo Dundee, flanking Muhammad Ali, and boxing cards of champions Roberto Duran of Panama City and Michael Moorer of Monessen.

> *"Roberto Duran was the little tough guy from Panama who knocked out horses as a teenager, quit school at the age of thirteen after having reached the third grade, won the lightweight title in 1972 from Ken Buchanan on a low blow, then refused to honor a return-bout clause of the contract, the man sportswriter Dick Young called "The Animal," (a term he would never dream of using to describe a black fighter).*
> **—From a story by Gerald Early, Cultural Definition of Prize-Fighting**

Mary Louise Conn and her son Tim, when she lived in apartment in Squirrel Hill. Below, she shows off picture of her and her handsome husband Billy Conn when they were young. The photo is on the wall in her apartment at Little Sisters of the Poor residence in Brighton Heights section of Pittsburgh's North Side.

Movie billboard of "The Pittsburgh Kid," starring Billy Conn and Jean Parker, is on wall at Tim Conn's home in Point Breeze. Lawrenceville's boxing champion Fritzie Zivic adorned cover of *The Ring Magazine*. Author Jim O'Brien is seen at Madison Square Garden during 25th anniversary of "The Fight of the Century" between Ali and Frazier on March 8, 1971.

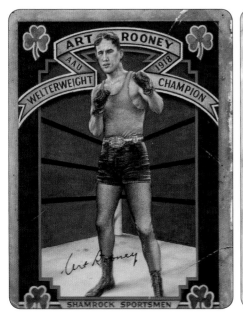 

Special cards honoring Pittsburgh fighters Art Rooney Sr. and Bill Conn were commissioned by Art Rooney Jr. and are shown here with Art's permission. Among those in attendance when Craig Street near where the old Duquesne Garden once stood was named in an honorary manner for Billy Conn included, left to right, Pennsylvania Boxing Commissioner Andy "Kid" DePaul, Pittsburgh writer and boxing historian Roy McHugh and former Pittsburgh heavyweight boxer and bartender/bouncer Art Swiden.

Jim O'Brien

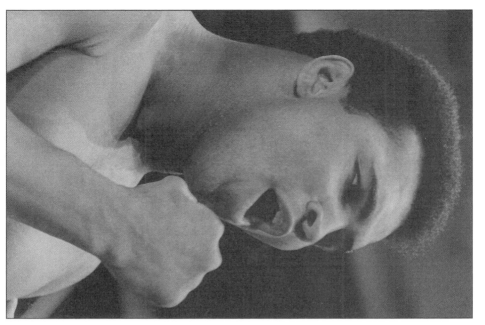

ALI
VS.
FRAZIER
"FIGHT
OF THE
CENTURY"

Muhammad Ali
To Harlem and back

Nervous perhaps, and in need of an audience, Muhammad Ali sent Stacks Edwards, the big man who sat on a chair outside Ali's suite at the Hotel New Yorker, in search of some sportswriters.

Edwards and I had hit it off—I always paid attention to the guys who accompanied and ran errands for the stars—and he invited me to follow him into an elevator with a few other fellow journalists. With Edwards aboard, we had to be a select few to fit in the elevator.

"I wasn't going to talk to anyone," Ali announced as we entered his room on the 25th floor on the afternoon of the day before his much ballyhooed "Fight of the Century" with Joe Frazier, "but I can't do it. A real champ doesn't run and hide. Bet you figured I'd be in the bathroom, scared to death, throwing up or something."

Picture this scene. I can't imagine Terry Bradshaw of the Steelers, for instance, calling the media to his room on the eve of a Super Bowl. He invited some of the support team of the Steelers to keep him occupied, to keep him calm. Bradshaw, to be sure, was nervous.

* * *

Over the next two hours, nearly non-stop as usual, Ali burned off some more of his energy...talking up a storm.

He mocked the man he was fighting for the heavyweight title the next night across the street—8th Avenue—at Madison Square Garden, which sits directly above Penn Station.

"Nixon'll call him if he wins," Ali said. "I don't think he'll call me."

He spoke of an early-morning walk in the rain through Harlem and his plans to return there for dinner later in the evening.

Again, I can't imagine Bradshaw taking a stroll through the streets of New Orleans or Pasadena prior to the Super Bowl, and strutting his stuff for the Steeler Nation.

"I spent one-and-a-half hours in Harlem," said Ali, "sitting on a garbage can, talking with wine-heads and picking up little babies. And where's Frazier?"

Later, I asked Frazier's manager, Yank Durham, what his Philadelphia fighter was doing that same day. "Relaxing, watching TV, playing his guitar, and talking over the telephone with friends from his hideaway. Both were doing their best to ignore a bomb threat, which was more ominous that what was on Muhammad's mind at the moment.

"That man down there," said Ali, referring to the people he came upon in his Harlem sojourn, "he's picking who he want, too. He got his reason.

"I win, they win. I lose, they lose. It's going to be a feeling in that house, I'll tell you."

Ali's own street poll shows 98 percent of the blacks are for him. "They like the idea of one man standing alone," he said. "They identify with my struggle. It's the same fight they're fighting every day—on the job and against the police.

"When you're the underdog, that's when every punch looks good. Everybody in his right mind who is black wants me to keep winning...to keep talking...to keep coming in their neighborhoods...to keep picking up their black babies. And anybody who thinks Frazier can whip me is an Uncle Tom."

Ali always painted Joe Frazier as if he were a white man or a white man's tool. It's true that most blacks were behind Ali, but it was also true that Frazier was more familiar with the black man's plight than Ali, and was, indeed, blacker than Ali in all ways.

Frazier felt that he was there to defend his title, and not to win a debate with Ali. He was there to fight, not to give a lecture, or to entertain sports writers.

Ali said he needed opposition to get his best competitive juices stirred up, "the villain writers," and "the evil expressions at ringside." He was fighting against everybody who picked against him. I picked Ali in the sixth, to stay out of harm's way, but I was wrong.

* * *

"He going to see all of his people against him," Ali said of Frazier. "I hope I'm the first in the ring so that when he comes in they'll boo. When I hear those things, it's better than four days in training."

Ali poked fun at Frazier's image on the TV screen in the room. A documentary on Frazier was being shown. "Is that the way he runs?" Ali said when Joe was shown jogging along a beach. When the announcer called Frazier the heavyweight champion, Ali shouted, "No, he ain't!"

Ali shadowboxed in front of the screen, giving his own rendition of what was on the TV screen. "Keep walkin' in, Joe," he said. "Ooooh, how am I going to get to sleep tonight? I'm so anxious to get at him."

Ali promised he'd do no talking in the ring the following night—March 8, 1971—and would do his best to fight Frazier to the bone. "It's too serious," said Ali. "This is a fight that's going to be watched over and over and over the rest of history. I didn't want to cheapen it, make it a clown match. I'm going to make it a clean scientific fight."

Looking back at this afternoon with Ali, I am reminded of why boxing was such a great beat. You got to know the people.

"There comes to mind the anguish when I read that the once magnificent heavyweight Cleveland 'Big Cat' Williams, who was nearly shot to death a few years before, was going to fight Muhammad Ali for the title, a hopeless mismatch."
—Gerald Early

Author Jim O'Brien at upper left has great view of Muhammad Ali's 15-round TKO of Oscar Bonavena. Referee Mark Conn pushes Ali back after he flattened the Argentine fighter a second time in the round. That's ABC-TV's Jim McKay at ringside with the bow tie.

Freddie Fierro, veteran trainer, on Billy Conn:
"He's the man whose Irish temper cost him the heavyweight championship. In the gym, Billy worked like a coal miner. That was Billy Ray's gym in East Liberty. Ray, who had worked with Harry Greb, taught Billy a left jab—the punch that made him famous."

Joe Frazier
He felt a debt to boxing fans

From *The New York Post*
November 27, 1971

Even if Terry Daniels didn't tell everybody he played football at Southern Methodist, you'd know when he says stuff like, "I know Joe Frazier is a great fighter, and a great champion, but he puts his pants on the same way I do; he's got only two legs, two arms and two hands—the same as I do."

Come January 15—the eve of the Super Bowl—Daniels may learn in Louisiana that coaches' clichés can sometimes be awful lies. For one thing, Joe won't be putting on any pants. Just boxing trunks. Daniels should have looked closer at those two hands or he'd have noticed a big difference between the two fighters.

A guy can get knocked out by Frazier's fists nowadays even if Joe never lays a hand on him in anger.

* * *

The other day at Jimmy Weston's restaurant, where plans were discussed for the heavyweight title fight, which will be shown on home TV, Frazier wore three rings that cost him $20,000. They were all fat rings, one he valued at $10,000—"a seven cluster," he said—and another held the five respective birth stones of his children. It was the best collection of jewelry I'd seen since the Crown Jewels in the Tower of London during a vacation in Europe last year.

It made the Mets' and Knicks' championship rings look like the simulated stuff they gave away as a come-on for the Muhammad Ali-Buster Mathis fight.

Frazier also owns five automobiles, including an El Dorado Cadillac but didn't say whether he has one of his children's birthstones set in the horn button on each.

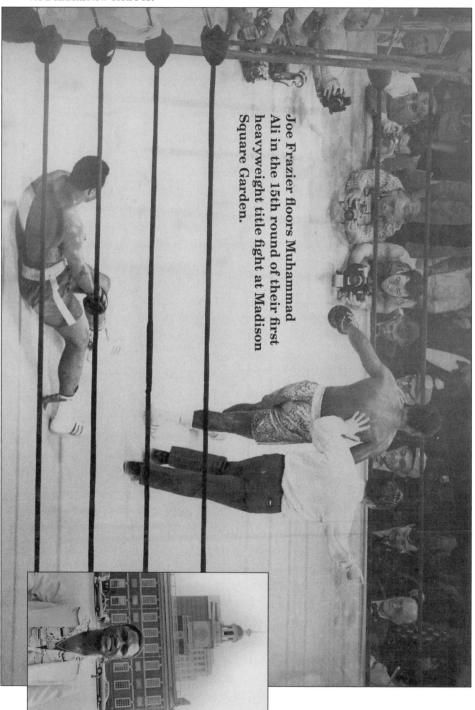

Joe Frazier floors Muhammad Ali in the 15th round of their first heavyweight title fight at Madison Square Garden.

Frazier is a rich young man. He probably has as much money as Terry Daniels' dad, who owns a multi-million-dollar construction business in Cleveland. Yet, he wants to get going again in the fight game. "I want to get back really bad," he said.

Gil Clancy, local fight manager and trainer, recognized this and helped put together this fight for the Century Telesports Network, which is guaranteeing Frazier $250,000 for fighting Daniels, who will get $35,000.

This is regarded as one of the greatest mismatches in boxing history. Daniels himself was in disbelief when this fight was proposed to him. They come from different backgrounds, that's for sure. Frazier was born the son of a sharecropper in Beaufort, South Carolina—also the hometown of one of my favorite authors, Pat Conroy—and Daniels led the good life as the son of a millionaire.

Frazier doesn't know if Daniels deserves such a shot at the title, but Joe's business is fighting, not picking opponents, and as he says, "I'll fight anyone they put in front of me."

Unless, he says, that man is one of his sparring partners. That, of course, is an obvious knock at Muhammad Ali, who took on Jimmy Ellis in his next-to-the-last fight. "I know too much about what makes them tick," said Joe, "and it wouldn't be fair to them or the public."

* * *

Frazier feels he owes the public an honest break. He doesn't think Ali's been giving it to them lately. "I respect the public," said Frazier. "Kids can't come to the closed-circuit TV shows to see fights, but this one is going into the homes. I want the kids to see what a heavyweight champion is made of, what makes him tick. Instead of what they may have read about what happened in Houston."

That was a reference to Ali's easy win over Ellis, knocking him out in the first round.

Frazier feels that Ali makes a farce of the fight game. "I don't want to con nobody," he said. "I'm a normal person, just like you. I don't think I'm better than the next guy. Clay does. He wants to be a great man, but as long as I'm out there, he's not going to be anything but Clay.

"He wants to be the champ, but he can't be anymore. People are finding out what kind of phony he is now. He'd like to be champ, but he can forget it. The next time I'll be shorter (the fight will end sooner).

"All the guys who've been in the ring with me ain't the same anymore, and he ain't the same."

Ali has been insisting that Frazier might never fight again, that he took such a beating in their March 8 (1971) match at Madison Square Garden. Medical reports did indicate that Joe had high blood pressure, but he says it had nothing to do with the fight. "Do I look sick?" asked Frazier, with a smile. "A couple of guys buried me but I'm alive. And I would like to stay young as much as possible—and live."

Daniels doesn't figure to mess up Frazier's future but he could make it interesting if he boxes with the same zest that he talks. Joe says he is not taking Terry Daniels cheap (lightly), but like Ali, he seems more directed toward the Rematch.

"I know the cat's a phony," Frazier said of Ali. "He forgets I'm black, too. I know what a brother's like. He talks about going to the ghetto. Hell, I was raised there. It's another thing to go visit and say hello and pose for pictures with little babies.

"I respect a fighter whether he's white or black. That color stuff is in the past. We don't have to have that hassle anymore."

Frazier won the fight by TKO in the fourth round. It was stopped because Frazier was flooring Daniels at will, and had left him defenseless.

Frazier fought six of his first seven pro fights in his hometown of Philadelphia and once in New York. In his eighth fight, he scored a third-round knockout over Don Smith in Pittsburgh. That made his record 7-0. He was 26-0 when he met Muhammad Ali to defend his title.

Howard Cosell
He and Ali teamed up
to be a comedy team

I was in the Manhattan apartment of Howard Cosell, the controversial New York sports broadcaster, and he instructed me to call my wife Kathie at our home on Long Island.

I did as I was told. Who could say "no" to Howard Cosell?

No sooner had I said hello to Kathie than Cosell took the phone from my hand. "Hello, Kathie," Cosell said as only Cosell could say. He had a different voice than Myron Cope, but it was just as distinctive.

"I want to tell you, dear, that I am here with your husband, Jim O'Brien, and I must tell you, dear, that you definitely married beneath yourself! This is Howard Cosell!" Then he chortled at his own joke. His profile resembled Dracula in the movie of the same name.

His beloved wife Emmy looked on with a smile. I am sure she had witnessed similar scenes many times in her married life, but she smiled just the same. No wonder Howard Cosell loved her so much.

That was sometime in the fall of 1970. In the summer of 1971, in early August, Kathie and I had breakfast at the Warwick Hotel, across the street from the headquarters of ABC Television, with Cosell. The Warwick Hotel is at 65 West 54th Street.

He told us of the death the day before of his good friend Horace McMahon, an actor famous for his role as the chief detective on "Naked City," a crime series that was a staple of Sunday night television on the ABC network from 1958 to 1963—our high school and college years.

We were driving home to Pittsburgh later that day and we tuned in to Cosell's nationally-broadcast radio show, and he devoted it to the death of his friend Horace McMahon.

I had met McMahon at many press conferences in advance of boxing events at Madison Square Garden. McMahon was a big boxing fan. I was as excited to see him at Toots Shor's as I would be to see Muhammad Ali, Joe Frazier or Joe Louis.

As we listened to Cosell reflect on his friendship with McMahon, Kathie turned to me and said, "It sounds exactly the way he told us the story at breakfast."

That was Cosell. That's the way he talked. He was always "on," as they say. I recall being with him in the news room at ABC Radio when he tore a story off the wire service machine about the death of an old baseball player. Cosell read the story, turning the long copy of it over in his hands in a dramatic manner as he speed-read it. He tossed it aside with great elan or flair. Five minutes later, he went on the air and told the story, without any script, without a flaw or hesitation in his delivery. He was a bright man.

In his biography of Cosell, author Mark Ribowsky wrote the following: "It was in the arena of boxing that Cosell demonstrated his genius. First promoting the careers of Sonny Liston and Floyd Patterson, he became most identified with the young Cassius Clay and it was this symbiotic relationship between the beautiful Muslim convert and the Jewish lawyer from New York that propelled both to superstardom. Even after Ali was stripped of his heavyweight crown, betrayed by the media who had previously anointed him. It was the fierce civil rights advocate Cosell who stuck in Ali's corner, making the case that eventually led to Ali's vindication."

One of my colleagues at *The New York Post*, Maury Allen wrote of Cosell: "He was a very big part of American culture, a cultural link from Jackie Robinson to Ali to Barack Obama."

Cosell was the star of "Monday Night Football" and some of the great boxing events of that era. He and Don Meredith and Keith Jackson teamed up as the broadcast team for the first year of "Monday Night Football." Jackson, who was happier to do college football, gave way the second year to Frank Gifford.

"Monday Night Football" was an idea promoted by NFL Commissioner Pete Rozelle and sports producer Roone Arledge. It was Arledge who convinced reluctant ABC powers to put the show on the air in 1970, the first year of football after the merger of the National Football League and the American Football League.

It became a national phenomenon, drawing 33 per cent of the TV viewing audience. Arledge brought in Chet Forte, a former All-American basketball player at Columbia, and he directed the show for its first 23 years. Every self-respecting pro football fan stayed up late on Monday night to watch the NFL offering.

They used twice as many cameras as had been used to cover other NFL games, one more announcer, stirring music, graphics and "instant replay." Cosell was the lighting rod that made it different. When he described fight action his delivery could tip the scales in favor of the fighter he was praising.

I was fortunate in my sports-writing career to be in the right place at the right time. Soon after I arrived in New York after one year at *The Miami News* where I covered the Dolphins in their final season in the AFL, I was assigned to be one of four reporters on the staff of *The New York Post* to cover the New York Knicks in the NBA playoffs. The Knicks went on to win the first NBA title in the team's history. The Garden was filled to capacity every game and there was an electric atmosphere in the building.

It was a great time to be writing about sports in New York. The "Miracle Mets" had won the World Series in 1969, and the New York Jets of Joe Namath had upset the Baltimore Colts in Super Bowl III, the AFL representative beating the highly-favored NFL entry. I was going to cover the Nets, and then the Islanders, at Nassau Coliseum near my home on Long Island.

My boss, sports editor Ike Gellis, a look-alike for the actor Edward G. Robinson, assigned me to cover Monday Night Football. I was the new guy on a veteran staff, and I had covered the NFL a year earlier in Miami.

It was a great beat. You only had to write features about the quarterbacks and running backs and receivers, or a standout defensive player, and you didn't have to write about the long snapper or the second-string guard or tackle as you do when you cover one team for a full season.

The day after a game in Minneapolis, I called the office to check in with Ike Gellis. "What was it doing weatherwise when you got to Minneapolis?" he asked in his usual gruff voice.

"It was raining," I replied.

"You didn't mention that in your story," said Gellis, more gruffly than usual. "You know, a lot of our readers gamble on those games."

None more than Ike Gellis. He's the one who really wanted to know it had been raining.

Host teams made a fuss over out-of-town media and I had a chance to mix socially with Cosell, Meredith and Gifford. My friend and booster from my Pitt days, Beano Cook, was one of the sports publicists at ABC-TV. A gent named Irv Brodsky handled publicity for Monday Night Football for ABC-TV, as well as "Wide World of Sports" and he was great to work with. Beano introduced me to all the right people. I was 28 at the time. I was in sportswriters' heaven.

Monday Night Football is not as big a deal these days because now it seems like there is a game on every night of the week. It wasn't that way in the early '70s. The other TV networks shifted their best shows away from Monday night so they didn't have to compete with the pro football offering. Bowling leagues were shifted from Monday to Tuesday night. Movie attendance was way down. A hospital in Seattle said no babies were to be born when Monday Night Football was on TV.

I remember covering the first game in the Monday Night Football series. It was played on September 21, 1970. The New York Jets beat the Browns, 31-21, in Cleveland.

I enjoyed an edge as a reporter for that game, especially in post-game interviews. Joe Namath, the pride of

Beaver Falls, was the Jets quarterback. I was our "Joe Namath man" at *The New York Post*.

Paul Zimmerman, one of the most respected pro football writers in the nation who would later write as Dr. Z for *Sports Illustrated*, was not one of Namath's favorites. Namath and I knew some of the same people back in Beaver Falls and Pittsburgh.

Some of those people were of questionable character as far as others were concerned, but Namath figured I had to be a good guy if I knew them. So once a week, on Zimmerman's day off, I was sent to the Jets' training facility at Hofstra University, to interview Joe Namath. It was only five miles from my home.

Namath, as well as O.J. Simpson, would later be analysts for brief stints on Monday Night Football. There was no more friendly and cooperative fellow in pro football than O.J. Simpson. Now he's in prison, a place a lot of Namath's high school teachers figured he might end up someday.

Myron Cope was talking to Howard Cosell when the Steelers hosted a 50th season celebration in 1982. Cope was telling Cosell about how big he (Myron Cope) had become as a sports broadcaster. Cosell, never one to miss a put-down, said, "Yes, Myron, in Pittsburgh."

Beano Cook was a life-long friend and admirer of Cope, but he loved to share that story. Cosell, of course, had told Beano about what transpired in Pittsburgh.

Cosell knew a good thing when he saw one, and he fell in love with Muhammad Ali. He'd get up close to the fighter and pepper him with questions, like a good trial lawyer in court, and taunt him if he didn't answer the question to Cosell's satisfaction.

He usually got the best of Ali. But Ali counter-punched pretty well, too.

Cosell came to Pittsburgh to serve as the emcee for the Steelers' 50th Season celebration. It was Cosell, after all, who branded Pittsburgh "The City of Champions" during the late '70s and it caught on.

Cosell, of course, might have said it best when explaining himself:

"Arrogant, pompous, obnoxious, vain, cruel, verbose, a show-off. I have been called all of them. Of course, I am."

Many New York sportswriters, especially Dick Young of *The New York Daily News,* couldn't stand Cosell, and were often critical of him in their columns. "He changed his name and he wears a wig," wrote Young, "and he tells it like it is."

Cosell turned against me after about five years. My sin was quoting boxing trainer Gil Clancy saying something critical of Cosell having to do with a fight in Zagreb, Croatia. Cosell was not nice to me after that. He turned on Frank Gifford and a few other co-workers.

ABC-TV Sports publicist Irv Brodsky shared a story with me once about Cosell raising hell with him during the Olympic Games in Munich because some writer in Milwaukee had written something negative about Cosell. Cosell was in Munich, but he knew what was written about him in Milwaukee in the previous day's newspaper. And this was before cell phones and iPads. In his self-description, Cosell forgot to mention he was paranoid and sensitive to the core.

Howard Cosell loved it when Art Rooney Sr., at right, finally won all those NFL championships.

Muhammad Ali
He almost moved to a home
in Mt. Lebanon

A chance meeting in February of 1996 with some old friends from the South Hills brought Muhammad Ali to mind.

We started reminiscing about how we originally met in New York at Ali's first heavyweight championship fight with Joe Frazier at Madison Square Garden on March 8, 1971.

We also talked about how Ali was all set to buy a home in Mt. Lebanon about the same time.

It had been so long since I had last seen Ruth and Pat McGrath of Mt. Lebanon. They had come out to Monroeville at a special reunion to say hello to Joe Greene, L.C. Greenwood, Dwight White and Ernie Holmes, whom they had gotten to know when the fearsome foursome was the cornerstone of the Steelers' Steel Curtain defense.

In fact, the Steel Curtain tag was first applied to the front four only, and later the entire defensive unit.

Die-hard sports fans, the McGraths had somehow gotten to know Ali in a similar manner. Pat was a real estate appraiser, and he had learned that Ali, who was then living in Cherry Hill, New Jersey, was looking to move elsewhere in the East, but farther away from the madness of Manhattan.

Through his contacts in the real estate business, McGrath made early arrangements for Ali to buy a home in the posh Virginia Manor section of Mt. Lebanon, one of Pittsburgh's most expensive and prestigious neighborhoods at the time.

He was interested in a six-bedroom home that sold for $195,000 then and would probably go for more than $1 million today.

Ali was a rather controversial sports figure, easily the world's most renowned athlete. He had rejected being drafted into the U.S. Army, insisting he had "no fight with them Viet Cong." He had changed his name from Cassius Clay—"my slave name," as he put it—to Muhammad Ali, and joined the Black Muslims.

This made people nervous about having him as a neighbor.

So there was opposition to the idea of him moving next door to some of the residents of Virginia Manor, forcing Ali to change his mind. He wanted to pick his own battles carefully. It was our loss, as I see it. He later bought a home in another neighborhood of Mt. Lebanon for a female friend of his. I know the couple that lives there now.

Pat and Dan Rooney were residents of Virginia Manor, but more recently relocated to Dan's boyhood home on the North Side, not too far from Heinz Field and PNC Park. His dad, Art Sr., often walked to Three Rivers Stadium from his home on North Lincoln Avenue. Katie and Jim Leyland lived in Virginia Manor but now live in Thornburg. Jan and Rocky Bleier live there, next to a home that was once owned by Rick Tocchet of the Penguins.

Ali would have been an addition to our label as "City of Champions," as TV sportscaster Howard Cosell called Pittsburgh in the decade of the '70s. Art Rooney Sr. would have cast his ballot in favor of Ali moving to Pittsburgh because he was a big fight fan and a former boxer in his heyday.

It was hard for us and the McGraths to realize it had been 25 years since we first met Muhammad Ali.

"The Fight of the Century" was the most exciting and electrifying sports event I ever personally covered as a newspaperman. I had just been assigned to the boxing beat—talk about good timing—at *The New York Post,* one of the city's three major dailies at the time.

No one had a better seat at The Garden. I was smack in the center of one of the ringside press rows. I could touch the canvas and feel the impact of the punches.

At the end of the grueling, non-stop punching duel, my ribs actually hurt. It felt like Ali and Frazier had belted me in the kidneys.

Within ten yards of me were the celebrity likes of Frank Sinatra, who was shooting photos for *Life* magazine, Burt Lancaster, Lorne Greene, Jack Kent Cooke and famous writers such as Norman Mailer, William Saroyan and Budd Schulberg. My wife Kathie was about 30 rows from ringside, in a seat near the singer (Supremes) Diana Ross, resplendent in fur and sequins and lots of make-up.

I smiled and frowned when I saw myself in my ringside seat in the film ESPN showed of the fight. How lucky I was to be there, I thought. How stupid I looked with longer hair and a Fu Manchu mustache. I should be more tolerant of our youth today. I have never been in a building where there was so much electricity. And everyone was dressed to the hilt; it was a show within a show.

"I remember the day after the fight," recalled Pat McGrath, "we were in an elevator at The New Yorker Hotel, and you were on one side of Ali and we were on the other side as we went down to the lobby."

McGrath also remembered Muhammad Ali visiting here and making good on a promise to his son, Pat Jr., paying an impromptu call on wide-eyed students at Mt. Lebanon High School. I know he also visited students at Schenley High School. "Ali was walking down the hallway at our high school and he spotted two kids fooling around in a biology class," said McGrath. "He patted them on the shoulder and said, 'Hey, that teacher is talking for your benefit. You better pay attention!' They nearly died.

"My son, Patrick, was about 15 at the time. Ali started asking people in the hallway, 'Where's Patrick McGrath?' Pat was in an English class on the fourth floor, we learned. Ali went to the classroom and knocked on the door. 'Is Patrick McGrath here?' he asked. 'Yes, sir,' someone said.

"The word spread and students started spilling into the hallway to get a look at Ali. He started sparring with one of young Pat's friends, Chip Jackson. After a while, Ali addressed everyone by saying, 'Education is the most important thing in your life. Now get back to class!' About 125 students went without a word back to their classes. He was quite a human being."

New York Post

Muhammad Ali conducts casual press conference at Manhattan's Marriott Hotel before his title fight with Joe Frazier, with sportswriters Jim O'Brien of *The New York Post* and Ed Comerford of *Newsday* at right.

Muhammad Ali and Pirates' slugger Willie Stargell spar playfully at 1974 Dapper Dan Dinner that was held at Pittsburgh Hilton, now Wyndam Grand at Point State Park. If Ali had moved to Pittsburgh he would have enhanced Pittsburgh's reputation as "City of Champions."

Muhammad Ali
The man nobody knows

R ufus Brassell, who's been employed to take punches in the gym from both Muhammad Ali and Jimmy Ellis over a two-year period from 1970 to 1971, was talking about the difference between the two men matched to fight at The Astrodome on Monday, July 26, 1971 in what they were force-feeding us as "The Inevitable Fight."

"Jimmy is easy to get next to," Brassell said. "Even when you're close to the other guy, he's over there and you're over here. You can get closer to Jimmy. You can communicate."

Rufus Brassell was a promising boxer I had known from my year (1969) working in Miami and I had covered some of his bouts. Angelo Dundee, who looked after all three of these fighters, had brought Brassell to me in Houston, and he was tuned in to our conversation. "That's it!" said Angelo. "Communication. You can't reach the other guy. No one knows him."

Angelo was talking mostly this way because he had made the choice to stick with Ellis, with whom he had worked for a longer time, and because he was his manager as well as his trainer. So he would be in the Ellis corner.

The exchange took place in the lobby of the Sheraton Hotel in Houston, a parking lot away from The Astrodome, another hotel away from the Astroworld Hotel, where Ali was staying. Brassell, Jeff Merritt and Johnny Hudgins, all sparring partners for Ellis, were sitting about, waiting for Jimmy to come down for dinner.

Brassell and Hudgins both went two rounds with Ali in Atlanta in exhibitions that preceded Ali's comeback bout there with Jerry Quarry a year earlier. They have worked with both combatants in Miami Beach's 5th Street Gym, but now they were both with Ellis.

So was Dundee, who had trained both fighters. So was Luis Sarria, somewhat reluctantly. He didn't want to be in either corner. Chickie Ferrara and Dr. Ferdie Pacheco were also in the Ellis corner. The cast was complete.

For the record, Ali's aides for this one were the incumbent Drew "Bundini" Brown and Wally Youngblood, who's been in his dressing room before, and Harry Wiley and Dr. John Holloman, trainer and physician, in that order to Sugar Ray Robinson.

The next day, in Ellis' dressing room, I asked Brassell to expand upon his remarks relating to the difference between Ali and Ellis. Brassell, a good-looking kid from Lima, Ohio, recalled the return of Ali to the 5th Street Gym, just before the first fight with Frazier.

"Soon as he came to the door," said Brassell, "he came down on Ellis. There was an air of friction from the start. Then he wanted Jimmy to come into the ring and box with him. He told him to be his own man. 'Don't listen to that Italian' he said, pointing toward Angelo. One day, when Angelo was away, Ali called Ellis into the ring. Ali had already boxed about five rounds. Jimmy came in strong and really went at Ali. Everyone hollered that Jimmy tried to take advantage of the champ.

"Most guys take sides in the gym. Just the way the public does. Everybody's waiting for the right bandwagon. Nobody knows the real Ali. I don't think he does. He's been pushed around from a very young age in boxing. I don't think he's had a chance to be himself.

"Now, there's a real human element about Jimmy. He likes people. He likes Ali, too. But he's more edgy for this fight than I've ever seen him."

The shift in supporting cast to Ali has given some new front-runners a chance to chase after Ali. It's all black, and this reflects a triumph for many of them. His sparring partners are Alonzo Johnson, from Rankin, a 1961 victim in Ali's eighth pro fight, and Eddie Brooks, for whom Ali has been falling down for two weeks in Houston.

Stacks Edwards, a 24-year-old record dealer from South Ozone Park in Queens, who pushes people to clear a path for Ali, and sat outside his hotel door in New York before the fights with Oscar Bonavena and Joe Frazier, is at Ali's side continuously. That's fine with me because Edwards treats me like a long lost pal.

277

Edwards, a big boy who came by his nickname honestly, and was sporting a big black cowboy hat since his arrival in Texas, believes he knows Ali.

"Maybe those other guys put him on a pedestal, and that's why they don't get close to him," said Stacks. "He's a human being...we argue about who's going to pick up the check at a restaurant.

"He's one of the nicest, most considerate guys. Angelo Dundee is one of the nicest guys I've ever met, and I don't even put him on the same level. I had him (Ali) in my neighborhood. No one believed he'd come, but he did. I'm not his peer—I don't have his money—but it doesn't matter with him. Anyone who picks sides is going to be a loser. You know, you don't see Jimmy Brown or Lew Alcindor or Diana Ross coming into the ghetto neighborhoods with the kids. They are big shot niggers. Ali...he's a man of the people."

Ali goes toe to toe with George Foreman after Ellis fight

After Muhammad Ali's 12th round TKO of Jimmy Ellis, he was approached by George Foreman, who had a microphone in hand.

"Hello, champ," said Foreman, moving in close to get a few words from Ali. Foreman was covering the fight for *Boxing Illustrated*.

"What are you doing here?" asked Ali. "Who are you, the colored Howard Cosell?"

George got a little testy when Ali added, "I'll get you."

"Bye, boy," said Foreman. "Don't let me see you in Houston anymore. This is my town."

"You serious?" asked Ali.

Later on, Foreman, believed to be a future contender for the heavyweight crown, said, "I don't care what he says or does. He can outdare me and outstare me. I want to know if he can outfight me. They gotta reckon with me now."

Jimmy Ellis
The other champ from Louisville

"He's always been knocking me."
—Ellis about Ali

A fter years of dismissing Jimmy Ellis as nothing more than his former sparring partner, Muhammad Ali was asking us now to regard Ellis as a formidable opponent in the ring.

On this day, Wednesday, June 2, 1971, at the Americana Hotel on 7th Avenue in midtown Manhattan, it was announced that Ellis and Ali, who both grew up in Louisville, trained in the same 5th Street Gym on Miami Beach, and were world champions in their own right, were going to meet in a 12-rounder July 26 at the Astrodome in Houston.

"He knows everything about me," said Ali, "and Ellis is getting a little better. I'm not like I used to be...not *exactly* like I used to be."

Ali's admission meant to lend credibility to Ellis' changes—and help sell tickets at the Astrodome—was unnecessary. Muhammad's mortality was revealed to all at Madison Square Garden on March 8 by Joe Frazier.

And, as far as Ellis was concerned, Ali was exactly like he used to be, if not in the ring, at least outside of it. Fifteen years had not changed him a bit in one respect.

Ellis was 16 and Ali 14 when they first met, at a swimming pool in Louisville. It was Ali who introduced the story about their original encounter.

"I had some tennis shoes and some raggedy trunks in my hand," said Ali. "We introduced ourselves, and here we were both on our way to compete in a local TV boxing show called 'Champions of Tomorrow.'

"I didn't know 'til we got there that we were supposed to fight each other. Well, I weighed 165 and he only weighed 149. My manager said he was too light and so he wouldn't let us fight. I walked out of my dressing room and went home mad. I didn't even get my four dollars."

Ellis was encouraged later to give his own version of the story. There was a slight variance.

"I knew I was fighting him when I met him," said Ellis. "A friend of mine named Danny Hall had fought him before, and Ali had beaten him. I was there and afterward I told Danny I could whip that guy myself. I had only three fights then, and Danny got mad at me for saying that.

"Danny was there when I met Ali at the swimming pool and he tried to put him on. 'Who you fightin'? Danny asked him. 'I'm fightin' some chump,' Ali answered. He looked surprised when he saw me later at the TV studio.

"He's always been a talker," Ellis went on. "He's always been predictin'. Always the Lip. He's always been knocking me. Why he put the bad mouth on me, I'll never know."

Two weeks after their first meeting, a match was made between Ellis and Ali, then called Cassius Clay. Ellis lost the first amateur fight, and later won a return bout.

JIMMY ELLIS

WBA HEAVYWEIGHT CHAMP

"I really beat him," Ellis said of his second fight. "No doubt about it. He's the greatest, but I always thought I could beat him."

Ellis had fought 36 times, and had 30 victories and six losses. His only loss as a heavyweight was to Frazier, the same man who dealt Ali his only defeat in 32 pro fights.

Ellis said he had beaten all of the top-ranked heavyweights, such as Floyd Patterson, Jerry Quarry, Oscar Bonavena and George Chuvalo the previous May. Yet many

280

people have a low estimate of Ellis as a fighter and this is what rankles him most.

"Everybody thinks I'm just a little bitty kid," said Ellis. "Sure, I was his sparring partner and I worked with him. I did my job. But I never hear about how he was my sparring partner, and was paid by me, when he trained with me during his suspension."

It was during his exile, Ali said yesterday that he grew angry with Ellis.

"Joe Frazier always said he wanted to fight me and he always mentioned my name," said Ali. "Ellis never mentioned me. He got with the power structure in keeping me down."

To Ellis, Ali cried out, "I told you this day was coming! Now we'll find out if you can beat me or not!"

Ali was guaranteed 45 percent of all income against a guarantee of $450,000 and Ellis 20 percent of income for what Bob Arum, president of Top Rank Inc., promoters of the fight, called their "inevitable fight."

"To be my sparring partner, he had to be good," said Ali. "If he was nothing, they wouldn't be paying him that kind of money. They ain't crazy."

Ali always insisted on calling Ellis his sparring partner. Ellis was a decent guy. I got to know him a little by my visits to the 5th Street Gym when I was covering boxing and the Dolphins for *The Miami News* in 1969, and later when I was on the boxing beat at *The New York Post*.

Ellis was an honest workman, and was WBA heavyweight champion in Ali's absence, yet Ali never let him forget his earlier undistinguished role in the ring.

It was a put-down, pure and simple, part of Ali's act for antagonizing anyone he went up against. Ellis said nothing in reply. Talking was always Ali's strength, not his. Ellis lacked Ali's charisma and color and showbiz banter, also his speed and skills, but he certainly deserved more respect.

"I never liked it," said Angelo Dundee, who had trained both boxers, and liked them equally. "I told Ali not to do it many times, but he wouldn't listen.

Autographed photo shows Jimmy Ellis battling with Muhammad Ali in title fight in Houston.

"It's been under Jimmy's skin a long, long time. It's really gotten to him. He's a quiet guy, though, and he's never said anything about it in public."

Ellis would get his chance to show he was more than Ali's punching bag.

It would appear that Angelo Dundee would be man caught in the middle on this match, but Dundee decided long ago that if these two men were to ever meet in the ring his place was in Ellis' corner.

"I have to work there," Dundee said. "I'm Jimmy Ellis' manager. I have to do it right."

Dundee was simply a hired hand for Ali, who was managed by Herbert Muhammad. Dundee drew a straight salary for his efforts in the fights with Jerry Quarry, Oscar Bonavena and Joe Frazier rather than a percentage of the purses.

When Ali was in training for the Frazier fight, there was a scene one day in the Fifth Street Gym that is now worth recalling.

Ellis was in the crowd and Ali challenged him to spar a round. Ellis refused. "I got a strange disease," Ellis said. "I only fight for money."

But Ali taunted him. "Ellis is scared," Ali announced to the crowd, "maybe if you help me..."

And then an A cappella chorus—singing without musical accompaniment—of about 200 voices chanted, "We want Ellis. We want Ellis." Ellis exited the gym.

There was more. "Once they went at it for a round when I was on the road," said Dundee, "and I heard it got out of hand. I was always afraid there'd be a flare-up in the gym. I wanted to see them fight, but only when they got paid for it."

Dundee, of course, was shrewd enough to know that such talk was good for drumming up business on their bout, one in which Ali would be a heavy favorite.

Dundee, Chickie Ferrara, Dr. Ferdie Pacheco and Luis Sarria, always the supporting cast for Ali, would all be in Ellis' corner this time. Drew "Bundini" Brown, assistant trainer and as Gordon Parks put it, "black angel" to Ali, would be the lone non-defector from Ali's entourage. Wally Youngblood was in Ali's corner as well.

Ellis first came under Dundee's wing in 1966 when Angelo invited him to Miami Beach to work as a sparring partner for Ali, then called Cassius Clay, who was preparing for a bout with Henry Cooper in London.

"I needed a guy of Cooper's stature with a good left hook," Dundee recalled, "and Ellis fit the bill. Jimmy will have to fight the fight of his life to whip Ali. Ali's a heck of a fighter, and I'm not going to change my tune about that. I'm not silly. But I think Jimmy's ready to fight the fight of his life."

Ellis assured everyone the morning of the fight that he was, indeed, ready to rumble with Ali. "If I beat him, I'll get a shot at Frazier and that's all I want. I have nothing against Ali. I hope that never changes. He's just in my way right now. There's no way around this.

"He's never going to change. He came in talking and he'll go out talking. To me, it's still Cassius Clay I'm fighting. The kid I knew and grew up with in Louisville."

"All the rocks have been thrown at me already. I don't think I deserved that. I don't have to hate him to want to beat him. And I believe I can.

Luis Rodriguez, once world welterweight champion, worked with both fighters at the 5th Street Gym. "Me, I don't like the fight," said Rodriguez. "Both guys are my friends...I don't want to see either guy get beat."

* * *

Ali defeated Ellis easily, scoring a 12th round TKO, stopping Ellis just 50 seconds short of the scheduled bout. Ali said after the fight, "I didn't want to hurt him.

"He's a nice fellow. A family man with children. He's my brother. I knew he could get killed, the look in his eyes. All it would have taken was just three more punches— bam, bam, bam. He was in critical trouble, what with my 230 pounds hitting him hard."

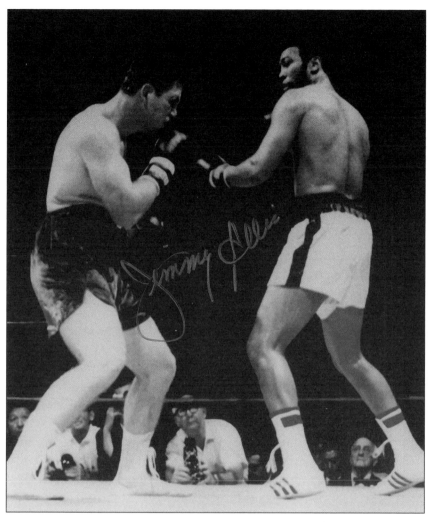

Jimmy Ellis, at right, won the WBA title by beating Jerry Quarry in a 15-round bout in Oakland on April 27, 1968. It was the final fight in an 8-man elimination tournament to determine a champion for the vacant heavyweight title. Muhammad Ali had been stripped of his title for refusing to be inducted into the U.S. Army.

"Eighty percent of success is showing up."
—Woody Allen

New Orleans
Still the best Super Bowl site

"I've already seen it!"
—Weeb Ewbank

I know New Orleans too well. I have visited the Crescent City at least a dozen times in my career. It's not a city you like at first glance; you have to get to know it.

It is a unique city, different from all others. I know its streets, its beats, its beauty, its bad side, its smells, good and bad. I've heard the music up close of Al Hirt and Pete Fountain and the iconic jazz band at Preservation Hall. Those gifted musicians are the heart and soul of this southern city at the tip of the Mississippi River. It is such a storied town.

I was with Barney Kremenko when we caught Pete Fountain's performance. Kremenko was the publicity director of the New York Nets of Julius Dr. J Erving, and we were in New Orleans for a game with the Buccaneers. Kremenko had been a newspaperman and covered baseball for *The World Journal.* He was the writer who gave Willie Mays his nickname of "Say, Hey." Kremenko was a character, a great story-teller, and a terrible driver. Once, we were driving down a one-way street the wrong way in San Diego. It was raining and Kremenko was trying to clear the window with his hand—from inside the car while he was driving. When I cautioned Kremenko that we were on a one-way street, he shouted at me, "I'm only going one way!"

I've dined on Oysters Rockefeller at Antoine's and had Creole Bloody Mary for an eye opener and Eggs Benedict for breakfast at Brennan's. I've had Hurricanes and Sazerac on different visits to Pat O'Brien's Bar & Restaurant on Bourbon Street in the French Quarter, and even raw clams on a shell at several different curbside restaurants.

I've walked the familiar streets framed by fancy railings on second-story balconies that were being shown on television round the clock in 2005, ever since Hurricane

Katrina came to town and tore it apart and flooded its homes and historic buildings. I've never been to Biloxi, or any place in Mississippi for that matter, so I couldn't relate to what happened there.

Through the years, New Orleans has been the best town to hold a major sports championship or title of any kind. I'd also been there to cover pro basketball games when the ABA Buccaneers and the NBA Jazz held court there. I saw Larry Brown and Doug Moe and Red Robbins and James Jones and Goose Ligon play there for the Bucs and I saw Aliquippa-born Pete Maravich score 68 points without a three-point field goal for the New Orleans Jazz against Walt Frazier, an all-pro and all-defense guard for the New York Knicks. That was in the Superdome back on Feb. 25, 1977. Maravich still holds every scoring record in the college ranks and that was done before the 3-point field goal was introduced. I drove a rented car from New Orleans to Baton Rouge to see him play at LSU with some other sportswriters when we were in the Crescent City to cover a Super Bowl.

I first heard about New Orleans as a child because the Pirates had a farm team there in the '50s called the New Orleans Pelicans and that's where the Pirates came up with Joe L. Brown and Danny Murtaugh.

Yes, I have the best memories of days spent in New Orleans. Everything was confined to a few blocks and you could walk to everything from your hotel. Headquarters for the early Super Bowls there was the grand Roosevelt Hotel. That legendary hotel was supposedly the inspiration for author Alex Hailey's 1965 novel *Hotel*. The streets were full of sights and sounds unlike any back home. There was a show of some kind on every street corner. Everyone was on the hustle. I've been to eight Super Bowls, but the three I attended in New Orleans prompts me to say it was the best site of all. No city had hosted as many Super Bowls as New Orleans. It's nine and still counting.

I remember walking down Bourbon Street behind Weeb Ewbank, the coach of the New York Jets, when the Super Bowl was played in New Orleans in 1970. His team had upset the Baltimore Colts in Miami to win the Super Bowl the year before.

A barker in front of a strip bar was inviting passersby to come into the bar to see Ricki Covette, billed as the tallest exotic in the world. She was 6-7, I recall. "See the biggest bust in the country!" the barker hollered to Ewbank. "I've already seen it," replied Ewbank. "It was my ballteam this year!"

I first visited New Orleans that year as a writer for *The Miami News.* I was covering the Super Bowl match-up of the Minnesota Vikings and Kansas City Chiefs. Lenny Dawson, who had been a quarterback for two seasons with the Steelers, led the Chiefs to a victory. I interviewed him before and after the game at Tulane Stadium.

One of the things I enjoyed the most about that first Super Bowl experience was having an opportunity to meet and talk to some of the great sportswriters and columnists in the country, such as Red Smith and Dave Anderson of New York, who would both win the Pulitzer Prize for sportswriting. I also met Milton Gross and Stan Isaacs of New York, Blackie Sherrod of Dallas, Edwin Pope of Miami, Furman Bisher of Atlanta, Jim Murray and Melvin Durslag of Los Angeles, Joe Falls and Jerry Greene of Detroit, Jerry Izenberg and Dave Klein of Newark, John Camichael, Brent Musburger, Bill Gleason and Ray Soens of Chicago, Hubert Mizell and Tom McEwen of Tampa. I sought them out and talked to them as much as I could. I admired these men.

I would later cover two Super Bowls at the Superdome, and the Steelers vs. the Saints in New Orleans. At my first Super Bowl, when the Kansas City Chiefs beat the Minnesota Vikings, I interviewed Lenny Dawson of the Chiefs, the game's MVP, in the locker room after the game. You could go to the locker room in those days. There wasn't a formal press conference staged mainly for TV purposes. In one of the Super Bowls in New Orleans, Mike Ditka, a former Pitt All-American end from Aliquippa and Carnegie, caught a touchdown pass in that victory over the Miami Dolphins. That same weekend, I covered a heavyweight championship bout in which Joe Frazier defended his title against Terry Daniels, scoring a third-round TKO.

I arranged to meet a former light-heavyweight champion who grew up in New Orleans, Willie Pastrano, at a local dive called The Bastille. We sat in a booth in a dark, dreary room and he was enthused about telling me about his glory days in boxing. I had spent time with him earlier in Miami. Angelo and Chris Dundee had ties with Pastrano as promoter and corner man and trainer, respectively.

The last time I was in New Orleans was in early April, 2003 when I went there during the NCAA men's basketball championship. I was inducted into the U.S. Basketball Writers' Hall of Fame, and I took my wife Kathie with me. That was a real honor. We rooted for Syracuse, led by freshman sensation Carmelo Anthony, as they won the NCAA title for Jim Boeheim's ballclub. "We have to root for the Big East," said Kathie.

She had been there with me once before. We toured the town, visited the Louie Armstrong Museum, and I took her to a hotel where Frazier and his sparring mate, Ken Norton, later a heavyweight champion himself, had trained on the top floor. I remember that Norton was helping Frazier prepare for the fight. I recall one day on the top floor of the Hotel Monteleone watching a trainer slam a medicine ball repeatedly into the stomach of Norton as he lay on a table. The trainer was standing over the table and slamming that medicine ball as hard as he could onto Norton's stomach. It was like a medieval torture chamber. It was tough to watch.

Famous writers had stayed there, at the Hotel Monteleone.

New Orleans was the hometown of Tennessee Williams and Anne Rice, and writers were always drawn there, such as Mark Twain, Erskine Caldwell, Sherwood Anderson, Eudora Welty. Truman Capote came into his own there.

We toured Royal Street and looked at the artwork, antiques and books that were displayed in one little shop after another. As I later watched the Hurricane Katrina coverage, I wondered what had become of all that stuff in the storm that has devastated the area.

I prefer my favorite images of New Orleans to the horrific photos and images that continue to disturb us. My New Orleans remains intact. Like Preservation Hall.

TWO OF THE GREATEST—Muhammad Ali always said he was the greatest, but he might have to get in line behind Jack Dempsey and Babe Ruth as far as the greatest sports figures of the 20th Century. Inset Billy Conn and Jack Dempsey.

Publicity photo

Joe Frazier poses in a proper costume for a fight with George
Foreman that was billed as "The Gladiators," set for New
York's Madison Square Garden on June 15, 1976. "I feel I am a
gladiator," said Frazier before the fight. "The way they fought—
thumbs up, you win; thumbs down, you lose; it's all over. There's
no in between."

Willie Pastrano
A last stand at The Bastille
with a former champ in New Orleans

From *New York Post* January 15, 1972

Whenever I was on the road with a particular assignment, no matter the sport, I tried to take advantage of where I was to find another story, one I was not expected to provide for the next day's newspaper. I liked giving them something extra so no one could complain about me doing so much free-lance work on the side.

Such an opportunity presented itself when I was in New Orleans to cover a nationally televised heavyweight championship fight between Joe Frazier, who was defending his title, and Terry Daniels.

Joe visited the Fair Grounds, a local race track, to see a horse named Joe Frazier. The horse tried to stomp on Joe's foot, but Frazier was quick enough to elude him, and felt it was a good warm-up to be ready for Daniels.

At his hotel earlier that morning, Joe was drawing his bath when he decided to call his family back in Philadelphia. Frazier forgot to turn the water off, and part of his suite was flooded as a result. He laid that $800 green and gold brocade robe which he wore for his fight with Muhammad Ali on the floor to soak up the water. "I'll get it dry-cleaned," he said when we questioned the wisdom of what he had just done.

New Orleans was a busy place because the Super Bowl VI match between the Dallas Cowboys and Miami Dolphins was also on the sports schedule that same weekend. I did a story on Mike Ditka who caught a TD pass for the Cowboys. Ditka had always been one of my personal favorites.

When you walk the streets of New Orleans you feel like everyone is out to take your money.

Willie Pastrano raises his arms in triumph after a 1964 fight. That's his trainer, Lou Gross, going after him.

"It's a hustle scene," said Willie Pastrano, once the light-heavyweight boxing champion of the world, who should know. He grew up in New Orleans. This is where they danced in the streets when he beat Harold Johnson for the world title. "There are a lot of people here now," Pastrano said of the Super Bowl scene, "and this town comes to life. And the town is hustling people."

I had gotten in touch with Willie Pastrano through Angelo Dundee, his former trainer. I was working for *The New York Post*, and I invited two friends of mine, John Crittenden, my former boss at *The Miami News*, and Roy McHugh of *The Pittsburgh Press* to join me, knowing they were such big boxing fans and they weren't in competition with me.

Willie was hunched over the bar at a place called The Bastille—"a little hole in the wall," as Pastrano put it, just off Bourbon Street. It had a phony façade of yellow shutters on a red surface and the way the blue lights played on it gave off the appearance of a stage setting for a Tennessee Williams play.

Inside, the color scheme was red and black, and the walls were papered with huge posters, some pornographic, others picturing the likes of Dracula, Fu Manchu, Albert Einstein, Elliott Gould and Frank Zappa.

It gives you a capsule look at the area about Bourbon Street at its worst. Once when I asked Art Heyman, a player for the Pittsburgh Pipers, to describe the décor of a similar place he owned on New York's East Side, he said, "It's Early American Vomit."

Pastrano was proud to tell us that he had beaten a heroin habit and that this had been the toughest battle in his long career. He weighed about 230 pounds and he had fought at 170.

Pastrano pinpointed the change in the city that comes with the Super Bowl and, to a lesser degree, the heavyweight title fight.

Pastrano got caught up in the frenzy like all the locals. "Last week, you'd go into spots on Bourbon Street and all the owners had long faces," he said. "Like a fight promoter's whose show loses money. Now everybody's happy.

"It's like Hong Kong this week. It's so heavy with people. Quite a few hustlers are in town. They come in from Alexandria and those places. Girls who walk the street in the daytime are walking in the night, too. That's how good business is."

An overweight Willie Pastrano has his girth measured for a laugh.

The hustle, indeed, was on. Unlike Las Vegas, where you expect to blow a bundle, here you wonder who is going to get it from you. Several hotel robberies had been reported that week. There was no action on the fight, so forget that.

On that afternoon, I came across three young men with musical instruments going into Jackson Square, playing "Gotta Travel On." It must have been their theme song.

"They gotta hustle," said another young man looking on with a girlfriend. "They gotta stay one step ahead of the cops."

The girlfriend wanted to know why, and he told her of an ordinance against hustling and obscenity. "Shucks," she said, "no more fun."

I saw the same musical trio at work later on, at the corner of Royal and St. Louis, and a crowd gathered to hear them play. The crowd threw coins into an open guitar case. There were a few silver or gold-plated men and women pretending they were statues—statues that moved now and then.

Black kids at the curb shined shoes on their knees and wanted to bet the customers that they could tell them where they bought their shoes. The hustle, as Willie warned us, was truly on.

"This town has a certain magic about it," Pastrano said. "It's like the Paris of the United States." I asked Willie why he was frequenting a dive like The Bastille. "The prices are right," he responded. "It's The Bastille. It's the last stronghold."

Frazier floored Daniels a few times and the fight was halted at 1:45 of the fourth round with Daniels in dire trouble.

Kathleen Churchman O'Brien

Author Jim O'Brien visited the Hotel Monteleone while in New Orleans for NCAA Final Four.

Roy McHugh on Billy Soose:

"In 1938 when colleges had boxing teams, Billy Soose, a Penn State fighter from Farrell, fought 16 times, knocking out his opponents in the first round in the first 15. The 16th, a glutten for punishment, lasted until the second round. In 1941, he decisioned Ken Overlin in New York for middleweight title. His manager, Farrell neighbor Paul Moss, was a Hollywood press agent. Soose lived with actors Dick Powell and Joan Blondell during a stay in Hollywood."

Ken Norton
He broke Ali's jaw

The first time I ever saw Ken Norton he was lying flat on his back on a slab or rubdown table on the top floor—an atrium—of the Hotel Monteleone overlooking the French Quarter in New Orleans. It's a grand four-star hotel a block from Bourbon Street. The sun was streaming through the skylight onto Norton's near-naked body.

He wore only skimpy gray undershorts.

Norton was not getting a rubdown. A huge black man was standing over him and repeatedly slamming a medicine ball onto Norton's stomach. Bam. Bam. Bam. The table shook every time the man slammed that medicine ball. A medicine ball, by the way, is like a basketball filled with lead pellets. Norton made no sounds. He just grimaced.

Norton was well built, even more muscular than Muhammad Ali or Joe Frazier, more of a body-builder type. I thought I was witnessing a scene from the days of medieval torture chambers. What had Norton done to deserve this punishment? Had he stolen a neighbor's chickens?

Norton was simply doing his regular agenda to toughen his body. As if absorbing shots from Frazier wasn't bad enough. Norton was working as a sparring partner for Frazier, who was going to defend his title a few nights later at the Rivergate Auditorium, on the eve of a Super Bowl contest between the Dallas Cowboys and Miami Dolphins at Tulane Stadium. That was the site three years later of the Steelers' first Super Bowl victory, over the Minnesota Vikings.

Frazier correctly predicted the Cowboys would defeat the Dolphins. No one asked Ken Norton what he thought. He was 28 at the time and I was 29. Norton had a five-year old son, Ken Norton Jr., who would someday star as a linebacker for both the Dallas Cowboys and the San Francisco 49ers. His son would be the only NFL player to win three Super Bowl rings in consecutive years.

Had Ken Sr. known that, surely he would have joined Joe Frazier in predicting the Cowboys would defeat the Dolphins.

When I took my wife to New Orleans for the NCAA Final Four in early April of 2003, I took her to the Hotel Monteleone and rode the elevator up to the top floor so I could show her where Frazier and Norton worked out for Frazier's fight with Terry Daniels, a 25-year-old contender (or pretender) from Willoughby, Ohio. The rooms were empty of people when we visited and used for storage.

There were some bags with concrete mix in them. Had they been there when Norton was lying on his back, surely someone would have stacked them on his chest.

Back in January of 1972, Frazier was such a prohibitive favorite that Las Vegas took no bets on the outcome of the scheduled 15-round bout. Frazier floored Daniels five times and won by a TKO in the fourth round.

Norton's name is inextricably linked to that of Muhammad Ali. Norton fought Ali three times and handed "The Greatest" the second defeat of his career, breaking Ali's jaw with a first-round punch. Asked in a 1992 interview what he thought he would be most remembered for, Norton replied, "Fighting Ali."

Norton was one of the best heavyweights in the business in the 1960s and 1970s. He did not grow up boxing or dreaming of becoming a boxer. He played football, basketball and track in high school in southern California, and earned a scholarship to Southeast Missouri State, which he attended for two years and then joined the Marines. It was in the Marines that he started to box and found he was good at it. He was athletic and had a devastating punch. Just ask Ali.

It was on March 31, 1973 that Norton won a 12-round decision over Ali in San Diego. He lost a 12-round decision to Ali in Los Angeles on September 10, 1973, and he lost a close split decision in 15 rounds to Ali at Yankee Stadium on September 28, 1976. I still have a red baseball cap with a patch on the front with Ali's and Norton's names and the date and site of the fight. It was given to the media rather

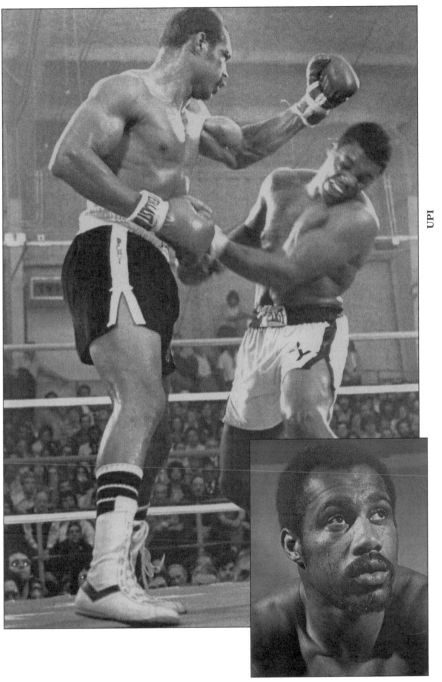

Ken Norton connects with a hard left to Jimmy Young's head while winning a 15-round split decision at Caesar's Palace Sports Pavilion in Las Vegas on November 11, 1977.

than a ticket to gain entry to the press section for that fight. Norton is the only heavyweight champion never to defend his title successfully.

I wrote the following story about Norton before his second fight with Ali:

From New York Post June 8, 1973

Ken Norton doesn't believe he broke Muhammad Ali's jaw in either the first or second rounds, as claimed, when he upset the former heavyweight champion. And he said so several times at a press conference in New York as he viewed a film of that fight.

"Maybe I did in the sixth round," said Norton, and later, as he watched himself slugging away at Ali in the final round, he added, "Maybe it happened in the 12th. But you can see for yourself watching this film, that it sure didn't happen in the first few rounds, like they said."

Ali's alibi for his weak performance steals something from Norton's enormous accomplishment. Ken would like to get credit for being the only fighter besides Joe Frazier ever to defeat Ali at that point. He reminds people that, in any case, Ali didn't break his own jaw. Ken Norton was the name of the fighter who did the damage.

Norton, a believer in positive thinking, voiced confidence before his first fight with Ali, and is talking the same way about the return match set for September 10 (1973) in Los Angeles.

"I beat Muhammad Ali once," he says, "When we fight again, I'll beat him again. Nothing he could say is going to change that."

Norton, along with his trainer, Eddie Futch, attended a luncheon yesterday at Gallagher's 52nd St., at which Norton received an award for his victory over Ali. Norton was not thought to have a chance against Ali, going into the fight, even though he had a 30-1 record. He hadn't fought any rated boxers and was a 5-1 underdog.

He thinks Ali psyched out a lot of his opponents in the past, but said he ignored him whenever Ali started talking to him, or staring at him. "It's like when you get bawled out by your parents," Norton said. "You see the mouth move but a minute later you couldn't tell what was said."

Norton was nearly signed to fight Jerry Quarry June 18, but his backers nixed the fight in favor of another with Ali. "What would be a better fight?" asked Futch. "Where would he take away more money?"

Norton, who never made more than $5,000 for a fight prior to his $50,000 payday against Ali, was offered $150,000 to fight Quarry at the Garden. "He's getting double that against Ali," claimed Futch. "He's rated over Quarry. Why should he go backward?"

Futch was credited with outlining the kind of fight Norton needed to defeat Ali. "I've watched Ali for ten years," said Futch, who's worked with Yank Durham in Frazier's corner through the years. "As far as I'm concerned, he's always had technical flaws. Ali's great speed took him over a multitude of technical mistakes."

Norton never gave Ali an opportunity to get going, pressing him from the opening bell, and breaking his jaw somewhere along the line, which had to hinder Ali's performance.

"Everybody's looking for him to be 24," Futch said of Ali as he watched the film being shown, "but Ali's 31."

Futch is also the reason that Frazier and Norton never fought since he worked for both fighters, and didn't want to have to make the kind of Solomonesque decision Angelo Dundee had to make in sticking with Jimmy Ellis, whom he also managed, against Ali, whom he served only as a trainer.

Norton is nearly as handsome as Ali, a little younger at 28, better built, and at ease on his feet, whether he's in the ring or simply talking about himself. He thinks he'd make a real nice champion, too.

"After I beat Muhammad Ali again," he said, "my paramount goal is to fight George Foreman for the championship."

* * *

Ken Norton was named "Father of the Year" twice by Los Angeles dailies and said "Dad" was the best title he ever had.

He was in the movies for a while and did motivational speeches, but ran into difficult financial times. Some of his friends, especially George Foreman, helped him out. He suffered a horrific auto accident in which he had his ribs and several other bones broken and incurred a brain injury as well that left his speech slurred.

He suffered several strokes and then a heart attack and died at age 70 on September 19, 2013.

Howard Cosell hooked up with young Cassius Clay and they became a TV comedy team in the mid '60s and into the '70s.

Ken Buchanan and Ismael Laguna
A great fight at The Garden

I have seen some great fights in my time. The Marvin Hagler vs. Tommy Hearns was as good as it gets. All three fights between Arturo Gatti, whom I had seen in several fights at Felt Forum in the bowels of the Garden beforehand, and Mickey Ward of Boston were real wars.

The fight between Scotland's Ken Buchanan and Panama's Ismael Laguna on Monday night, September 14, 1971, was a better boxing exhibition than Al-Frazier earlier in the year, even if it lacked the frenzied excitement of the celebrity crowd of "The Fight of the Century."

Ismael Laguna may have been my favorite name for a fighter.

Unlike Ali or Frazier, Laguna was not that friendly or cooperative with the press, but that may be because he didn't speak English well, but Buchanan did his best to answer questions and help the promotion.

They had both trained at Kutcher's Country Club by Kiamesha Lake in the Catskills, and I had been there for a week to watch their final workouts. Laguna was looking forward to the fight. In the week prior to the fight, he said, "I love it. I love to dance. I feel happy to see my people. A lot of people proud of me."

About 500 people from Panama paid about $500 apiece to make the trip to New York to support the kid from Colon. "I feel like I'm back in Panama," Laguna allowed when he surveyed the scene at the Garden. Laguna had never lost in five previous fights at the Garden.

Once their bout began it was an all-out war.

After a while, Ken Buchanan confessed, he could not tell whether he was hearing the sound of bagpipes or the beat of bongo drums in the distance. "Maybe," he said, "they mixed it up."

It was just as difficult to determine whether Buchanan or Laguna was going to win the lightweight title match at Madison Square Garden the evening of Monday, September 13, 1971.

For those little guys, game as can be and backed up by crowd-stirring bands alternately playing music between rounds from their native countries—Scotland and Panama—were both mixing it up pretty good. This was to determine a champion in the 135-pound division. It was tough to sort out all the punches—they flashed back and forth, forth and back—to score the fight, or to know whether the deep cut above Buchanan's left eye, or Laguna's legs, would victimize one of the fighters first, and stop the exciting scuffle short of its scheduled 15 rounds.

I pulled a white handkerchief out of my back pocket at one point, and wiped the perspiration, spit and blood off my forehead which was this close to the canvas edge. Buchanan kept the title, winning a unanimous decision, but he was a bloody sight for his own sore eyes when he stared into a dressing room mirror afterward.

Dr. Edwin Campbell, physician for the State Athletic Commission, examined Buchanan's cut before the 13th round, and again before the 14th, and said he would have stopped the fight if a world's championship had not been at stake.

Buchanan was coming on strong at that stage, but blood was fast filling his left eye, and blinding him. It was "misty," he said, as misty as a morn on the heather lands in his native Edinburgh.

Buchanan, in turn, thought referee Jimmy Devlin, was going to stop the fight in the 14th, when he left Laguna sitting on the ropes, then reeling about the ring. Laguna's legs may have betrayed his body, but his heart kept him going. He survived the onslaught and even came on to win the final round, on Devlin's card at least.

Devlin, who looked like he put in a long day's work at a meat packing house—the kind heavyweight champ Joe Frazier, who took a bow before the fight—used to work in back in Philadelphia—scored the fight nine rounds to six in favor of Buchanan. Judge Tony Castellano scored it 8-6-1 and judge Harold Lederman made it 10-5 in favor of the Scot.

Cain Young, Laguna's manager who put up a $100,000 guarantee to get Buchanan to come to New York, disagreed with the decision, and felt the fight should have been stopped when Buchanan bled profusely; in the 12th, and accused Dr. Campbell of being part of the "machine" geared against Laguna, or any black man for that matter, getting a fair shake under such circumstances.

Young yelped that it was no different than what had happened in San Juan, Puerto Rico less than a year before, when Laguna lost his title by a single point in a split decision. Laguna would have seemed to have an edge with the fight staged in Puerto Rico. In this latest scrap, there were six rounds in which officials disagreed as to the winner.

Buchanan complained of a sore back after the brawl. Laguna got him good there, and often hit on the break. "I feel like I did when my mother had given me a beating," Buchanan said. It was simply a bloody good fight.

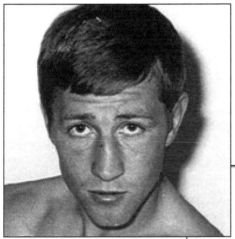

KEN BUCHANAN

ISMAEL LAGUNA

Earnie Shavers
Punching a clock for a living

Earnie Shavers remembered Hill Creek Park in Youngstown, Ohio, as a lot of hills. That's where he often did his roadwork while learning the ropes as a professional boxer in the late '60s. One day, Shavers started collecting rocks as he ran through the park. "I hadn't made any money for such a long time," he recalled. "I thought maybe we stopped using money. I started thinking maybe we'd be trading stones like in the olden days. I thought maybe I'd buy some steak with the stones."

Shavers was set to slug it out with Jimmy Ellis this night, Monday, June 18, 1973, at Madison Square Garden in the biggest fight of Shavers' career. It was a long, hilly climb to get to this iconic venue.

He also remembered the monotony of working on the assembly line in the General Motors plant in Lordstown, Ohio, just outside his hometown of Warren where he went to work at age 21. That was in 1967, the same year he began boxing as an amateur.

Another automobile came along every minute. Earnie would put the front bumper in place, and somebody else bolted it in place. A bumper every minute. "Once in a while we got a break," said Shavers. "Once in a while the line broke down, which is what we prayed for."

Shavers remained on the assembly line nearly three years. Then he quit to devote full time on boxing. He hooked up with Dean Chance, once a Cy Young Award winner at the peak of his major league pitching career, who also dreamed of making it big in boxing, and Earnie was put on a weekly salary of $125. That was $40 to $50 less than Shavers had made on the assembly line. I was making $200 a week as a sportswriter in Miami that same year.

Shavers believed he could be a champion someday, and it would be worth the sacrifice. His wife went along with his dream. She also went to work, as an inspector at a

HARDEST HEAVYWEIGHT PUNCHER IN BOXING HISTORY

Earnie Shavers of Warren, Ohio was some puncher. He was thought to be one of the hardest-hitting fighters of all time.

Coach Jack Schricker, at left, poses with pugilists from Pitt's 1935 squad. The Panthers were in a four-team league that included Carnegie Tech (now Carnegie Mellon University), Duquesne University and John Carroll University of Cleveland.

GM-affiliated company, because there were four daughters at home to be fed and dressed.

As a pro boxer, Shavers had been making between $6,000 and $7,000 a year for three years. "A lot of sacrifice," said Shavers, "and nothing to show for it. Not yet, anyhow." Boxers are a breed apart from athletes in other sports. They haven't been spoiled since they were schoolkids. They've grown up in a real world, where a man puts in 40 hours a week or he doesn't collect on payday. They haven't lived a cocoon-like existence like pro football, baseball and basketball players. Bill Russell once remarked that most athletes have been on scholarship since they were in the eighth grade, pampered and fawned over, but it isn't that way with most boxers.

They are more attuned to the problems and successes of Everyman, and it shows in the way they behave and befriend people, in their vocabularies and life styles.

George Foreman, the heavyweight champion at the time, came out of the Job Corps to win greater glory. Joe Frazier, the youngest of 13 children, went to work as a South Carolina field-hand at age 8, dropped out of high school after nine grades and wound up in Philadelphia as a married 16-year-old with a job in a slaughterhouse. There have been some exceptions. Muhammad Ali never worked a day in his life. But, generally, boxers come from hard-labor backgrounds.

Jimmy Ellis' first pro fight was in 1961. But it wasn't until 1967, when he knocked out Johnny Persol at Madison Square Garden, the upset that was to lead him, eventually, to the championship of the World Boxing Association, that Jimmy let his membership lapse in the Louisville cement masons' union.

Ellis quit school in the 11th grade and was a cement finisher at age 16. He nearly lost a big toe to a jackhammer which bit through his work boot. "You learn to take care of your family—that nobody gives you nothing," said Ellis. "It makes you wise taking care of your money, too. You don't throw none of it away."

Angelo Dundee, who managed and trained Ellis, knew what it was all about. He was an inspector in a Philadelphia aircraft factory for six years before he followed his older brothers to the boxing gyms to take up the cornerman's trade. "Boxers are the easiest-to-handle athletes in sports," said Dundee, "because they have been baptized in other things."

Archie Moore, who was helping prepare Shavers for his match with Ellis, said, "Boxing's the real one-on-one sport. Boxing is the most gut-level sport."

Ellis didn't remember his cement-finishing days as the worst of times. "You're out there in nice weather sometimes," he said, "in a T-shirt and work pants, the wind blowing, smelling things, seeing the people walking by. It's better than looking at a machine all day."

Jimmy was now 33 and if he didn't get beat by Shavers his services as a boxer might be in more demand. "I won't jump out no windows." Said Ellis. "I can always go back to cement. It's a living."

I picked Ellis to win this fight by a knockout in the 8th round. Shavers didn't see it that way. Shavers scored a first-round knockout and picked up $12,500 for his payday.

Talking about Ellis, Dundee said, "He walked into a beauty, no doubt about that. I didn't want him to mix it up with Shavers so soon."

"One punch did it," said matchmaker Teddy Brenner. "It was not like he hurt him, got him in trouble and finished him off. One punch changed the whole ball game."

"It's a damn shame," said Ellis. "I should have boxed more. I should know better. It's a damn shame."

Shavers got knocked out by Jerry Quarry in the first round of a fight on December 14, 1973.

He twice fought for the title, but lost to Muhammad Ali and Larry Holmes. His career record was 74-14-1, with 68 KOs to his credit.

Jimmy Cannon
Nobody asked me but...
Cannon was in a league of his own

According to my Muhammad Ali wristwatch, it was 8:55 p.m. According to the TV listings, in five minutes Ali would be defending his World Heavyweight Boxing title against Belgium's Jean-Pierre Coopman in a televised bout from San Juan, Puerto Rico. It seemed a good time to turn on the TV.

It was Friday night fight time once again. Time to look sharp, feel sharp and be sharp, or so I thought.

Hold on, though. Ali and Coopman weren't in camera view, and wouldn't be for more than an hour. CBS-TV was stalling, as usual, trying to build up interest in a fight that had failed to grip the public's interest, and to sell some automobiles, stomach settlers and, of course, shaving kits and blue razor blades.

Instead of Ali and Coopman, we had to settle for Phyllis George and Brent Musburger superimposed on the home screen. Was Super Bowl XI here already? Phyllis was wearing a yellow dress, and Brent was beautiful in a mauve—or lilac—tuxedo. They were dressed for a ball if not a boxing match. They chatted about the upcoming fight as if they really knew what was going on.

They had become pros at that. "You can smell the anticipation in the air," Musburger began. Maybe he really did know what was going on; maybe he knew we'd be witnessing and smelling a real stinker if we stuck around another hour.

Then he said to Phyllis, "You'll never forget your first heavyweight championship fight. There's nothing like it." Phyllis nodded and cooed, "Yes, you can feel the electricity."

She may have read that line from the notes in front of her.

If Phyllis is smart, though, she'll forget her first heavyweight championship fight. It was very forgettable. Ali put

Coopman away in the fifth round. Ali has also been guilty of filling time. No wonder they loved him on Madison Avenue.

Watching Phyllis and Brent talk about boxing, and the big fight we were about to watch, I remembered the scene in Houston in July of 1971. Boxing was my beat for *The Post* back then, and I was at the Astrodome before Ali's fight with Buster Mathis.

That's where I got my Ali wristwatch, a souvenir of the event, that was given to the regular boxing writing corps.

Mathis was about to spar one afternoon, and a public relations man picked up a microphone at ringside and began extolling Buster's boxing credentials. Let's just say he was exaggerating a bit. He was also wearing a silver tie.

I was in the heralded company of Jimmy Cannon, a New Yorker who may have been the best sports columnist to come down the pike, paving the way perhaps for another wonderful wordsmith named Jim Murray. Both Irishmen, just for the record.

Jimmy Cannon was sitting in great pain next to me. The PR man was causing Cannon the great pain. Cannon, a little guy who was a giant in the newspaper business in his heyday, screeched, "Who the hell is that guy?"

"Shelley something or other," I replied.

Then, reverting to his famous "Nobody Asked Me But..." Cannon commented, "Never trust a PR man with a microphone at his mouth." Better yet, he added, "Never trust a man who wears a silver tie. Shelley is a name that invites suspicion"

No wonder I loved Jimmy Cannon. He could be insufferable and irascible, but he was worth the price of admission. His list of complaints could fill a book. He was like a man who couldn't get rid of a bunion on his big toe. But it was worth waiting for the golden nuggets of a newspaperman who could really write well. And he had spent time on the Left Bank in Paris with Ernest Hemingway during World War II, and with Joe DiMaggio at Toots Shor's and the Cotton Club and Copacabana. More about Jimmy Cannon later. Stay tuned. Never trust a woman in a yellow dress, either, or a man in a mauve tuxedo.

These two were only the first of a phalanx or commentators CBS-TV sent our way. It seemed like they were out to have a bigger reporting cast than ABC-TV had for recent Winter Olympics coverage, if that were possible.

Haywood Hale Broun and Jack Whitaker were the best, offering some good imaginative commentary, and Broun on the beach with Ali in an interview may have been the evening's best moment.

Tom Brookshier and Pat Summerall looked smart in white tuxedos but sounded dumb when they described the fight action. They may have been the best announcing combination in pro football, but they were as ill-suited for this event as Coopman and their white tuxedos.

During the preliminary, when Alfredo Escalera stopped Jose Fernandez for the WBC junior lightweight championship in the best fight of the night. Brookshier said to Summerall during some spirited action, "They've got something going in there we don't know about."

After the main event, Brookshier was talking to Ali's trainer, Angelo Dundee, about the speed of his man's punches. "They're so fast," Brookshier said, "if you knew what they were, you couldn't describe them."

Said Dundee: "I know what they are."

So did Don Dunphy, the veteran boxing announcer who sat mostly silent beside Brookshier and Summerall throughout the evening. What a waste of talent, someone knowledgeable about the fight game with a compelling announcing style. He was busy scoring the fight for CBS-TV when he should've been calling the punches. Dunphy could provide the dramatic delivery necessary to enliven even a dull fight like this one.

Summerall said to Dunphy after the fight. "I was interested in your comments earlier on Ali." So were a lot of people, Pat.

The first time I laid eyes on Jimmy Cannon he was sitting in the VIP section at Toot Shor's Restaurant in midtown Manhattan. Joe E. Lewis and Walter Winchell's secretary were seated back there, too, and Shor introduced me to them, and to his wife, whom he called "Baby Doll." She had been a dancer with the Ziegfeld Follies.

I was the new sportswriter in town and Toots Shor took a liking to me. Sportswriters once spent a lot of time late at night at Shor's, but those days were long gone, and Shor was happy to have a new disciple at the bar.

One day I was coming to a press conference at Shor's to promote the first Ali-Frazier fight and I saw Joe E. Lewis on the same street—West 52nd Street—as Shor's and then Joe Louis, the great fighter, at Shor's. I remember telling my wife Kathie that sort of experience was what was so great about New York. "You could see Joe E. Lewis and Joe Louis on the same street."

Joe E. was being helped out of a bar called Jilly's that was owned by a friend of Frank Sinatra. It wasn't noon and Joe E. Lewis was drunk and needed to be helped to a waiting car at the curb. The bar's owner Jilly Rizzo was killed in a car accident in Palm Desert, California when a drunken driver struck his vehicle which exploded into flames on impact. It happened on Rizzo's 75th birthday.

When I got to the press conference, which was held on the second floor of Shor's, I saw a familiar face at the top of the stairs. It belonged to Horace McMahon, who had starred in the TV series "Naked City." That series, which ran from 1958 to 1963 on ABC-TV always concluded with the iconic line: "There are eight million stories in the Naked City...this has been one of them."

*   *   *

Howard Cosell was not popular with most media types in New York, and that included Cannon. Cosell embraced me early on because I was new in town, and had no reason yet to dislike him. He would turn on me later on, as he did everybody in the business.

"If Howard Cosell were a sport," Cannon wrote in his column, "it would be roller derby."

They tell a story about how this man with a long beard and long hair came into the newsroom one day when Cannon was at work. The man proclaimed that he was Jesus. "I've heard a lot about you," said Cannon without missing a key on his typewriter.

I met Jimmy Cannon and talked to him for the first time at a restaurant on Treasure Island, a resort community this side of St. Petersburg, Florida. This was in the spring of 1972. I was assigned to cover the Mets in spring training, and I would be switching with Maury Allen to cover the Yankees after the All-Star Game. Allen loved baseball and grew up with the Giants and Dodgers as well as the Yankees, and was one of the best at writing about it. Cannon and I were in St. Petersburg to write about the Mets of Gil Hodges. My wife Kathie and I had an apartment on Treasure Island for six weeks. What an assignment. Hodges died on the last day of training camp and was replaced by one of his coaches, Yogi Berra.

I spent as much time as possible with Cannon. I learned from Joe Durso of *The New York Times*, one of the most dapper sportswriters I ever met (There are no dapper sportswriters these days), that many of the sportswriters avoided or ducked Cannon's company because he was a pain in the ass, a reformed alcoholic who expressed unhappiness about so many things.

That was fine with me. I can be selfish and I liked having him all to myself.

I was used to such behavior because Milton Gross, our lead columnist at *The New York Post*, could be just as fussy and hard to please. I can remember how Gross would give

314

a waitress a stern eye and say, "I want my coffee hot-hot." Now I find myself offering the same sort of instruction to waiters, about soup as well as coffee.

I was in a restaurant with Cannon one night before the Ali-Mathis fight and he ordered prime rib. He was quite specific about how he wanted it. And what he didn't want. I memorized his order, just in case. Then he went to the bathroom. While he was gone, the waitress came back to our table to check on something. I told her, "Listen, I'm going to do you a big favor. Please get this man's order right, just like he told you. Otherwise, he will give you a bad time."

She smiled and left the table.

Cannon came back and seated himself. The waitress came back. "Sir, how do you want your steak?" she said.

I started to slink under the table so I wouldn't get hit with any of the shrapnel when Cannon roared. "Sweetheart, prime rib is not a steak! Now please pay attention..." Then it got worse. He was like that all the time.

It may have contributed to the fact that Jimmy Cannon was a lifelong bachelor. Dave Anderson, who later won a Pulitzer Prize for sports writing at *The New York Times* and admired and enjoyed Jimmy Cannon, said Cannon "was married to his column."

Cannon wrote a column once about Joe Namath of the New York Jets, who came out of Beaver Falls to become more famous than most athletes, "It all comes down to a man being great at something," wrote Cannon.

Anderson suggested that line belonged on Jimmy Cannon's tombstone when he died in 1973. I had visited Cannon at Bellevue Hospital in Manhattan when he was recovering from a stroke. As I was coming down the hallway of the hospital toward his room, I could hear Cannon telling a nurse about Wilt Chamberlain. He said that Chamberlain, a 7-foot giant of basketball, once said, "Nobody loves Goliath."

Cannon died at the age of 63, same as my dad.

I always took advantage of being in the company of elder sportswriters, people I could learn something from, just to hear their war stories.

Cannon not only knew Joe DiMaggio ("the loneliest man I ever met," he once wrote of the Yankee Clipper), Joe Louis, Vince Lombardi and Eddie Arcaro. After several daily newspapers went out of business in New York, there was a long period where Cannon was a nationally syndicated columnist, but with no daily outlet in New York. "I hate not being able to read my stuff in a newspaper," he complained.

Some of his best lines:

- "The higher the girl's heels the skinnier her legs figure to be."
- "If I had a choice of drinking partners it would be Winston Churchill."

It was tough being held up to such a standard, but I know I was a good listener and I took notes. And I didn't drink around him. Jimmy Cannon liked that.

Cannon helped change my career, in a sense. Once while we were both covering one of Ali's fights, and Cannon was into his 60s, I saw him chasing after Muhammad Ali in a hotel lobby.

Ali had enough of sportswriters that afternoon and was leaving us behind. Cannon kept after him, "Muhammad, Muhammad," Cannon cried out. "Jimmy Cannon. Jimmy Cannon."

I remember the scene like it was yesterday. I told myself I never wanted to do that. I wasn't going to be an old man, chasing after any athlete, begging for his time and attention, calling out his name, calling out my name. Like that would make a difference.

Ali kept going. I got out of the daily newspaper business early, leaving *The Pittsburgh Press* in 1984. I was 42 at the time.

One time Jimmy Cannon and I were at ringside for a sparring session in Houston. LeRoy Neiman, the great sports artist, did a sketch of us sitting there together. Neiman could fill up a book with such sketches in a hurry. I wish I had asked Neiman for that sketch. A British journalist came by and bellowed, "Jimmy Cannon. Jimmy

Cannon. Still at it. Jimmy, how come you don't retire and rest on your laurels?"

Cannon was obviously annoyed. "Maybe," he said to the Brit, "I don't have as many goddamn laurels as you do."

After the Brit went by, Cannon asked me, "Who was that prick? Laurels...my ass!"

Some other Cannon chestnuts:

- "Time is a vandal and the young ballplayers should enjoy what's happening to them today, because a lot of times famous men quit baseball and it's like they fell off the rim of the world into some sort of obscurity."
- "Joe Louis was the greatest heavyweight I ever saw and Ray Robinson the best all-around fighter. Joe Louis was a credit to his race—the human race."
- "We have a tendency to write about the past, to let time telescope on us. A sportswriter is entombed in a prolonged boyhood."
- "My great hero in sports, when I was a kid, was Pie Traynor. He played a wonderful third base for the Pittsburgh Pirates, and was particularly good against the Giants. I think the name fascinated me. I never heard of a guy named Pie before, except there was a homely girl in our neighborhood who we called Pieface."
- "A lot of writers think that ballplayers like them. But ballplayers are amused by writers and think of them as necessary evils. One thing I know about ballplayers. They never thank you for the praise. But they really complain if you rip them. They think they are entitled to good stories."
- "The trick of interviewing is to start with the easy questions and some small talk. You warm up slowly, then you drop the bomb, and if the guy doesn't answer, the interview will be almost completed. I save the tough questions for last because I don't want an empty notebook."

- "I would much rather be Ernest Hemingway than Babe Ruth or Red Grange. Hemingway, after all, was a sportswriter."
- "I think the great athletes are lucky that they have met me."

From Jimmy Cannon collection

Jimmy Cannon, at left above, interviews Joe Louis at Toots Shor's Restaurant in New York. Below, Cannon looks like he's in a staring contest with Smokin' Joe Frazier, with New York Post writer Jim O'Brien refereeing the confrontation. Frazier's manager, Yank Durham, is seated in background.

George Kalinsky/Madison Square Garden

George Foreman
Winning Olympic title still his biggest thrill

Before he was a pitchman for hamburger grills and naming his five sons George and becoming an ordained Christian minister, he was one of the most feared yet endearing heavyweight boxers on the planet. It was always fun to be around George Foreman. He had a great sense of humor and an easy smile, which helps explain why the five boys of his 12 children are all called George, from George to George V.

I met him for the first time when he was training at Gil Clancy's Gym in Manhattan. That was in June of 1976. I had a chance to interview him on June 7 at Nassau Coliseum, about five miles from my home on Long Island. I covered all sports activity at the Coliseum, starting with Dr. J and the Nets of the ABA and the Islanders of the NHL. The Nets won two ABA titles there, and the Islanders were putting together a team that would win four consecutive Stanley Cups after I returned home to Pittsburgh.

Winning an Olympic gold medal was more of a thrill, he told me on June 7, than becoming heavyweight champion of the world.

He was getting ready to fight Joe Frazier the following week—on June 15—in a 12-round bout to determine the next logical contender for Muhammad Ali's title.

Ali took that title from Foreman on October 30, 1974, knocking him out in the eighth round in Kinshasa, Zaire. Foreman had won the title back on January 22, 1972, knocking down Frazier six times before flattening him for good in the second round at Kingston, Jamaica.

"That was a tremendous accomplishment, as big as there is for most men," said Foreman, who was hardly like most men, reflecting on defeating Frazier. "Joe Frazier is one of the toughest men who ever lived. But it wasn't as exciting as winning the Olympic gold medal. It wasn't even close."

319

Foreman first came to international fame by winning the gold medal in Mexico City in 1968, defeating the Soviet champ, Jonas Cepulis, and waving a tiny American flag rather than a black-gloved fist. John Carlos and Tommy Smith of track & field fame chose to give Black Power salutes on the victory stand in those Summer Olympics. I had a chance to hear John Carlos explain what he did—at the Heinz History Center on July 18, 2016—and he came off as an alright dude.

"I think the Olympics was the greatest thing that ever happened to me, without a doubt," said Foreman. "After I won that particular fight—there was so much tension; I had won four different fights—I had come to somewhere out of nowhere.

"No one expected me to get that far in the amateurs. I didn't have that much experience. I had 25 fights total, including the gold medal fight. And after winning, to stand on the platform and have the gold medal put on your neck… the playing of the National Anthem…

"I mean, it just lingered, the whole spectacle just went through me." Even so, the 27-year-old boxer from Marshall, Texas said he could understand and appreciate the feelings of some of the outstanding collegiate basketball players who chose not to try out for the U.S. Olympic team that would compete in Montreal that summer. "It's different for football and basketball players," explained Foreman. "They start off as popular heroes in junior high, and the fans and coaches begin petting them. All through high school, someone is babying them. They're getting by as far as their school grades are concerned, and so forth.

"Then comes college, maybe new cars and some money. They're not begging for a whole lot. With me, you're talking about a man who'd never had his picture in the papers prior to the Olympics, period. Those guys are spoiled.

"Guys like O.J. Simpson and Kareem Abdul-Jabbar have been taken care of all the way along, ever since they started wearing a jock-strap. There was more emotion involved in it for me. Everything all happened in a year."

* * *

Foreman floored Frazier twice in the fifth round and Eddie Futch, Frazier's cornerman, stepped onto the apron and told the referee to stop the fight.

Foreman was a big favorite with the American sports public in those days. To read over his remarks it's easy to determine that George Foreman could talk well and was a winning personality.

It led, in time, to him being the spokesman for the George Foreman Grill. He was on TV all the time pitching that grill. It sold over 100 million units worldwide. He sold the naming rights to the grill in 1999 for $138 million.

At age 45, he made a comeback in boxing in November, 1994 and regained a portion of the heavyweight title by knocking out Michael Moorer of Monessen to win the WBA and IBF titles. Foreman, for sure, was not Everyman.

He sparred that day on Long Island as part of the press conference at Nassau Coliseum before his rematch with Frazier. He sparred four rounds with three different opponents, Cookie Wallace, Ernie Lassiter and Scrap Iron Johnson—there's a great name for a sparring partner—and he did some shadowboxing and hitting the big bag.

Foreman made an unusual request of the onlookers at Exhibition Hall at the Coliseum.

Holding his heavily-taped hand high over this head to get attention, Foreman said, "I have to practice beating up people, and getting beaten. There are certain things that annoy me, that make me mad, and I want to get in practice for that, too.

"There are some things I want you to chant while I'm working out, like Frazier...Frazier...Frazier. Then Ali...Ali...Ali. Then boo...boo...boo."

Urged on by Foreman's sparring partners at ringside, who acted as cheerleaders when they weren't sparring with George, the 150 or so fans on hand hollered abuse at Foreman from then on, screaming that Frazier and Ali will beat him, terrific encouragement.

321

Foreman smiled through it all. It seemed to add zest and pop to his punches. "A boo to a monster is like a cheer for the good guy," Foreman explained afterward. "I'm the monster for this one.

"You see, Joe Frazier lost to me, and people have a thing where it's just instinctive to go for the underdog. So I want to be prepared for that, too, so it won't bother me."

Foreman finished his career with record of 76-5, with 68 KOs to his credit. He worked as an analyst at ringside for HBO Boxing for 12 years, leaving in 2004.

"When I knocked Frazier out and won the title, it was like a dream."
—George Foreman

Author Jim O'Brien interviews George Foreman and his trainer Dick Saddler at Gil Clancy's Gym in Manhattan. O'Brien had talked to Saddler back in November 1968 when he was working with Sonny Liston for a fight in Pittsburgh.

Roberto Duran
He was unreal at his best

There was a commotion down the hallway. I went to see where the noise was coming from. When I was a kid, we had a neighbor who had chickens in a coop in their yard three doors away down an alley called Gatelodge Way. That's what the noise down the hallway sounded like.

I was staying in a hotel in Cleveland with the Steelers who had beaten the Browns at Cleveland Stadium in a pre-season game the night before, Saturday, August 9, 1981. I don't remember the name of the hotel, which is just as well. There was a lot going on in Cleveland that weekend. I planned on taking it all in. Baseball's All-Star Game would be played there that Sunday afternoon and Roberto Duran, once one of the most feared fighters in the game, was scheduled to fight Mike "Nino" Gonzalez at the Cleveland Public Auditorium that night. I still have the program from that matchup. It was billed as "The Comeback." Both events would be on national TV.

Dave Parker of the Pirates hit a solo home run as the National League beat the American League 5-4. Pete Rose was the leadoff hitter for the National League and the Pirates were represented by Parker, Phil Garner, Bill Madlock and Mike Easler.

This was Duran's first fight since his shameful defeat in a welterweight title fight with Sugar Ray Leonard—the infamous "No Mas!" fight. This came five months after he had beaten Leonard to take the title. In the eighth round of the rematch, Duran, frustrated and angry, threw up a glove in the air and quit. *No mas.* The phrase has since become a sports cliché, and many have never forgiven Duran for saying it. The "hands of stone" had been stilled.

Back at the hotel and the noise down the hallway...

I went to see what was going on...

People were screaming in Spanish inside this suite and I swear I could hear chickens screaming as well. I knew these rooms were ones occupied by Duran and his entourage, mostly Panamanians from his hometown of Panama City. There was a cockfight going on inside that suite. It was an event that was not listed on the Cleveland sports calendar for that weekend. I saw animated men with dollar bills in their upraised fists, hooting and hollering.

I didn't have a press credential for this sports event and I was turned away at the door. I didn't press the issue. The Panamanians wanted no part of a reporter in the room. The notebook in my hand must have given me away. I didn't see Roberto Duran and I don't know if he was in there at the time.

I had never experienced anything quite like this in my journalistic career. But it's one of the reasons the boxing beat was always interesting. Imagine what the maid found when she came to clean that room later in the day.

Duran defeated Gonzalez that night.

I had seen Duran at his best and worst. I was at Madison Square Garden when Duran made his American debut. That was on September 13, 1971 when he TKOd Benny Huertas of New Jersey in the first minute of the first round. Duran must have hit Huertas with all he had for that minute, turning his head into a speed bag right from the bell. I had never seen a fighter with such fury.

John Sculian wrote of Duran's debut: "Duran is called Manos de Piedra. He has just what his nickname says he does—hands of stone. He won 69 of his first 70 fights, knocking out 55 targets. The zest for violence remained, waiting for Duran to put together his two-fisted attack and flee Panama for Madison Square Garden. When he finally arrived there, in December of 1971, the crowd belittled him as a skinny fraud until he knocked Benny Huertas still as death for six minutes. From that night on, people began to understand what Duran's hands were made of."
In late summer 2016, a movie about Duran's life came out called "Hands of Stone," and it explored his rags to riches story, and how he turned being mean into making money.

Duran returned to Madison Square Garden, at age 22, when he met Ken Buchanan of Scotland for the lightweight championship of the world in 1972. I was at ringside for that one as well. Buchanan was a classic boxer from the old school, but he was no match for Duran. Referee John LoBianco pulled Duran off the helpless Scot in the thirteenth round.

A writer named Richard O'Brien—no relation—recorded it this way: "Buchanan complained afterward that he'd been fouled at the finish, which was rather like a man who had just been run over by a train griping that the conductor had been rude to him. Duran had the title."

O'Brien also wrote: "There has never been a purer fighter than Roberto Duran."

I was also at ringside when Duran defeated Edwin Viruet at Nassau Coliseum on September 17, 1977. I was responsible for covering all sports activity at Nassau Coliseum. It was a new building when I moved from Miami to New York in the spring of 1970. I covered the Nets and the Islanders for two straight winters—going back and forth between the two—getting on and off airplanes almost on a daily basis. The Nassau Coliseum was not Madison Square Garden, and the Islanders and Nets now play at the Barclay Center in Brooklyn, but it was a good beat for me in the '70s. The Nets would win two ABA titles with Dr. J and the Islanders, under the direction of general manager Billy "Bowtie" Torre put together a team that won four consecutive Stanley Cups.

Duran was just 5-7 and weighed between 130 and 160 pounds in his ring career. He fought as a lightweight, a welterweight and a middleweight and held titles in all three divisions. He was a savage fighter, who had rage and skills to back up his snarling attack. His last fight was a loss to Ray Leonard in 12 rounds on December 7, 1989.

All told, Duran defended his lightweight title twelve times, scoring eleven knockouts. After one of those victories a TV commentator asked Duran if he was aware that his opponent had been taken to a hospital.

'I did not hit him right," said a sweaty but steady Duran. "If I hit him right, he would be in the morgue, not the hospital."

Larry Holmes
He learned how to box from Ali

It was difficult to watch. When Larry Holmes fought Muhammad Ali it was a mismatch. Ali had announced his retirement after previous fights with Leon Spinks, losing one and winning a rematch, and had not fought for two years when he made an ill-fated comeback against Larry Holmes.

They fought in Las Vegas and the bout was stopped in the 11th round, Holmes winning by a TKO. That was on October 2, 1980. He had hit Ali almost at will. When it was over, Holmes had tears in his eyes. Howard Cosell, who called the fight from ringside for a TV audience, asked Holmes why he was crying.

Holmes muttered something about admiring the man so much, but didn't finish his thought. He was crying because he was upset with dealing so much punishment to a man he admired and credited with teaching him so much about boxing. Ali had helped him and had been a good friend. The student had just beaten the teacher so badly, never a good thing.

Ali had backed off rather than dealing further punishment to Jimmy Ellis and Buster Mathis—"I didn't want to bust him up; he has family," Ali said after both of those fights. Larry Holmes did not back off of Ali. He just kept hitting him.

Ali said afterward that he had been taking some medications and they drained his energy. He said he was not himself. Ali's trainer, Angelo Dundee, stopped the fight after the tenth round, wanting to save his fighter from further punishment. It was the only time Ali failed to go the distance in a fight. Three of his five losses came in his last four fights. Joe Frazier and Ken Norton were the only boxers to beat Ali at his best. He lost to Leon Spinks but beat him in a rematch.

Ali had one more fight after his setback by Holmes, losing a 10-round bout to Trevor Bobick at Nassau in the

Bahamas. Then he quit for good. But, as it developed, he had stayed too long in the ring, taken too many punches. He'd pay dearly for that. He suffered from Parkinson's disease the last 30 years of his life.

Cosell should have understood how Holmes was feeling. Cosell had been among the famous visitors to the Deer Lake Training Camp in Pennsylvania where Ali had established a hideaway to train for his fights after his banishment from boxing for refusing to be inducted into the U. S. Army. That was in 1970. Holmes came on the scene when Ali was training there.

The camp is still intact, with many of Muhammad Ali's artifacts still present on the grounds. There are huge stones, for instance, that have names painted on them in black: Jack Johnson, Floyd Patterson, Jack Dempsey, Rocky Marciano, Sonny Liston, Joe Frazier, Sugar Ray Robinson and Joe Louis. I am not certain if Larry Holmes has a rock with his name on it.

They were all men Ali admired. They were all boxing champions, among the greats of the game.

Even Elvis Presley visited the place. They tell a story about when Elvis and Ali dropped into a local antique store together the owner nearly fainted when he saw them coming through the door.

That's where I first saw Larry Holmes, a hired hand in the training camp. He was among the boxers who were there to train with and spar with Ali in 1971.

It's twenty minutes from Reading, 30 minutes from Allentown, an hour from Philadelphia, and two hours from New York City. I traveled there from New York City in February of 1971 the first time before Ali's first fight with Frazier and for other fights as well. I had also gone to boxing training camps in The Catskills before other fights.

I was writing for *The New York Post*, in my second year on the staff, and had drawn the assignment a year earlier of covering boxing. Talk about good timing.

I didn't talk to Holmes at that camp, but I do remember him. He was from Easton, Pennsylvania. He was big and gave an honest effort in the ring. Outside the ring, he looked bored and lazy—that's because his eyes were always half-closed—a little slow on the drawl when he did speak to anyone. He often used a piece of straw for a toothpick.

It was not a good first impression, but that was probably my fault. Holmes turned out to be an all right guy.

I took him for granted. He was just part of the scene, like the many log houses scattered about the site. Ali liked the solitude of the sylvan setting.

Holmes had fought once in Pittsburgh. That was on November 6, 1981. He rose from a seventh-round knockdown—during which he staggered into the turnbuckle in a corner of the ring—to stop Renaldo Snipes in the eleventh round.

He had several business interests in Easton. He owned two restaurants, a night club, a training facility and slot machines. He had moved from his birthplace in Cuthbert, Georgia to Easton in 1954. His father abandoned the family and moved east, coming home about every three months for a visit, and the Holmes family was living on welfare.

Larry Holmes dropped out of school in seventh grade and went to work at a local car wash for $1 an hour. Then he drove a dump truck and worked in a stone quarry.

*   *   *

Larry Holmes was crying again on Friday, June 3, 2016 when he learned that Muhammad Ali had died at age 74. Ali had been rushed to a hospital in Scottsdale, just outside Phoenix, and died from septic shock, not from Parkinson's disease. He had been diagnosed with that illness 30 years earlier. Holmes was now 66 and still living in Easton.

Gareth A. Davies, a boxing correspondent, spoke to Holmes after he heard the bad news.

Here's what Holmes had to say about Ali "never knowing when to quit."

His remarks are reprinted here:

"Did Muhammad Ali not know when to stop? Did he know when to stop taking punches? Did he go on too long? I'll answer all those questions.

"People won't like me for this. They'll say, 'you're jealous of him. You envy him.' But I don't. I loved that man.

"Number one: He did not know when to stop taking punches and he never knew when to quit. Boxing is about 'hit and don't be hit.' What happens is your mind makes a date your body can't keep. And you have to learn to accept that.

"Ali aged young, but only because of the beatings over the years. They made him old before his time. Three fights with Joe Frazier, one with George Foreman, three with Ken Norton; those fights would have killed most people. He got hit and hit and hit—and hit in training, too.

"You don't take punches to the side of the head to prove how tough you are. I started working with Ali in 1971. I trained with him for four years as a sparring partner and he tried to prove every day how strong he was, taking punches to the head, to the body. I told him, 'Don't take no punches, the body is not made for punching.' And he took 'em just the same.

"But I didn't hit him like that. Frazier, Foreman and Norton hit him hard like that. Frazier didn't like him. Ali called Joe 'ignorant' and slow, but Ali had a way of throwing you off key, off your game. And that's why he did that. Frazier has gone, Ali has gone. Only me and Foreman left now.

"Ali did me some favors. I asked him to do some things for me and he did them and never asked for anything in return. He went to a school for me, and to a prison. He came to say hello to my Mom. When I was working for him as a sparring partner, at the end of each week he would pay me. Sometimes there was a bonus of a few thousand dollars.

"I went all over the world with him. I went to Zaire with him, to London with him. He and I became good friends. I learned a lot from sparring with him, Ken Norton and Earnie Shavers. After a while, I figured if I could take their punches maybe I was good enough to go out on my own. After all, I was in there against the best. I saw Ali a few months ago at the Boxing Hall of Fame and he didn't look too good. He didn't walk, he didn't talk and he was shaking a lot."

Angelo Dundee
Sent letters and cards
that I kept in my files

There were three men in the sports world who would write to me on occasion, just to keep in touch or to answer questions I posed in my own correspondence with them. They were Art Rooney, the owner of the Pittsburgh Steelers; Marques Haynes, "the world's greatest dribbler" for the Harlem Globetrotters and Harlem Magicians; and Angelo Dundee, the trainer for Muhammad Ali and other champions.

September 9, 2003

Dear Jim:

Merci for sending *Pittsburgh Proud*. I enjoyed it.

I had the pleasure to meet Jack McGinley and Art Rooney as boxing promoters in 1949 or 1950. Juste Fontaine at Hickey Park. I came in with Johnny Williams. It was a great fight—a great night. Fontaine won decision.

Jack and I have been friends ever since—Art must have been great fite fan as a lot of great fighters came out of Pittsburgh.

Thanks again,

Sincerely, Angelo Dundee

331

September 21, 2005

Just the way Angelo wrote the three-page hand-written letter. He had his own punctuation style.

Dear Jim:

A joy talking to you—just like being with you and having a Cuban sandwich at the Puerto Sagua Restaurant on Miami Beach—Pittsburgh has a history of developing good fighters—Zivics—Conn—(Ezzard) Charles came from Cincy but was handled by Becker Brothers—Chris handled him early on—Jake Mintz then Tom Tannas—Dusty Bettor handled Bob Baker

49-50 I was in N.Y.—Came to Pittsburgh in 49 with Johnny Williams to box Juste Fontaine in Hickey Park— Art Rooney and Jack McGinley were promoting—I used Ted Crystal as corner man—was great fite Juste won a decision—I handled a kid from Pittsburgh—name was Bill Bassio—felt good about it as he boxed in main event in Madison Square Garden and won over Pat Marcune— Another kid from Pittsburgh was Mike Koballa—a good fighter boxed Kid Gavilan distance and also had a win over Carmen Basilio at Eastern Parkway

Came to Pittsburgh with Ali—boxed Charlie Powell— sold out Civic Arena during an ice storm

I can do more talking to you—if you can send me some specific questions and I will do my best to give you the answers—

The reputation of Pittsburgh fighters a way back—all the managers and trainers knew they were in "tough" going to Pittsburgh—Talented tough fighters

Stay well – Always
Angelo

Author Dick Schaap on Angelo Dundee:

"He was a great guy and a great trainer and a great student of his sport."

From the
Corner
of . . . . .

Angelo Dundee
INC.

Dear Jim:

First of all, thanks for being so nice—which is par for the course with you—for sending that stuff to me. The pic of you and Ali...that is Hugh McIlvaney in the middle. He's from London, England.

Second, Puerto Sagua is a Cuban restaurant and is still there when I go to the 7th Street Beach Gym (we moved the gym since you were here). I go there for my usual Cuban sandwich and café con leche—

Last nite I was with Dan Marino Sr. They were having a Dan Marino Foundation Dinner. Dan Jr. was there. Joe Rose, Kim Bokamper, Jim Kiick and about 300 fans +

Fond memories of Pittsburgh—when I was a little kid in Philly—my uncle Frank Lucia would visit us from Pittsburgh. And, by the way, the family name for us was Mirena. My brother Joe became a boxer and took the name Dundee and Chris and I followed in that respect. We would give Uncle Frank a bed by himself. Brothers Jim and Frank and I slept at the foot of the bed. His snoring kept us all awake.

1949 I went to Pittsburgh with Johnny Williams. He boxed Juste Fontaine at Hickey Park. Promoters were Rooney & McGinley. Ted Crystal local worked with me

Next visit was when (Ezzard) Charles fought (Jersey Joe) Walcott—I had a four-round fight I was with a heavyweight just after Walcott knocked out Charles with a left hook—

Next Pittsburgh experience—Muhammad boxed Charlie Powell—streets were frozen with ice and we sold out (Civic Arena)—It was so cold I couldn't cross the street to go to a drugstore from our hotel

Legendary boxers Harry Greb—Sammy Angott—The Zivic Brothers—Billy Conn—and three fighters from the area I worked with were Mike Koballa, Bill Bassio and Joey LaQuatra—

I recall you coming to the gym. It was a joy to see you and I could see you liked boxing—

Dan Marino Sr. is a real fight buff. Knows fighters. I met his son when he first came to play with the Dolphins. The first time I ran into him at a sports affair I told him we may be related as the family name was Mirena and I have always been friends with Dan—he is such a nice guy—

I met Bob Baker when I was in N.Y. His manager Dusty Bettor fine man and we're talking 48-49-50—

While in Pittsburgh had the pleasure of knowing Al Abrams—Roy McHugh—Myron Cope. Ali used to call Cope Mickey Rooney.

I still stay in touch with Don Elbaum—he is making matches in Philadelphia. He was a remarkable guy—if a fighter would not show he would step in and fight!!!

Pittsburgh fighters have always had great reputations for their talent—out of town managers were always leery of bringing their boxers to fight them—they knew they would be tough—

Hope this is enough cannon fodder—if more is needed just fire away—Always, Angelo

P.S. The pics you sent were great

Helen and Angelo Dundee

Chris Dundee and Red Holzman
Thankful for having met these good men long ago

"This would be a great life if it weren't for the damn games."
—Red Holzman

A couple of obituaries caught my eye and my heart back in late November of 1998. Red Holzman and Chris Dundee died within four days of one another, and I was saddened by their passing, but exhilarated by the wonderful experiences I had shared with them in my formative years as a sportswriter in New York and Miami before that. I was witness to great things in their company, and learned from them.

Holzman was the head coach of the New York Knicks when they won NBA titles in 1970 and 1972, something they have not done since. Dundee was a boxing promoter in Miami who booked over 1,000 fights in a 40-year career and, along with his kid brother Angelo, helped bring the world one of boxing's biggest personalities, first a kid out of Louisville named Cassius Marcellus Clay who morphed into Muhammad Ali.

Holzman was 76 when he passed and Dundee was 91. Both had led full and satisfying lives and both knew how to smile. Both were always available, and so was Angelo Dundee and you couldn't get Clay or Ali to stop talking. They were all a sportswriter's dream. Chris Dundee was the consummate showman, bug-eyed like his kid brother, he was always promoting something. Holzman had a more laidback approach, and had less to say, but knew when to open the locker room door, even after a difficult loss, and never got in the way. He did his best to give you something you could work into your story.

Holzman and the Dundees are all celebrated in their respective Halls of Fame, and they were some of the great

George Kalinsky/Madison Square Garden

Red Holzman coached the Knicks to two NBA titles in early '70s.

From Pacheco photo collection

Fight doctor Dr. Ferdie Pacheco is flanked by Angelo and Chris Dundee.

guys in the world of sports and the business I was fortunate to be in as a sportswriter.

I was lucky enough as a young man to live in Miami and New York, two exciting and challenging cities, most different from Pittsburgh and yet they offer clues and comparisons as to why Pittsburgh is such a special city. I think you have to have lived in and worked in other cities to appreciate Pittsburgh. I spent a summer in Philadelphia, a winter in Louisville and Kansas City while in the Army, nearly a year in Alaska while in the military service, so I know some other cities well as well. Too many media types in Pittsburgh knock cities such as Philadelphia, New York, Buffalo, Cleveland, Chicago and Atlanta, who've never spent more than a weekend in any of those places.

At a Thompson Club sports banquet, I once preceded Myron Cope to the microphone and I quoted Ernest Hemingway saying, "If you are lucky enough to have lived in Paris as a young man then wherever you go for the rest of your life, Paris goes with you, for Paris is a moveable feast."

Then I added to it, "You can say the same thing about Pittsburgh."

To which Cope cried out in a theatrical display of anguish from his seat below me, "Geez, now O'Brien is comparing Pittsburgh to Paris! Has he gone nuts?"

Everyone laughed and, of course, so did I.

Cope could have appreciated my experiences with the Dundees if not Holzman. Cope had spent time with the young Cassius Clay and wrote a classic magazine piece on him, and he spent time with Chris and Angelo Dundee while doing the interviews and research on that prize-winning piece.

The Dundees and Holzman always had an open door to their respective offices, a quick smile, wonderful stories and words of wisdom I still cite in conversations with my friends and students, and they were often generous with their time and thoughts.

"See the ball!" Holzman would holler. "Pass with a purpose! You coach in practice and you let them play in the game." Coaches would be wise to follow Holzman's how-to-do-it methods.

Holzman and Chris Dundee were part of the two most magic experiences in my early years in the newspaper business.

Covering the Knicks in the championship playoffs of 1970 and the Muhammad Ali vs. Joe Frazier fight in 1971, billed as "The Fight of the Century," were my all-time greatest assignments. Madison Square Garden was filled with over 18,000 fans for all the Knicks' games and there were even more for the most famous fight in boxing history.

Harvey Araton, the outstanding sports columnist for *The New York Times,* ranks the Ali-Frazier fight and the seventh game of the Knicks-Lakers championship series in 1970 as his personal two top sports events, and he watched them both as a young fan not as a sportswriter. He saw the fight on closed-circuit TV and the deciding basketball game by sleeping outside the Garden to get a ticket at the last minute. In my last years at *The Post*, Araton joined the staff as a promising young writer. He later wrote for the *New York Daily News* and then *The Times.*

I was at center ring-side for Ali vs. Frazier, my face just two feet from the apron of the canvas floor of the ring, or square jungle as it was often referred to in those days. I had one of the four best seats in the house of the most celebrated championship fight in boxing history. I sat next to Nat Fleischer, the founder and editor of *The Ring* magazine, the bible of boxing. I read copies of *The Ring* magazine in my youth and had copies stacked high on my night stand alongside issues of *Sport* and *Sports Illustrated.* My boss, sports editor Ike Gellis, and his boss, managing editor Paul Sann, sat off to my right with Milton Gross. Larry Merchant had to sit several rows back because Gellis and Sann were sitting at ringside even though neither would be covering the fight or writing any stories about it. Go figure... I remember that some insider at the Garden had given Sann some goalies' equipment from the Rangers for someone in his family, and it was stuffed in his back pockets making the back of his suit jacket flare out. That was referred to as a perk or payola. For *The Post* execs, it was simply business as usual.

I moved from Pittsburgh to Miami in 1969, in the second year of my marriage to Kathie Churchman, and shortly after my father, Dan O'Brien, had died at age 63. I was 27 years old, and went there to cover the Miami Dolphins in their final year in the American Football League and to cover the boxing beat. That's also where I drew the assignment to write a weekly column about the American Basketball Association for *The Sporting News* even though I did not cover the ABA's Floridians franchise.

The brothers Dundee, Chris and Angelo came to Miami in 1950 and began promoting boxing matches at the Miami Beach Auditorium, now known as the Jackie Gleason Theater of Performing Art. The Jackie Gleason Show was staged in this setting.

"Chris Dundee was a promoter's promoter," wrote Howard Kleinberg, my boss's boss at *The Miami News* when I came there in 1969. Kleinberg had the boxing beat as a young sportswriter before moving up in management ranks at the afternoon newspaper in town.

"There was not a fight he did not try to convince me that this was a match made in heaven. I don't recall that Chris had a press agent, as he always personally delivered by hand to our newsroom announcements of upcoming matches. Chris Dundee remained a lovable guy—even when he had to shut down his gym."

John Crittenden, Kleinberg's successor as sports editor, liked boxing, too. He assigned me to cover the local boxing scene in addition to covering the Dolphins as my primary beat.

Chris Dundee promoted bi-weekly boxing shows on Miami Beach. He and his brother Angelo ran the Fifth Street Gym, where Muhammad Ali, then called Cassius Clay, had trained. Ali and I both got our boxing education there. Kleinberg called it "The University of Boxing." I asked Angelo why they took me into their boxing world and embraced me.

"You were a new kid in town and we took you under our wings," Angelo Dundee would tell me in 2005 or 2006, when I called him on the telephone at his home in Weston, Florida, where he was a neighbor and friend of Dan Marino and his dad, Dan Marino Sr.

"You liked boxing and we always welcomed anyone who loved what we loved. You frequented the gym a lot and got to know everyone there. We took you to lunch at the Latin restaurant near the Fifth Street Gym, and let you into our inner sanctum. We liked you and you were an eager student. We had some good times, didn't we?"

I called Angelo Dundee because I was thinking about him for some reason while visiting my daughter Rebeccca O'Brien at her apartment in Woodland Hills, California. I sat on a cement bench at the intersection of Owensmouth and Irwin, and the next thing I knew I was back in the Fifth Street Gym with Angelo and all the characters who populated the place. Angelo answered the phone himself when I called on my cell phone. He sounded happy to hear from me. He'd have sounded happy, of course, if I were an IRS tax agent.

One of those colorful citizens of the Fifth Street Gym was Lou Gross, a trainer from New York, who referred to some of the other gym rats as "shoemakers" because Lou didn't think they belonged in the same company or class of elite trainers as him and Angelo Dundee. Another New York transplant was Moe Fleischer. Both combed what remained of their hair for maximum coverage of their otherwise bald pates. They loved to corner reporters and journalists and tell their boxing tales. Champion boxers such as Luis Rodriguez and Jimmy Ellis often worked out there. It was a real sweatbox in the Miami heat.

Floyd Patterson frequently trained there for fights in South Florida.

My favorite Lou Gross story was about how he was assigned once by the Dundees to keep watch on the hotel door of Willie Pastrano, a hard puncher from New Orleans they trained and a boxer good enough to win the world's light-heavyweight title while under their guidance.

340

Pastrano had a propensity for sleeping with women, and he wasn't choosy. "He would screw anything," gushed Angelo Dundee. "Even chickens, rats and snakes if they'd get too close to him." Gross agreed with that gross assessment.

"I'm doing my best to watch that no one gets into his room," said Gross, looking away like he was still on alert. "And yet when I cracked open the door in the middle of the night just to make sure he was sleeping okay, I see him on top of this woman in his bed. There was a belief that boxers should not have sex on the eve of a fight because it would weaken them. So I screamed at Willie. 'Don't come, Willie! Don't come!' But I was too late. Willie came early."

No wonder I loved and was always willing to listen to guys like Lou Gross. They were right out of central casting in Hollywood from the folks who made movies out of books by Budd Shulberg, such as "The Harder They Fall" and "Requiem for a Heavyweight," movies with stars such as (*I used "like" when I first wrote this sentence and then remembered Myron Cope screaming that it should be "such as" instead*) Humphrey Bogart and Marlin Brando and washed-up boxers such as "Two Ton" Tony Galento, "Jersey Joe" Walcott, "Slapsy" Maxie Rosenbloom and Max Baer Jr. in the background.

Bogart played the role of a former sportswriter Eddie Willis who was hired to help promote a charade of a fight in "The Harder They Fall." Willis made sharp cynical comments: "Powder-puff puncher and a glass jaw. That's a great combination."

My ties with the Dundees provided an introduction to Ali later on. The Dundees were delighted that I was from Pittsburgh. Chris had worked on some boxing promotions there, and recalled a stay at the old Pittsburgher Hotel. He had worked with Art Rooney Sr. and Barney McGinley Sr. and Jack McGinley Sr. on some boxing shows in Pittsburgh. The Rooneys and McGinleys owned parts of the Pittsburgh Steelers (and still do). So Dundee and I shared some stories about some Pittsburgh sports personalities. Chris and Angelo were the best one-two combination in boxing circles.

One time a ring rascal named Don Elbaum brought a fighter named Mert Brownfield to Miami Beach for a fight with a big heavyweight prospect named Al Jones. The Dundees thought Jones, a well-built 6-6 southpaw, had a chance to be something. But Jones broke his hand about four times in a couple of years and that stopped him short of his goals.

Brownfield was from McKeesport, my wife's hometown. My mother, Mary O'Brien, was visiting us at the time and came to the fight. We were rooting for Brownfield. He had his hair slicked down with lots of pomade. It appeared to be ebony black. Jones jolted him with an early hard punch to the forehead and suddenly Mert's hair stood up—black and burned-out blond like dried-up corn stalks in a farm field—and that was the beginning of the end for our boy Brownfield. His shock of hair became a brown field.

Months later, we learned that Brownfield took a few bullets in his arm in a neighborhood shooting. Boxing and bullets seem to be a one-two punch.

Chris Dundee invited me to join Elbaum, who was out of Erie, Pennsylvania and a boxing guy you just had to love if you were a sportswriter interested in the game. Elbaum and I were guests of Chris in the health club at the famous Fontanbleu Hotel where boxers such as Beau Jack and Levi Forte held forth as a shoe shine stand operator and doorman, respectively, and colorful characters were in abundance.

A health club attendant named Dan instructed Elbaum and me, both as naked as the day we were born, to line up against a tiled wall in the health club, and face him. He advised us to cover our privates with our hands. He then played a strong water hose on us, to stimulate our blood flow, I believe, at least that's what he told us. Remember how the police sprayed protestors in the Civil Rights movement in the '60s? Now you get the picture. I think Dan enjoyed firing that strong spray our way. There weren't computer action games in those days to satisfy thrill-kill instincts. "I haven't been sprayed like this since a short stay I had in the slammer once," said Elbaum, who viewed the world through mostly winced eyes. Is it any wonder I loved the boxing beat? It had the best characters to be found in any sport, and they were always available, always eager to sell their sport to anyone who'd lend an ear. Elbaum later had a pretty good heavyweight boxer named Earnie Shavers, who could hit as hard as anybody in boxing at the time, and worked with Don King to line up promising talent King could promote and hustle. Shavers, King and Elbaum all served time for some mischief, murder in King's case.

Once, a few nights before Ali's fight with Oscar Bonavena at Madison Square Garden, Angelo Dundee invited me to stay in his room and to sleep in the bed beside his at the Loew's Midtown Motor Inn in Manhattan. Talk about getting a behind-the-scenes look at a sport...

I remember him fielding a phone call from Hank Stram, the head football coach of the Kansas City Chiefs and someone I had gotten to know while moonlighting as a spotter in the press box at Municipal Stadium during my ten-month military stay in Kansas City in 1965, and when I covered the Chiefs against the Minnesota Vikings in the Super Bowl in New Orleans in January of 1970. I visited with Willie Pastrano at a dive called The Bastille in New Orleans while covering a later Super Bowl in New Orleans. Dundee was discussing an upcoming Chiefs' game with Stram, sitting on the edge of his bed.

During that hotel stay in New York, I recall getting up before dawn one morning when Ali was scheduled to run in Central Park as part of his pre-fight training. Louis Sarria, a quiet black Cuban and master masseur and corner assistant to Angelo Dundee, was with us as we went down the hall to wake up Ali.

Sarria knocked on Ali's door, and Ali called out, "We're off today!" Sarria didn't say anything—he seldom did—he just rolled his luminous dark eyes. And we all retreated to our rooms and went back to bed. No one protested or tried to convince Ali that he better get on the road for a good run in the park.

On the day of the fight with Bonavena, Ali rode away with his entourage in a shiny black limo to go to the Garden.

I walked up 8th Avenue to a subway stop. As I descended the stairs, I could hear a lot of hell-raising on the platform below. Ali and his loyal followers had left the limo in favor of taking a subway train to the Garden. Anything to surprise people and cause a commotion.

Drew Bundini Brown, who was Ali's ambassador of good will and constant sidekick and noise-maker, was shouting to one and all, "Ali is a man of the people! He gets down with the people!"

You should have seen the amazed looks in the eyes of the strap-hangers when Ali got onto the subway train. Imagine that scene. Guys coming and going to work and there's Ali appearing out of nowhere and standing among them on a subway train. Once we got to the Garden, Ali held the door back firmly as his entourage entered the building through the employee and press entrance, so they wouldn't have to pay their way in. They paraded in under Ali's extended right arm.

I was the only reporter to witness this sequence. It was hours before the main event so I went down into the bowels of Penn Station, located directly below Madison Square Garden, and wrote a piece for *The New York Post* about what I had just witnessed. I was sitting on a bench pecking away at my portable typewriter, working while waiting for my wife Kathie and our friends, Helene and Bob Wishnev, to come in on the Long Island R.R. from East Rockaway. I recall a bum coming up and checking on my activity, looking over my shoulders, wondering why the hell someone was typing in a train station. I gave him a few bucks and asked to be left alone.

A writer always worries about what kind of story he is going to be able to produce under deadline at any sports event, and especially a Super Bowl or big fight, and I felt a great deal of satisfaction knowing I had sent in a story to the office via Western Union no one else would have before the bell had even rung to start the Ali-Bonavena fight, Ali's last tune-up before he fought Joe Frazier for the heavyweight championship of the world. I felt comfort in knowing I had already gotten a jump on the competition, like Pittsburgh

Oscar Bonavena lands a solid right-hand punch to the throat of Muhammad Ali in their December 7, 1970 bout at Madison Square Garden. Jim O'Brien and Jim McKay are ringside observers.

boxer Fritzie Zivic striking a low blow at the beginning of a bout just to get warmed up for the war ahead.

I was 28 when I moved from Miami to New York, from *The Miami News* to *The New York Post*. I was immediately assigned to be part of a four-man team covering the Knicks in the NBA playoffs. Leonard Lewin was the main beat writer, and columnists Milton Gross and Larry Merchant supported his efforts, and they all taught me a lesson or two as the new guy in town. I picked up the loose ends and was under no pressure whatsoever, just to do the best I could with what was left for me.

I covered all sports teams in New York that were managed by the likes of Gil Hodges and Yogi Berra (Mets), Ralph Houk and Bill Virdon (Yankees), Al Arbour (Islanders), Emile Francis (Rangers), Weeb Ewbank (Jets), Alex Webster (Giants), Lou Carnesecca and Kevin Loughery and Rod Thorn (Nets) and Holzman (Knicks).

All were reserved, decent men, much like Chuck Noll, whom I would meet when I came home to cover the Steelers in 1979, when they won their fourth Super Bowl in as many outings.

I recall a day in New Orleans with Holzman and the Knicks on February 27, 1977. It was mid-afternoon and I was in my room at the Hyatt Hotel that is attached to the Superdome, enjoying a shrimp cocktail and some potato chips, a cold soft drink, and one of my all-time favorite movies "One Flew Over the Cuckoo's Nest," starring Jack Nicholson. I thought I had died and gone to heaven.

When the movie was over, I left my room and went down the hall to Holzman's suite and knocked on his door. I wanted to share my exhilaration with the Knicks' coach. Frankie Blauschild, who teamed with Jim Wergeles as public relations men with the Knicks, answered the door, talking to me and reminding me of a lookout at a speakeasy. "Whattaya want?" he asked me. I told him I wanted to see Red Holzman, his boss. Blauschild had a bum leg and always walked with a hitch, and he led me across the carpeted surface to see Holzman. Frankie moved like Igor, the man who helped Dr. Frankenstein unearth a corpse in a cemetery to create his monster.

I told Holzman of how impressed I was with my surroundings, and getting paid to tag along with his team to cities such as New Orleans. Holzman was sitting in a chair in a suit and had a drink in hand. He smiled at me.

"This would be a great life," he offered, "if it weren't for the damn games."

That's one of the great sports observations of all time.

That night in New Orleans, "Pistol Pete" Maravich, one of my all-time favorites, led the New Orleans Jazz to a victory over the Knicks. Playing against Walt Frazier, the finest defensive guard in the NBA, and the likes of Earl "The Pearl" Monroe, Maravich scored 68 points and wowed the crowd with his ball-handling wizardry.

His dad, Press Maravich, who played for the Pittsburgh Ironmen in the original NBA before he became a high school coach and then a college coach, and his attorneys, Pittsburgh-based Lester Zittrain and Aliquippa-based Arthur Herskowitz, had front row seats for the spectacle. Pete's sister was at courtside as well to witness his historic performance.

I remember that when we returned to New York, I saw Walt Frazier pulling out of a garage next to the Garden in a two-toned beige and brown Rolls Royce, and hearing young fans hollering for him to stop and sign autographs. But Clyde kept on driving, slowly but surely. Then the kids turned angry and started shouting "68! 68! 68!" just to remind him of how Maravich had manhandled him a few nights earlier. Like Frazier would soon forget...

When I was getting ready to leave New York and come to Pittsburgh to write for *The Pittsburgh Press* in the summer of 1979, I received a phone call out of the blue from Red Holzman.

"I hear you're leaving town," Holzman said. "Are you trying to sneak out of town without saying goodbye?"

Frankly, I was surprised to hear from Holzman. I didn't know him nearly as well as I knew Nets' coaches Kevin Loughery and Rod Thorn, for instance. I had played tennis with them and sportswriter Doug Smith several times on road trips.

Holzman invited me to come to his tennis club on Long Beach and play some tennis and have a goodbye drink or two. For the record, he beat me and he told me some terrific stories, and he signed a book I brought with me that had been written about Holzman by Leonard Lewin, a colleague of mine at *The New York Post*.

Holzman signed it for me with this message: "To Jim O'Brien, once just a sportswriter and now a friend. Red Holzman." I still have it on my bookshelf with other signed books, one signed to me by Muhammad Ali.

Thanksgiving was on the horizon when I heard about Holzman and Dundee dying. Press and Pete Maravich and Angelo Dundee have all died as well. I have to be thankful for the times I spent in their company and watched them at work and play. I'm glad they came my way.

Racial contrast made for good box office in boxing. Even with Joe Louis, certainly the most beloved of all black boxing champions during the 1930s and 1940s, his most important and most publicized fights were those against Max Schmeling, "Two-Ton" Tony Galento, Billy Conn, and the final bout of his career with Rocky Marciano, all of whom were white."

—From a story by Gerald Early,
Cultural Definition of Prize-Fighting

Conley's
A bar in Pittsburgh where boxing is still a hot topic

A life-size image of Billy Conn peers out from a dimly-lit corner at the customers lined up along the long bar in Conley's at 5245 Butler Street in Upper Lawrenceville—or the 10th ward as locals call it—just past Allegheny Cemetery and before you get to the zoo in Highland Park.

Conn strikes a classic boxing pose just to the left of a picture of Conn and Joe Louis sitting together in U.S. Army uniforms in the early '40s, one of Conn sparring with the great Henry Armstrong somewhere near Pittsburgh, and a color likeness of John Wayne, the ultimate western hero.

There's another one nearby showing Fritzie Zivic pummeling Armstrong in their first fight, the one Zivic won in 1940 to take the middleweight crown.

These remain important people in Conley's. There are also framed and often water-stained photos of Fritzie Zivic, a world boxing champion who lived in Lawrenceville, and Joey Diven, one of Conn's closest companions, once billed in a *True* magazine profile by Roy McHugh as "Pittsburgh's Greatest Streetfighter."

It just so happens that Joey Diven served as the godfather for the bartender, Geary Conley, who inherited the place after his father, Ray B. Conley, died two days' shy of two years earlier, August 4, 2014. Geary showed me a photo of his baptism. "I think I was the best-looking baby in Pittsburgh," he said, with a dark shadow of a three- or four-day beard on his chin. The woman in the photo, Geary told me, was his Aunt Tess. Geary's eyes gleamed behind glasses when he made that boast.

Geary Conley couldn't have been a better host. He served me two cold bottles of I.C. Light and refused payment. "It's on me," he said. Geary was wearing a gray Pittsburgh Penguins T-shirt. There was another bartender helping him, so no one went dry. He wiped off the bar in front of me. He asked me if I wanted a glass. I didn't need a glass. So he put a paper coaster down and placed the bottle on it. I had a feeling I was getting preferred treatment.

My blood pressure probably got back to normal because Conley was so kind, quick to show me the pictures of boxers and baseball fields and such that are everywhere on the walls. He even turned some lights on. When I arrived, the only thing that was well lit was the pool table and nobody was playing pool. I felt like an outsider when I walked into the bar and everybody at the bar studied my movement. I thought I should have brought my bodyguard, Big Tom McGuire. I did just that when I visited The Corner Restaurant out near Beaver Falls just over a year earlier. That bar was for stand-up guys only because there were no bar stools.

The long bar at Conley's was filled from one end to the other, with from 16 to 20 customers at any one time. They were all men. One woman accompanied by a man, both black, came in just before I left. "My dad didn't permit women in his bar," said Geary.

I stood with my back to the wall and a tribute to the late Art B. Conley. I like to have my back to the wall in most restaurants and saloons, but especially on this afternoon at Conley's. I told Geary it had to be one of the busiest bars in Pittsburgh at that time—between three and four o'clock on a bright, sunshiny afternoon. It was 88 degrees and humid, so the beer tasted good.

Three of the men wore doo-rags, colorful handkerchiefs, red or blue, tied behind their heads, and they all took an interest in me when I entered their domain. I felt different, a real stranger, like someone walking into a bar with too few bullets in a John Wayne movie. I'd have felt better if John Wayne had walked in with me.

In truth, it looked like a lot of bars my father frequented when I was a kid in Glenwood and Hazelwood in the mid-50s. There were 34 bars in a one-mile stretch from the Glenwood Bridge to Hazelwood Avenue, not all of them on the main street, Second Avenue. I counted them when I was delivering the morning newspaper. I used to go get my dad to bring him home for dinner. A buddy of mine told me he used to go to Tom and Tuds in Aspinwall to drag his dad home, even on Christmas Eve.

So I should have felt right at home, my wife told me when I told her about my day, when I visited Billy Conn's wife, Mary Louise, at the Little Sisters of the Poor Home on the North Side and then Conley's in Lawrenceville, not far from where my mother lived for 20 years at St. Augustine's Senior Apartments. But I didn't. I had a notebook and a camera and I was taking notes and taking pictures so people were paying attention to me. When the word got out that I was a writer, I became popular.

A guy came down and introduced himself as being from Garfield. "I'm from Harry Greb Country," he said, with more than a hint of pride.

I gave him a quick quiz to see if he was really from Garfield. I mentioned Frank Gorshin. "The Riddler," said my newfound friend. I told him Bill Hillgrove told me Gorshin lived in an exclusive block. "Yeah, that was Kincaid," said the man from Greb Country.

He also knew Hillgrove and Phil Musick, friends of mine in the media who grew up in Garfield and were proud of it. I asked him about Billy Neumont, who had been a boxer and once came out of Cavanaugh's Bar to take a joyride in a fire truck that was sitting at the curb.

Neumont missed the left turn from Penn Avenue onto Atlantic Avenue and ran right into St. Lawrence O'Toole Catholic Church. He's more known for that than any of his boxing feats. Turns out Billy Neumont was this guy's godfather.

Now what are the chances that I go into a saloon in Lawrenceville while working on a boxing book and I come across one guy who had Joey Diven for a godfather and another guy who had Billy Neumont stand in for him at his baptism? It was probably held in the same church that Neumont would later strike with a fire truck. What a parlay.

"Billy Conn used to call Billy Neumont 'Kid Cautious,' because of the way he boxed," said Geary Conley.

I hope you are starting to get a feel for Conley's. Geary Conley showed me a photo that had his father and Al Quail, another Pittsburgh fight fixture in the old days, both wearing police uniforms in the company of Golden Glove boxers from the Bellefield A.C. Quail was the boxing coach at the A.C. I met him in my teen years.

"Quail was really the toughest street-fighter in Pittsburgh," said Geary Conley. "Billy Conn used to come in a lot, and so did Fritzie Zivic until he opened his own bar just a block from here. I overheard Conn talking to a guy at that table over there one day, and the guy asked Conn what he would do if he had to fight Quail in the street.

"I'd call in sick," Conn is reported to have said. "I'd make the odds even if Quail were going up against King Kong in a street-fight."

Quail was an Irishman who came out of Brookline— that may be redundant—and turned pro in the mid-30s. He had a record of 31-16-3 and often sparred with champions Teddy Yarosz of Monaca and Billy Conn of East Liberty.

Geary also told me that Cavanaugh's, which was in Garfield, was owned by a city policeman as well. "It wasn't permitted for cops to own bars," said Geary, "but my father did whatever he wanted to do. I guess Cavanaugh did, too. My father had a bar for 40 years."

There was a poster-size and nicely framed tribute to his late father on the wall where I was standing at the far end of the bar as you come through the front door. There was one black man sitting alone at the first table when I came in, so apparently he felt comfortable and safe in his surroundings.

I read a review of Conley's in a report called "The Great Pittsburgh Bar Crawl," in which the anonymous author attempted and, admittedly, failed to visit every bar in Pittsburgh in a year's time. Here's what he had to say about Conley's:

"This is one of those bars you aren't going to go to unless you live right near it. Well, even if you live near it we're still not sure if you should go there. It's not that it's

352

terrible. It's just that it's an average dingy dive bar on a street with a lot of great options."

Now I would never write such a wicked review because I told Geary Conley I'd be back in the fall to personally sign a book for him. Some of the customers asked me when the book would be out.

I asked Geary Conley what was the favorite adjective of his customers and he was stumped. What do you think?

They used the f-word to describe the realtors who were peddling homes in Lawrenceville that you could get for $35,000 ten years ago that are now commanding $135,000 or better. They didn't use their favorite adjective when they referred to Children's Hospital, but the price of empty lots and row houses—now called townhouses—went way up when the hospital replaced St. Francis Hospital in the neighborhood.

"Now you got Hipsterville here," complained one customer, who tossed a few f-words into the most casual of conversations. "All these foo-foo shops and stores."

Art Conley boxed for Johnny Ray, who trained Billy Conn. They all went to Florida to train once upon a time. Geary, who is 58, also boxed and he ran a boxing club of his own in Sharpsburg for years. He grew up in Lawrenceville but now lives in Shaler,a suburb north of the city.

When he was young, he trained at a gym at the Boys Club on Butler Street in Lawrenceville and later with former boxer and union leader Joe LaQuatra, whose photo from his boxing days is on the wall in the back room of Atria's Restaurant & Tavern in Mt. Lebanon.

"If I had the money I'd still be running a gym," said Geary Conley. "It gets kids off the streets and keeps them busy. Boxing gives you the best workout of all. I've played baseball and basketball, but neither of them give you the physical workout that boxing does."

Why do you love it so much?

"I just think it's in my blood," he said. "I grew up with it. Hey, we had world champions coming into Conley's. It has a history about it, a legacy."

He showed me a picture of kid named Blaise—"I can't think of his last name," he said. "Something Italian. He was a real quiet, backward kid, but he turned out to be a good boxer. That happens. He won a state amateur title."

The storage room in the back of the bar looked like it could use some housekeeping. My wife Kathie would get hives if she saw it. She also tells me that I have become a snob. "No one from Glenwood or Hazelwood should be a snob," she often reminds me. She grew up in the White Oak section of McKeesport and believes I married up.

There was a sign near the front door that said SMOKING PERMITTED. That was one of the draws. There could have been a sign that said SWEARING PERMITTED.

"Here's why people come here," said a little guy near me at the bar, wearing a white T-shirt. He held up two $1 bills and waved them. You can buy a bottle of beer or a shot of whiskey for $2, and there are $1 drafts available. Conley point to a 24-ounce can of Pabst Blue Ribbon (that once sponsored boxing on TV) that costs $2.25. Those were half the prices most bars charge for drinks, one third of the price at Pittsburgh's sports venues. I was the only guy at the bar drinking an Iron City Beer product. That beer used to be brewed in Lawrenceville.

"You should have been here yesterday," said Geary Conley. "It was like a zoo in here. Those guys get their checks the first of the month. That's when we're really busy."

He told me he used to have even more boxing photos but he gave some to Jimmy Cvetic, a former Allegheny County policeman and poet who runs boxing gyms about town. Cvetic called them "non-profit gyms." Michael McSorley, who stops by Conley's on occasion, also got some photos for his Conn-Greb Boxing Gym in Oakland.

"We sell the cheapest beer and drinks in Pittsburgh," said Geary Conley. "My dad used to keep the prices low. You should have met my dad. He'd have liked you. He knew the history of boxing in Pittsburgh and loved to share his stories."

When I left, one of the guys in a red doo-rag reached his right hand high over his head and gave me the kind of handshake I don't think I ever experienced before. "Be careful, pal," he said in parting.

When I was leaving Lawrenceville in my car, I saw a man who had been in Conley's. He was standing, leaning like a statue against a white garage door. His eyes were squinted in the bright sunlight. He looked like he was sleeping standing up, or just sobering up for the walk home and a match with his wife at the door.

From Conn Family collection

Fritzie Zivic, at right, whose nose was broken so many times it became squishy, makes fun of Billy Conn, who proudly wears a patch on his battered nose.

Art Conley, at right, loved to see Billy Conn come into his bar in Lawrenceville.

J.T. Thomas
Steelers' former cornerback says
Ali pointed way for young blacks

People often ask me what Steelers were my favorite subjects and are often surprised by my answer. J.T. Thomas is near the top of the list.

Dwight White may have been the best interview—he had a good story and he told it with great passion. He called me "Bookman." He was followed closely by Mel Blount, Terry Bradshaw, Moon Mullins, Jerome Bettis, Hines Ward, Brett Keisel, Mike Webster, Frenchy Fuqua, Ray Mansfield, Joe Greene, Dwayne Woodruff, Mike Wagner, Andy Russell, Rocky Bleier, Randy Grossman, Paul Martha and Neil O'Donnell. Franco Harris didn't have much to offer when he was playing ball, but he is much better these days.

Thomas never disappoints me. He always has good stories and he peppers his responses with big words and a smile to punctuate his points. There is a strong spiritual side to Thomas that is appealing. I knew he had been active in civil rights demonstrations as a high school and college student in the South so I thought I'd ask him about Muhammad Ali and what he meant to him.

"Muhammad Ali gave us the courage to stand up for ourselves," said Thomas, age 65, talking over the telephone from his home in Monroeville. "We were trying to find our identity and he showed us the way."

Thomas, No. 24, was paired with Mel Blount at the corners in the Steel Curtain Defense and they were rated the sixth best cornerback combination in NFL history.

He was the team's first draft pick from Florida State in 1973, spent nine seasons with the Steelers (1973-1981) and was a member of three Super Bowl championship teams, and finished up with a year (1982) with the Denver Broncos. He had to sit out the 1978 season with a serious illness.

J.T. Thomas is a terrific speaker.

J.T. Thomas (No. 24) assumes stance in Steelers' secondary.

As a student at Lanier High School in Macon, Georgia, Thomas received military training, and he was in ROTC as a student at Florida State. "It was a no-brainer," he said of his ROTC involvement. "We received $15 a month in laundry money as football players. ROTC students received $140 a month, plus we had use of a Corvette if we had a date or something special to attend."

I was caught off guard by the Corvette perk. "Some Florida State alumnus who loved this country made it available to us," said Thomas.

He said he enjoyed going to military balls.

Thomas was a pioneer as a student. He was one of the first black students to integrate a previously all-white grade school in Macon, and he was the first black on a football scholarship at Florida State. He made these decisions on his own with his parents' approval.

Thomas said there were pictures of important people in his boyhood home, starting with Jesus Christ. "In our neighborhood, you might see a picture of Joe Louis, or President Kennedy, Reverend Martin Luther King Jr., Jackie Robinson," said Thomas. "In our college, in the rooms of the black students, you were more likely to see posters of Muhammad Ali and Malcolm X, Rap Brown and Stokely Carmichael.

"We weren't told about black heroes in grade school or high school. We learned about the Roman Empire, Constantine and Hannibal, but blacks were kind of left out of our history lessons. They didn't mention the slaves showing up in Jamestown in 1619, or mention that a preacher named John Brown was an abolitionist bent on ridding the country of slavery. We missed that part.

"My heroes came out of the era I was living in. I was in marches in Macon. I remember when Dr. King came down from Atlanta and that Rev. Ralph Abernathy would lead the way with him. I was living in Georgia and I can tell you that Georgia was not in the United States.

"After we won some Super Bowls, they had a day for me in Macon, Georgia. I was given a key to the city by the mayor, Ronnie Thompson. When I was a youngster in

Macon, Ronnie Thompson was the police chief and he was known as 'Machine Gun' Thompson. I mentioned when I received the key that I had been with blacks who were sprayed with hoses and worse by the police when Thompson was the chief. It was all on tape; we could see that. It was a tough situation in Macon."

At one time, Thomas had considered a military career. "I was one of the best students from a physical and mental aspect in our military programs in high school and in college," he said. "During my junior year at Florida State, I was asked to sign a contract to enter the military as a second lieutenant.

"But that gave me pause. So often at Florida State, we had the flag flying at half-mast because one of our former students had been killed, serving as a second lieutenant in Vietnam. They were always on the front lines. Fifteen of our trainers were killed in Vietnam. This was in 1969. I said, 'Wait a minute. Let's re-think this.' It was a tumultuous time. There was a lot of unrest on college campuses. We were all going through a metamorphoses. I was marching with the protesters every week. And they wanted us to sign on the dotted line. I'm starting to think that flag at half-mast could be for me.

"We heard there was going to be a lottery to determine a draft order, so I wanted to see how I fared in that respect. My number was so high I knew I was never going to be drafted. That very day I turned in all my military uniforms and gear, except for my shoes.

"I remember Muhammad Ali saying he had nothing against them Viet Kong. He said no Viet Kong were calling him nigger, and he didn't see why he should want to kill them.

"That got our attention. We felt the same way. Hey, most of the white students at our school wanted no part of the Vietnam War. It was not a popular war."

Thomas then told me something that I had never heard before, but it makes some sense. He said Muhammad Ali was the first rapper, speaking his peace in a poetic manner, in a sing-song way. I asked him to define what made a rapper.

"In the black community, you had to know how to rap," he said. "It was a way of talking. It was something that was indigenous to the black community. You had to say something with alliteration. When guys were playing dice, for instance, they were rapping as they tossed the dice. It was part of the culture.

"Ali was a public rapper. He was rhyming his reasons for being unhappy with the system. The black community bought into that. They were hearing what he was saying on TV, and they embraced what he was saying. I was 11-12-13 and we were marching. Our parents were hesitant to do it because they feared losing their jobs. They don't send old men to war, remember. They send kids who don't know any better.

"I was playing piano for an all-black choir that began to be part of community activities," he recalled. "The theme for our town was Macon is on the Move. I said we had to be moving faster.

"Ali cleared up a lot of stuff for us. A lot of times you don't see what you don't see. After Ali started talking, now you see the obvious. There were so many distractions. He eliminated a lot of the distractions. What is the real why? Why are we fighting? Why are we really fighting? Lot of times we don't get the real why. He had a way of getting to the issue. He explained what the real issue was. Muhammad Ali made us proud to be black young men, and we were on the move."

> *"Boxing is a lot of white men watching two black men beat each other up."*
> **—Muhammad Ali**

Martin Smith
Recalls when Muhammad Ali
paid surprise visit to Schenley High

Construction workers were busy tearing out the innards of the magnificent building that was once Schenley High School in North Oakland, just below The Hill District, and they were doing the same to the heart and soul of Martin Smith. "I hate to see them doing this," said Smith, age 62 and retired, as he stood just inside the three doors at the north entrance of the still elegant edifice on North Bellefield Avenue and Bigelow Boulevard. "It was a great school. So many famous people went to school here and it should be preserved."

The building is, after all, designated a local and national landmark by different historical societies. Smith said he would never forget the day when Muhammad Ali paid a surprise visit. That was on May 18, 1970. "I think one of his advisors suggested it would be a good public relations gesture for him to visit a predominantly black school while he was in Pittsburgh," said Smith. He said Ali arrived in a big orange-colored luxury car with white leather seats, and some students went to the windows to see the car.

"We moved to the auditorium and Ali addressed an impromptu assembly."

Smith closed his eyes when he was next to me and when he studied the interior walls and noted missing murals and statuary, and saw how the wall coverings in the once-grand entryway were torn and tattered. This was Thursday, August 18, 2016. Gone were the tapestries and paneling of its storied past. The inside had been stripped of all personality. It was being scrubbed of its originality.

The interior of the triangular building designed by Edward Stotz was being reconfigured and a story being added to accommodate 160 to 180 apartment units. When it opened in 1916, Schenley High School was said to be the first million dollar school building and one of the top ten school buildings in the U.S.A. It was built for 1800 students and 70 teachers, had state-of-the art classrooms and labs, and a 1600-seat auditorium. It was closed in 2009 because of mounting maintenance bills and asbestos deterioration.

Smith stood with his young grandson, Dominic Sapp, and surveyed the scene. We had to get out of the building because it was nearly 5 o'clock and the workmen were calling it a day. They had looked the other way when we passed by a NO ENTRY sign on the front doors.

"Our students went crazy that day," Smith said of Ali's visit. "He was everybody's idol. Our principal Mr. Outen did his best to keep some order in the hallways and to get us into the auditorium. Class was over and everyone was getting ready to exit the building, when Ali appeared.

"Muhammad Ali addressed us. He told us Joe Frazier was going to be the first black astronaut. He said, "You're going to see the launching. I'm going to send him into orbit.'

"Ali came out on our front lawn and he playfully sparred with some boys. One kid, Derek McLaughlin, got a small cut over his eye and he came to school for the next two days without any bandage on it. We think he pulled the scab off so it would look like a fresh wound. There were no cell phones or digital cameras in those days so everything is just in the memory of the day. It was absolutely fantastic."

I had met Smith in downtown Pittsburgh a few weeks earlier and he mentioned Muhammad Ali coming to his school. I told him I wanted to talk to him. I preferred doing it in person, at the scene, and not on the telephone. I don't want to start taking short cuts. He wore a red and black golf shirt because those were the school colors.

He was on time for our 4:45 p.m. meeting. He told me he lived on Dunseith Street, alongside Trees Hall Swimming Pool on the upper campus of the University of Pittsburgh. He mentioned that Schenley alumni included Andy Warhol, George Benson, Bob Prince and Bruno Sammartino.

Warhol was the famous pop artist who has a museum named in his honor on the North Side, Benson was a famed jazz musician, Prince was "the Voice of the Pirates" for 28 years, and Bruno Sammartino ruled the professional wrestling world for more than a decade in the '60s and

'70s. Dan Marino's father, also Dan Marino, played on the Spartans football team.

Pro football players Larry Brown and Darrell Dinkins were once Spartans, and so were NBA players Maurice Lucas, Kenny Durrett, DeJuan Blair and D.J. Kennedy, as were college standouts Petey Gibson, Jeep Kelly, Kelvin Smith, Sonny Lewis and DeAndre Kane, and Cleveland Cavaliers' owner Ted Stepien. Other famous musicians were Ray Brown, Walt Harper, Stanley Turrentine, actors Bill Nunn and Benjamin Tatar, opera singer Robert Mosley, Nobel laureate Clifford Shull, and Derrick Bell, the first African-American professor at the Harvard Law School.

They won City League and PIAA titles in basketball under coaches such as Willard Fisher, Spencer Watkins, Fred Yee and Fred Skrocki.

Smith told me a story about Dick Vitale coming to his home to recruit his brother, Kelvin Smith, to play basketball at the University of Detroit. "He told my mother that no one else would offer Kelvin a scholarship," said Smith. "My mother cussed Vitale out pretty good and chased him out of the house."

Kelvin was recruited by Tim Grgurich to come to Pitt. He could walk across the street to the Pitt Field House. DeJuan Blair could also walk from his home near the VA Hospital to the Petersen Events Center. Kelvin came to Pitt with Sonny Lewis and Wayne Williams from the 1975 state championship Schenley basketball team.

They had a large swimming pool and a small gym when I was playing CYO (Catholic Youth Organization) basketball in the late '50s. I took advantage of the small court—someone would get a rebound and four dribbles later they would be over the midcourt line—and my best scoring effort of 26 points. No wonder Kenny Durrett and Maurice Lucas were among the City League leaders in scoring. They later put in a new bigger gym.

There was a movie filmed at Schenley High in 2015, *Me and Earl and the Dying Girl,* a coming-of-age debut novel written by Schenley grad Jesse Anderson.

A view from the sky of Schenley High School.

I bid Martin Smith goodbye and walked down Centre Avenue and made a left on Dollar Street to take in some sparring sessions at the Conn-Greb Boxing Club in the Royal York Apartments. Michael McSorley Jr. would be waiting for me.

Martin Smith shows his grandson Dominic Sapp the former Schenley High School where he saw Muhammad Ali during his student days as a Spartan.

Craig
Wolfley

STEELERS STRONGMAN—Craig Wolfley loves all kinds of combat. He played offensive guard and tackle for the Pittsburgh Steelers from 1980-1989 and with the Minnesota Vikings from 1990-1991. In addition to football, Wolfley competed in weight lifting, boxing, sumo wrestling and martial arts. In 1981, he placed fifth in the World's Strongest Man competition. In 1985, Wolfley placed second in the first professional sumo wrestling tournament ever held in North America. In 2002, he lost a four-round boxing match to Eric "Butterbean" Ech—"now that was really stupid," he said. He also holds a black belt in Jiu Jitsu. He operated a martial arts studio in Bridgeville for many years and coached and trained boxers for Golden Gloves competition.

Conn-Greb Boxing Club
Michael McSorley Jr. swaps punches with his prospects because he loves his gym

"I like the grunginess of it."
—Gregg Rudolph

Isteeled myself for my second visit to the Conn-Greb Boxing Club in August of 2016. I had been there a month earlier and was nearly knocked out by the overpowering and pungent gym odor as I entered the large work-out room for the first time. It was like getting a punch in the nose from Billy Conn or Harry Greb, or both at the same time.

The Conn-Greb Boxing Club is located at the bottom and backend of the Royal York Apartments, still a tony address on Bigelow Boulevard in the Oakland section of Pittsburgh. It was built and owned and operated by McSorley Real Estate.

You get there through an indoor parking area and you walk up a slippery oil-stained slope to the second floor. The bathroom for the boxers is on the third floor, I learned, just down the hall. It's not pretty, but it works. The walls are covered with posters from boxing shows. Most of the tenants don't know the gym is there. Or the bathroom.

"We try to stay under the radar," said Michael McSorley Jr., who operates the gym, and is a descendant of the building's original owner, who frequented the P.A.A., the Duquesne Club and The Field Club.

It's down at the end of Dollar Street, but that is definitely misleading in the case of boxing. It's also a dead-end street, which is more appropriate, but it keeps some young men and women off the streets and that's a blessing. Yes, I saw a woman there in training. It's a block and a half east off Centre Avenue from the still beautiful building that was once Schenley High School, but has been abandoned since 2009. The school supposedly was the first $1 million dollar school building in the country.

The famous Park Schenley Restaurant occupied space at the other end of the building at the Royal York Apartments, but it's been closed for quite a while, too.

Once you're in the gym you get used to the foul smell. The ever-smiling handsome face of Michael McSorley Jr., who turned 44 on August 14, 2016, who runs the gym and teaches young men how to handle themselves in and out of the ring, makes a visitor feel welcome.

After a third visit, I wanted to be a part of the place. I wanted to skip rope, but feared I might fall and make a fool of myself. I was sweating in a short-sleeved shirt just being at ringside. I had to step back quickly a few times to avoid being hit by sparring boxers. I wanted to be close to the action, to better judge how hard they were hitting one another. I hadn't been in a gym in a while, and I was surprised by the sound and power of the punches.

McSorley gets in the ring, wearing special gloves that are like miniature catcher's mitts, and has his fighters throw punches into those mitts. He moves them around in a studied way and the boxers strike them again and again. McSorley is big on body punches. "You don't chop a tree down by starting at the top," he is fond of saying.

"You chop away at the trunk and then it falls down. It's the same thing in boxing with body shots. All of my fighters are trained to go to the body. By doing so, you wear your opponent down, for them to drop their guard. Then they are open for head shots."

There are all kind of motivational messages scrawled on the beams overhead. THIS IS YOUR LIFE. WORK HARD. YOU ONLY LIVE ONCE.

The fighters are all friendly and, to a man, they tell me they love the gym, admire McSorley, and are having a good workout and having fun. "I love it" is a frequent response to the question—"Why are you here?"

Everyone greets me with a handshake, a smile, and a welcoming word or two. Tom Prine, an "investigative writer" from the *Tribune-Review* shows up in an off-white suit, looking much like Tom Wolfe, the wonderful writer and book author from New York. He tells me he boxed in a

From the photo album of the Conn-Greb Boxing Club

gym when he was a kid. He was one of two men in the room wearing a tie. "Nothing to investigate here," one of the boxers told him. "We're on the up and up."

Tom Wolfe would have a field day describing the gym and the people in it. They would love Tom Wolfe. And share their stories. The other man wearing a tie was McSorley's partner J.J. Richardson.

Boxing people are like that. They take writers, even sportswriters, into their bosom and they love to talk about boxing. McSorley knew that I knew my stuff. I could identify all the posters on the wall of famous Pittsburgh boxers of the past and some of the present-day or recent vintage pro boxers from elsewhere.

I even identified a photo he had on the wall even though he did not know the two men captured in it. They were Charles Cooper and Chick Davies in their Duquesne University days. Cooper, a Westinghouse High School grad, was the first black ballplayer to be drafted into the NBA, back in 1950, by Walter Brown, the owner of the Boston Celtics, and Davies was a successful coach at Duquesne University (1924 to 1945, and then 1947-1948). In 1946, he directed Homestead High to a state championship in basketball. McSorley seemed pleased to learn about this. "I wondered who they were," he said, "and now I know."

It's near a photo showing Jack Dempsey with Knute Rockne, the world heavyweight boxing champion with the fabled Notre Dame football coach.

There were a dozen images of Billy Conn and an equal number of Harry Greb covering the once-white brick walls, along with similar photos of Charley Burley, the great fighter from The Hill who had a hard time getting fights because he was black and because he could make an opponent look bad with his defensive skills and shiftiness. There were exposed pipes lining the ceiling, and old rugs here and there, and a boxing ring on the floor in the middle of the room, with a row of six or seven seats for ring fans.

By coincidence, I came upon Kelly Burley, one of the young boxers toiling in the gym during my first visit who was the great nephew of Charley Burley. He looked good to me during a brief sparring session. McSorley said he'd have to wait and see how dedicated the kid was before he pronounced judgment on him. Burley went back to school at Penn State where he is on their boxing team. McSorley said they have fights with IUP and Clarion University. There are about 80 colleges that have revived boxing programs, most with unpaid coaches. McSorley introduced me to every fighter in the gym and gave me a big buildup, and encouraged them to talk to me. He pointed out a kid named Evan Billings, from Central Catholic, that he thought had potential. He told them to tilt their head and not to come in with a squared-face, easier to slip punches and to counter-punch.

McSorley seems to take special pride when a kid from Central Catholic shows up at the gym. He wrestled and played lacrosse in his student days at Central. "I was very honored to be inducted into the Central Catholic Hall of Fame in 2012 for the 'Distinguished Young Alumni Award.'"

I asked him how he first got involved with boxing. "During my freshman year at St. Michael's College in Winooski, Vermont, the school's athletic facility was closed for repairs. Seeking another place to work out, I stumbled upon a nearby boxing gym and became hooked.

"I started competing in Vermont's Golden Gloves. I competed in their state championship in 1994. I lost in the final."

McSorley sent me a series of e-mails during the time I visited his gym. One day I complimented him on how well he wrote. He said, "I was an English major." No wonder I like this man.

* * *

There were photos of Rocky Marciano, and fight cards featuring Sugar Ray Robinson, Marvin Hagler, Tommy Hearns, Mike Tyson, Evander Hollyfield, Roberto Duran, etc. There was a print of a painting of Billy Conn. And McSorley resembled him in a way. He liked the comparison I offered. The posters are the wallpaper of the Conn-Greb

Boxing Club.

There was a mixture of black and white fighters at work in the gym. The speed bag was missing because somebody broke it so there was no familiar rat-a-tat-tat sound in the gym. The windows hadn't been cleaned in a while, but at least they were open on this second visit. It was 82 degrees outside and as humid as a summer day in Miami so it provided little relief.

"It smells different this time," I said for openers. "What happened?"

McSorley stifled a laugh, but said with a smile, "We had a cleaning session here last week. I guess it was pretty bad."

I asked McSorley if his wife ever stops by. "Joan hardly ever comes to the gym." I thought that was understandable. "But she is fully supportive of what I'm doing. I am very lucky."

Certain cities have a distinct blend of sounds and smells. New Orleans and Memphis and Miami come to mind. But boxing gyms are all the same and always have been. I visited six boxing gyms in New York City the month before "The Fight of the Century" pitting champion Joe Frazier against Muhammad Ali for a six-part series in *The New York Post* about what life was like for the majority of boxers who didn't have the same talent or money of Ali and Frazier. I found that it was a far cry from Madison Square Garden, even though one gym was within walking distance of the sports mecca.

*   *   *

McSorley told me there was some feuding going on in Pittsburgh boxing circles. I assured him that was nothing new to the game. There had been a boxing show at the Roberto Clemente Bridge that week pitting local boxers against boxers from Cuba. McSorley and his fighters were not involved. Overall, he's optimistic about the state of boxing in Pittsburgh.

"There are currently a lot of gyms popping up which is a good thing," he said. "Exciting fighters like world-ranked Sammy Vasquez Jr of Monessen have brought a lot of interest locally to the sport. He's a welterweight (147-pounds). I don't train Sammy; I serve as his cut man. We do have a lot of tough MMA (Mixed Martial Arts) guys transitioning into boxing as well. I don't think MMA has hurt boxing on the amateur level at all. In fact, I think it's helped it."

McSorley shows up from a day of selling real estate at 5:30 on weekdays, except for Friday, and he always looks good. He handles commercial and residential leasing of properties and manages them as well for Sterling Land Company. He sheds a dress shirt in favor of a T-shirt, this time a green IRISH GERRY COONEY shirt he shows me that a sporting goods sales rep had given him recently.

Michael's great-grandfather, John McSorley Sr., came over from Ireland to Canada and then came to America. He built a number of buildings around the East End of Pittsburgh, including the Royal York Apartments and the King Edward Apartments at the corner of Craig and Bayard midway between the gym and Michael's alma mater, Central Catholic High School. Michael's dad is a Central and Notre Dame grad, and was grand company when we sat together at a boxing show at the Events Center of the Meadows Casino & Racetrack in late August 2016.

Duquesne Garden, the mecca for boxing in the days of Conn and Fritzie Zivic, was in that same neighborhood, in the shadow sometimes of St. Paul's Cathedral. It was razed in 1956 to make way for apartment buildings. Motor Square Garden is still standing not far away in East Liberty. The Hunt Armory, where boxing bouts were also held, is still standing on Emerson Street near Sacred Heart Church in Shadyside. Gregg "The Lumberjack" Rudolph,who runs Watson Chevrolet in Murrysville by day, was there for a workout. He wore a black T-shirt with this message across the chest: KILL OR BE KILLED—Pinnacle Boxing. Pinnacle promotes local fights at places like the Union Hall on Butler Street in Lawrenceville.

"There's no air moving in here," said Rudolph, who competes in boxing and MMA competition. "It's an old-school boxing gym. I like the grunginess of it. It gives you the 'Rocky' theme. Everything is dark and grungy. If you want to get better, this is the place." Rudolph said he knew most of the contemporary boxers pictured in the gym, and he learned about the old-time guys from McSorley. "Mike Tyson was my favorite fighter of my life," he said. "I met him in Las Vegas and it was like talking to a real person. I try to mimic my style after him. I met Floyd Mayweather and he's just as obnoxious as they say he is. My record is 6-0 as an amateur and I'm looking to my first pro fight in May."

A middleweight named Gerald Sherrell showed well in a sparring session, and McSorley said that Sherell (3-0, with 2 Kos) would be on a card at the Casino Meadows in North Strabane, not far from my home, on the last Saturday of August. He said he and J.J. Richardson managed Sherrell in the Integrity Fighter Management LLC.

I was impressed with the punching power of a light-heavyweight named Dustin Echard (14-2, with 12 KOs) from Washington, West Virginia. McSorley said of him, "He hits harder than a mule kicking downhill."

* * *

Matt Leyshock was the first one in the gym during all four of my visits in July and August of 2016. He is quiet and serious, and trains fighters there. He is 33 and he runs Pinnacle, the fight promotion company that does MMA and pro boxing shows. Leyshock owned a gym of his own on the South Side, but he had closed it down.

He had a young man named John Antonitis in the ring and he had a wicked punch and a winning smile for a sportswriter at ringside who offered him a compliment about his skills.

Leyshock has large tattoos on his arms, as do several of the fighters, and they are more visible when he extends his arms to block punches or to make a point about movement and reaction or footwork. He and McSorley swabbed a touch of grease on the gloves of two combatants before they started to swing at one another. It makes the blows more glancing and less likely to cut skin. There is a lot more involved in boxing than just punching each other. That's why the sport has always been called "The Sweet Science."

There's even a sanitizer spray just inside the door, and a sign saying it's required for everyone in the gym to use, even visiting sportswriters. I'm certain Billy Conn and Harry Greb never used sanitizer spray in their day. McSorley dons thin black surgical gloves when he adjusts a mouthpiece or touches a fighter's face. We're smarter now.

McSorley says he likes to get prospective fighters sparring early, to see if they can take a punch as well as deliver one. "I'm not a masochist," he said, "but I think it's important to learn in a hurry if a kid wants to mix it up, and how serious they are about taking up boxing."

As Fritzie Zivic liked to say, "It's boxing. It's not playing the piano."

One kid who probably wouldn't mind a piano accompaniment to his workout was Aidan Shovlin of Oakland, who had spent a lot of time in boxing gyms and dancing studios in his youth. His parents own the Shovlin Academy of Irish Dancing in Dormont. So he could do some high stepping. He won a Golden Gloves title at 122 pounds earlier in the year. He had graduated from Sacred Heart Grade School—Billy Conn's alma mater—and would be a freshman at Central Catholic High School—Michael McSorley Jr.'s alma mater—in the fall.

He hadn't been in the gym in a while because he was studying for his entrance exams for Central. I told him I had been in 1F and 1S as a freshman and sophomore at Central. There were 12 freshman classes and 10 sophomore classes in 1957 and 1958. That's how many kids wouldn't make the cut after their freshman year.

I transferred to Taylor Allderdice midway through my sophomore year where there were just as many smart kids but a more relaxed discipline. I had the best of both worlds as schools went, the best Catholic and the best public high schools in the city.

"I love this," said Shovlin, who showed a lot of discipline and hard-striking punches on target during his session in the ring with McSorley. There was a relative newcomer to the gym, a little guy from Lower Burrell, up near New Kensington, Domenic "The Honeybadger" Mazotta. "He's a local MMA star," said McSorley in his introduction.

Nicknames are easy to come by in boxing circles.

McSorley speaks well of Jimmy Cvetic, a long-time fixture on the Pittsburgh boxing gym circuit. "Jimmy has run PAL (Police Athletic League) gyms for decades," said McSorley. "He's also a well-renowned poet, and does readings in book stores and coffee shops in Bloomfield and Oakland.

"As we speak, he is in LA doing a reading. Actor Nick Nolte flew him out there and Nolte is narrating some of Jimmy's poems for an event. I hear Jimmy plans to come back by train. He's having some health issues."

He mentioned that Teddy Mrkonja ran the Pittsburgh Boxing Club on Rt. 51 in Brentwood and does a good job.

I asked McSorley what the paydays were like for local pro boxers.

"It depends on what level they are fighting at," McSorley said. "For a new pro, the club circuit level shows do not pay much. Fighters typically get a percentage of their gross ticket sales. However, if a young upstart gets offered a dangerous fight out of town, they wouldn't have to sell any tickets and the purse could be for a little bit more money. For world-ranked guys like Sammy Vasquez, the nationally-televised bouts prove much larger paydays."

McSorley slipped that question pretty niftily, like all the boxers in his gym when I asked them similar questions. I still have no idea how much money they can make.

What do amateurs get for their bouts? "Amateur fighters do not and should not ever get paid," said McSorley. When I was a young man they might give an amateur fighter a gift certificate or a frozen turkey for a fight.

I asked McSorley if he boxed as an amateur and how he learned how to coach boxing.

"I boxed as an amateur while I was in college at St. Michael's College in Vermont," he said. "I trained and worked out at several different gyms over the years and picked up what I learned from several different trainers over that time. One of the guys that I learned the most from was former Pittsburgh middleweight contender Johnny Morris. Johnny was a friend of my dad, and he later worked for our family business."

When I asked him if there was anything else he wanted to share, he said, "Our gym is committed to producing a world champion and I know that will happen. Nothing worthwhile in this life comes easy. We all know that it is a very tough road that takes a ton of dedication and personal sacrifice. We honored Billy Conn and Harry Greb by naming our gym after two of the best fighters out of the East End. Harry Greb is undeniably the best fighter to ever live. His stats speak for themselves. Tim Conn, one of Billy Conn's sons, has become a friend and he has given us a lot of images of his father, even some signed stuff, to make sure we honor Billy Conn in a proper fashion.

Michael McSorley Jr. resembles "The Pittsburgh Kid," Billy Conn.

Kelly Burley, a student at Penn State, is the great nephew of legendary Charley Burley from The Hill.

Jordon Roussos
A Greek-Italian heavyweight

When I saw Jordan Roussos striking a heavy bag, smiling through a clear mouthpiece and a red protective boxing headgear that had CONN-GREB across the face of it, I thought of Rocky Balboa, as played by Sylvester Stallone who scripted and directed the great "Rocky" movie series."

I could hear the theme song in my mind. Roussos might have as well. He laughed when I mentioned the Rocky likeness. "I'm part Italian, on my mother's side," he said. "But my dad and my name are Greek."

If the late Baldy Regan, the mayor of the North Side, were promoting him as a fighter, Roussos would be Italian in some towns, and Greek in others, depending on the major ethnic make-up of the community where the show was being held. The nationality of a fighter has always been important in boxing promotions.

Roussos is easy to cheer for. He's a big guy, 6-5, 245 pounds, but he's lost about 70 pounds from his peak weight. "Working out in a gym and spending your day looking after kids at a day-care center will help you lose weight in a hurry," he said.

When I asked him where he was from, he said Crafton, and that prompted gym operator Michael McSorley Jr. to scold him. "Crafton? Don't tell him that. Tell him Aliquippa. It makes you sound tougher."

Roussos resides with his girlfriend and their dog in Hopewell, which borders Aliquippa. "I live in the good part, where the old people live," he said. He grew up in Carnegie.

I had heard Roussos saying something about watching the Little Cougars practicing football. I knew that former Steelers' coach Bill Cowher once played for the Little Cougars and then at Carlynton High School.

Roussos lettered in four sports—football, wrestling, baseball and track at Carlynton High School and he played football at Bowling Green State University, and had a tryout with the Seattle Seahawks. He signed as a free agent with the Seahawks and went to their rookie camp and stayed around six weeks before he was cut. He had played defensive line in college, but was switched to offensive line as a pro prospect, and that could not have helped his chances.

"I wanted to lose some weight; I was over 300 pounds which is good for an offensive lineman, but not so good when you're finished with football. I thought I'd try boxing. I'm young enough that I can still do something in this sport."

He was wearing an Iron City Beer T-shirt, and knee-length trunks that looked like the ones worn by the New York Knicks of the NBA. He told me he had a degree in education and was working on a teacher's certificate, and that he had spent the day looking after little kids at a day-care center. "Those kids give you a good workout," he said with a smile. "The regular schools aren't open now, so I am hoping to get something as a teacher in the fall. I do a lot of subbing at different schools in the area.

"I'm a competitive person," Roussos told me when I talked to him while he was skipping rope at the Conn-Greb Boxing Club. "I get anxious if I'm not doing something physical. I like this; it's a great workout. I wish I had better results (8-4 at the time), but I know I can get better. I am just learning how to box. Michael is the best coach I've ever had."

I watched one session in which McSorley moved around the ring and blocked or fielded punches from Roussos. Some of them sounded ominous.

McSorley had donned a protective black-ribbed shield similar to the kind worn by baseball umpires and entered the ring to absorb some body shots from this promising heavyweight boxer who had quite a punch. It had to hurt, protective shell and all.

"Surprisingly, that protector gives pretty good protection," said McSorley. "However, over the years I have sustained an abdominal hernia, and most recently, in January (2016), I had to have surgery for a detached retina. Both of these injuries were sustained in training my fighters."

Why do you subject yourself to that?

"The pain is temporary," he said. "Too many fighters focus on head shots, and I want to teach them to go to the body."

Kevin Smith and Kevin Gorman, two other *Trib* writers, had recently written stories about Roussos.

After Roussos had won a Western Pennsylvania super heavyweight title, he told Smith, "It has an aspect of feeling like a cave man and hitting things really hard. But for the most part, I like to think I am an artist and appreciate it for its beauty."

McSorley had told Smith: "I always liked a fighter who played other sports. It takes a certain amount of discipline and work. He has a lot of attributes you can't teach, like toughness."

Kevin Gorman found out Roussos' middle name was Aristotle. "I'm a thinker," Roussos told Gorman. "I'm into a lot of ideas. I always liked combat sports, so I thought I'd try this. I want to be a winner at whatever I do."

JORDAN ARISTOTLE ROUSSOS
He loves the Conn-Greb Boxing Club

Bernie Stein
Boxing stories from Art Rooney Jr.

A rt Rooney Jr. never disappoints me. Mention a name out of the past and he provides a story. He is like his father in that respect.

I was talking with the second son of the Steelers' founder, one of five sons of Kathleen and Art Sr. His brother Dan, the president emeritus of the Steelers, was the first born, followed by Art, Timmy, and the twins, Pat and John.

We were talking about boxing on Friday morning, August 12, 2016. Art was in his office in Upper St. Clair, where he looked after the family's real estate interests. Art had included a chapter about boxing, and his father's interest and involvement in the game, in his memoir, *Ruanaidh— The Story of Art Rooney and his Clan,* with the editorial assistance of former *Pittsburgh Press* writer Roy McHugh.

Art Jr. had become an art collector, commissioning portraits of some of the greatest Pittsburgh Steelers, several of his father, and many of them are on display in his office. It looks like some kind of Hall of Fame. Art Jr. had recently turned his attention to having artwork done on some of Pittsburgh's greatest boxers. I had given him a book earlier that had some boxing artwork done by the late Marty Wolfson, who had worked with me on some of my earliest books about Pittsburgh sports.

I mentioned Bernie Stein. He is 75, a year older than me, but if I were to see him somewhere on a street in Pittsburgh tomorrow, he would address me as "Mister O'Brien." He was always super polite and eager to do something for you. He was one of Baldy Regan's best students in that respect. I was always impressed at how respectful Baldy's sons were with his friends.

Art Rooney Jr. was ready with a story. "My father had this little box of his own besides the press box at Three Rivers Stadium, which he'd share with a friend, usually a priest and his friend and driver, Richie Easton, who drove a truck for *The Press.* Don't refer to Richie as my dad's chauffeur; Richie didn't like that. He's gone now, but he'll know.

"There was some noise in the press box, and someone informed my father that there was a scuffle taking place in the hall behind the press box, and Bernie Stein was involved. My dad rushed out of his box, and went to see what was going on." Art Sr. once told me if he were a sportswriter he'd go to the losing locker room first because that's where the action is.

"Stein had roughed up a guy who didn't belong in the press box and wouldn't take no for an answer. My dad was disappointed that he missed it. He said he wanted to see Bernie Stein in action." Art Rooney had been a rugged presence on the North Side long before Bernie Stein showed up. He was, in fact, an amateur boxing champion.

Bernie Stein and Paul Tomasovich used to help Baldy Regan run off play-by-play sheets and statistics when that was done on a Ditto machine. Remember those and the dark blue ink that often smeared? It's much easier to do that task these days in the digital age. I first met those three in the press box at Pitt Stadium during my days as the sports editor of *The Pitt News* in 1961 and 1962.

They did the same service for Beano Cook at Pitt that they did for Joe Gordon at Three Rivers Stadium. They were the friendliest of fellows. "Howya doin', Brother?" Regan liked to say in the way of a greeting. He also liked to say, in reference to anyone going from rags to riches, "Only in America."

Tomasovich told me that he wasn't there the day Stein took a shot at a noisy guy who knocked some kind of machine off the wall, maybe a soap dispenser, in the media area at Three Rivers Stadium, and then swore at Bernie Stein when he stepped in to see what had happened. "Tom O'Malley told me what happened, and I heard the guy shouldn't have sworn at Stein like that."

> *"Life is like boxing in many unsettling respects. But boxing is only like boxing."*
> **—Author Joyce Carol Oates**

* * *

All three of those fellows were Pittsburgh sports legends. Stein started out as a football star at nearby Allegheny High School and won a Golden Gloves boxing title in 1958, and boxed as an amateur in Pennsylvania, Ohio and West Virginia, with Regan in his corner. Baldy wouldn't let him turn pro. "You're a good high school fighter," he told Stein.

Regan was a close friend of the Rooneys and had been a classmate and friend of Art Jr. during their respective days at North Catholic High School on Troy Hill. Paul Tomasovich was known as "The Babe Ruth of Softball" on the Pittsburgh sandlot circuit and the star of Skip's A.C. that won a national title in the sport. He was from Greenfield and was famous for launching Ruth-like blasts over the fences at Magee Field, not far from his home on Greenfield Avenue.

He later was a much-respected sports official, refereeing football and basketball games, and maintaining order in gyms not familiar with order throughout the city and region. He was also known as the father of seven daughters. That had to be fun.

"Stein was a little guy," related Rooney, "but he patrolled the sideline during the game, making sure that only properly credentialed people were on the sideline. We had a big guy doing the same. His name escapes me."

I suggested Jim Boston. Rooney rejected that. Paul Tomasovich? Again, that wasn't it. How about Joey Diven? Bingo!

"That's it," said Rooney. "He was about 6-5, 300 pounds and liked to fight."

Indeed, Joey Diven liked to fight. He was a friend and regular sidekick to Pittsburgh's most popular fighter of all time, the great Billy Conn. They frequented a few bars and nightspots in Pittsburgh, and put the fear of the Lord in a lot of people.

"It was an interesting situation to have such a little guy and such a big guy keeping things straight on the field," recalled Rooney.

382

Bernie Stein receives 1958 AMA "outstanding boxer" trophy from his mentor Baldy Regan.

Roy McHugh on Billy Conn:

Of the Pittsburgh champions, Conn was the most picture-perfect.

He was fast with his hands and fast on his feet. He boxed in the upright classic style, and had what the French call elan. Light heavyweight champion at 21, by virtue of beating Melio Bettina, he insisted on moving up to heavyweight ranks because "that's where the money is."

Sure enough, his two fights with Louis netted him more than $400,000, in the 1940s a pretty fair bundle.

Regan was a born promoter. He sponsored a lot of sports activity in Pittsburgh. Back in March of 1972, he brought the Irish Olympic boxing team to Pittsburgh on St. Patrick's Day to fight local amateurs at the Civic Arena. The Irish won eight of the ten fights.

That promotion was recalled when Cuban fighters came to Pittsburgh to fight local amateurs at the Roberto Clemente Bridge on the North Side in August 2016.

Regan was also responsible for bringing Eddie "The King" Feigner to Pittsburgh a few times. Feigner was thought to be the greatest softball pitcher and showman of all time, and barnstormed the world with his "King and His Court" team, playing against local teams. Feigner and just three other players would play your team and, like the Harlem Globetrotters, win most of their games. Feigner was from Walla Walla, Washington.

Baldy formed and coached a Pittsburgh Steelers basketball team that played in charity games throughout the tri-state area. He groomed Tom O'Malley Jr., the son of a *Pittsburgh Press* advertising executive, to take his place in booking games and getting the Steelers to show up on time, and the team is still active.

One of Regan's best promotional efforts was with Bernie Stein. He booked him for fights everywhere a ring could be put up, and he even changed his name and ethnic background to suit the local situation. If a town had a lot of Italians, Bernie became an Italian and became Bernie DelCastro or something like that. Otherwise, he was Bernie Stein, the Jewish boxer, even though he wasn't Jewish.

* * *

"Have you heard about Mike Hogan?" Art Jr. asked me.

That stumped me, at first, and then I remembered reading about Mike Hogan in Rooney's book. Art Sr. promoted Mike Hogan in his boxing days. Only Hogan's real name was Joe LaQuatra, later a union official in Pittsburgh. His boxing picture appears on the walls of a few Pittsburgh saloons to this day. And he attended Dan McCann's "Coaches Corner Luncheons" in the fall.

"My dad thought Irish boxers were more popular at the gate in those days," said Art Jr. "So Joe LaQuatra became Mike Hogan."

Bernie Stein had a busy weekend one November back in 1959. He was 17, and he was definitely overbooked. He was to fight in an amateur boxing tournament at the South Side Recreation Center that could run from Wednesday through Friday. Only problem is that Bernie was booked to play halfback that same Friday night in a City League Football Championship game at South Stadium. That game had been delayed a week because a playoff had to be held when two teams tied for a division title.

Bernie was hoping he could win the championship by Thursday night. He was described in a *Post-Gazette* report as an "athletic half-pint from the Northside." Yes, that's the way North Side, as we know it today, was written in those days.

Stein was a star 135-pound halfback at Allegheny High. They were going to play Westinghouse High School for the City League football title. Stein won his title but, alas, Westinghouse was too strong for the Allegheny football team and took the championship, as it often did when Pete Dimperio from my hometown of Hazelwood was the coach.

Bernie not only won the 135-pound class, but he was named the Outstanding Boxer in the A.M.A.A. (Allegheny Mountain Athletic Association) Junior competition that was sponsored by the Knights of Columbus. Stein was said to be the "most popular" amateur fighter in Pittsburgh by the local scribes.

Regan used his connections to get Stein a scholarship to be on the boxing team at the University of Wisconsin. Boxing was a popular sport on the Wisconsin-Madison campus. The NCAA had a bracketed tournament, just as it has today for basketball, and the tournament was being held in Madison in 1960.

One of the Badgers' best boxers, a New Yorker by the name of Charlie Mohr, took a shot in his helmeted-head in that tournament and went into a coma and died eight days later. That was the end of boxing as an NCAA-sponsored sport. The school was going to honor Stein's scholarship, but he left and returned home because he went to Wisconsin to continue boxing.

Pitt had a boxing team from 1930 to 1939 under a coach and former amateur boxer named Jack Schricker. They competed in a four-school boxing league that included Carnegie Tech, Duquesne and John Carroll of Cleveland.

"It was always an adventure hooking up with Baldy," Stein said when I sat in the food court at Ross Park Mall and interviewed him about ten years ago, when I first thought about writing this book. "We had a lot of fun together and we accomplished a few things. I enjoyed my association with the Steelers and Mr. Rooney—Art and Dan—were always in my corner."

*   *   *

I told Art Jr. that I had received a phone call that same morning from Jack McGregor, a former State Senator from Pittsburgh and one of the founding owners of the Pittsburgh Penguins.

"This is a voice out of the past," began McGregor, age 82 as of September 2016, when he called me from Bridgeport, Connecticut, where he has lived in recent years.

McGregor told me he had written a book about anecdotes from his days with the Penguins, and that he wanted to send me a copy. He said he was re-reading my book on Art Rooney called "The Chief," and enjoying it immensely. Those were his words, not mine.

McGregor is a graduate of Yale and Pitt Law School so it was nice to know that such an educated man was enjoying one of my books.

"As we're talking," I told McGregor, "I see you as you looked in the mid-60s."

Bernie Stein won the featherweight title in 1958 Golden Gloves Boxing Tournament.

Bernie Stein, right, cuts loose at Butch Bargainer in Pittsburgh Golden Gloves action.

Bernie Stein, age 75 in 2016, as seen at Ross Park Mall with his wife Pat.

"I like that," he responded.

"I tried so hard to get Art Rooney to join us in our investor team in the Penguins," recalled McGregor. "He was a hockey fan, but he said the National Football League would not permit him being involved with another pro sports team. The rules in that regard have since changed. But he said he would help me any way he could and he was good for his word."

McGregor and his partners bought the Penguins' NHL franchise for $2.5 million. Art Rooney bought the Steelers' franchise in 1933 for $2,500.

"He came to our games often, and answered any questions I had where his counsel might be of value," said McGregor. "He also helped me get elected as a state senator. I was a Republican candidate against an incumbent Democrat. Art was a staunch Republican but he was a close friend of our mayor, David L. Lawrence, who later became the governor of our state. Lawrence, of course, was a Democrat. He got Lawrence to look the other way and not oppose my candidacy by getting out the Democratic vote for my opponent."

McGregor, who was a handsome young political figure who drew comparisons to Jack Kennedy, served as a state senator representing Allegheny County (the 44th District) from 1963 to 1973. His brother Jim became a judge in the Allegheny County court system.

"I can still picture being with Mr. Rooney in the press room at the Civic Arena in those early days of the Penguins, and the Hornets before that. Beckley Smith Jr. and I did some Hornets games on WEEP Radio that last year for the team (1967)," I told McGregor.

"I remember this one night when Mr. Rooney was wearing a dark suit, and he was smoking a cigar in the press room," I continued, "and he got ashes on the front of that dark suit, and I just casually dusted the ashes off the lapels of his coat, like I was looking after my grandfather."

McGregor told me the current Penguins' ownership had been very kind to him and kept him in the picture. He said he had been invited to attend a reunion of the living

388

Jack McGregor and Jack Riley show off the Penguins' original mascot. Penguin Pete made his debut in February of 1968 season and, alas, died of pneumonia in November of that year. The ice crew at the Civic Arena was blamed for keeping his nest area too warm. Dr. Cyril Wecht did not do an autopsy to determine the cause of Pete's death. He was replaced the following year by a second Penguin on loan from the Pittsburgh Zoo. This one was named Re-Pete. Below, McGregor with Mario Lemieux.

members of the Penguins' first team (1967-68) that would be held in October of 2016. He mentioned it was a shame that Jack Riley had recently died. Riley was the Penguins' original general manager and the man who picked the team colors that were the same as his boyhood team, the Toronto Argonauts of the Canadian Football League (CFL), because Jack Riley enjoyed such reunions and always had good stories to share.

"They have asked me to drop the first puck prior to the game that night," said McGregor. "That's quite an honor."

* * *

"I know my father was a fan of Jack McGregor," said Art Rooney Jr. "Hey, I remember being in the back room at Atria's in Mt. Lebanon, with all those Pittsburgh boxers pictured back there, when you had a book-signing party there years back.

"Someone at the bar that day said to me, 'You're Dan Rooney's brother aren't you?' And I responded, perhaps too quickly, "No, I am Art Rooney's son!' The whole bar went quiet. Perhaps I protested too much."

Art Rooney Jr. wrote about boxing in his book, *Ruanaidh—The Story of Art Rooney and His Clan*, **edited by Roy McHugh.**

Tom O'Malley Jr.
He learned from his Dad,
Baldy Regan and Bernie Stein

Tom O'Malley Jr. is the manager of the Pittsburgh Steelers basketball team that always has a better record than the football team with the same personnel.

O'Malley's main responsibilities are to book games for his team throughout the tri-state area during the off-season for football and to round up the players for each game and get them to the site on time. I believe he promises at least seven Steelers, some current and some from past rosters.

They play in fundraisers at school gyms against teachers, policemen, firemen and anybody willing to challenge a heavyweight basketball team. Ben Roethilsberger comes on occasion, and Hines Ward and Bret Keisel could bring it, and Louis Lipps would play if they were short on Steelers. They get a few hundred dollars per game and the rookies are especially eager to make some pocket money.

O'Malley was groomed for this job by Baldy Regan, who first put together such a team, with the blessing of Dan Rooney, but not necessarily the endorsement of the reigning Steelers' head coach. Regan was known as "the mayor of the North Side," even though his only official title was District Magistrate at an office on Perry Highway across the street from Perry High School.

And Baldy was often in the company of Mike Kearns, Bernie Stein and Paul Tomasovich, all wonderful Pittsburgh characters, who worked in press boxes at Pitt Stadium and Three Rivers Stadium, turning out play-by-play and stat sheets.

Stein was also in sideline security along with Joe Diven. They were the Mutt and Jeff of Steelers' security, and were something of a Steel Curtain before there was a Steel Curtain. Stein was about 5-5, 140 pounds and Diven was 6-5, 280 pounds. Stein was a Golden Gloves boxing champion and Diven was known as "the world's greatest streetfighter."

O'Malley had not seen Stein in some time when I contacted him in August of 2016 at the Bob Purkey Insurance Agency in Bethel Park. O'Malley was also mentored by Purkey, a fine pitcher for the Pirates and Cincinnati Reds in the '50s and '60s, and took over his business when he died.

Another influence was his father, Tom O'Malley, the actual mayor of Castle Shannon and an ad executive at *The Pittsburgh Press*. When I was a copy boy in the classified ad department of *The Press* in 1959 and 1960, the elder O'Malley was an ad salesman. He was also a pleasant fellow and lots of fun.

He reminded me of a combination of Red Buttons and George Gobel. How could a guy go wrong if we were taught the tricks of the trade by so many standouts? When I asked young O'Malley—an eligible bachelor forever—of his memories of Bernie Stein, he said, "He was a fine athlete at Allegheny High School and he won some Golden Gloves titles in Pittsburgh. He was one of Baldy's first proteges and they were also best friends.

"He went to the University of Wisconsin on a boxing scholarship, but the school dropped the sport after one of his teammates died following a fight (even though it was eventually determined he did not die from fight injuries). Bernie came back home after his freshman year.

"He and Baldy got back together and he was Baldy's first assistant with the Steelers' basketball team in the early 1960s.

"Bernie got a job as a driver with Pittsburgh Brewing (probably through Baldy's buddy, Dan McCann, the leading sales representative at the Iron City brewery, until he retired). Bernie eventually ran the merchandising department for the sales and promotional staff.

"Bernie was also on Baldy's staff with Mike Kearns in the press box before Baldy brought me on in 1969. That was Chuck Noll's first year, and the Steelers were playing at Pitt Stadium. Bernie stayed on for a couple of years after we moved to Three Rivers Stadium and then Dan Rooney requested that Baldy move Bernie to help secure the field.

"Bernie was stationed outside of the walkway from the underground tunnels from the locker rooms and press gate to the field. Bernie would check the field passes of people coming onto the field and, if they didn't have a proper pass, send them off the field.

"If Dan Rooney saw someone on the field that didn't belong there he would call Bernie on his walkie-talkie—this was before cell phones—and tell him where the person was on the field and dispatch him to remove the culprit!

"One time after the 1979 World Series, Willie Stargell and two of his teammates came onto the field before the game. Bernie said they didn't have proper passes, but he let them go on the field anyway. I guess a World Series MVP gets some perks!

"Bernie could be tough when necessary, but he was one of the quietest and most unassuming persons you would ever want to meet. He was always a true, humble gentleman who loved his wife and four daughters and all his grandchildren."

I always had the same perception of Bernie Stein. He was always respectful and polite and addressed me as Mr. O'Brien. In that respect, he was like all of Baldy Regan's sons. They behaved like military academy cadets. Baldy was one of those guys who always made you feel like a big deal.

O'Malley said he had a favorite story involving Baldy, Bernie and Tom's dad. They were going to the Steelers' first Super Bowl in New Orleans. The original plan called for Baldy and Bernie to room together, and Tom Sr. and Tom Jr. would share a room.

Just before they departed Pittsburgh, Baldy told them his wife Alice was coming along, and could Bernie stay with the O'Malleys.

"That was fine with us," said O'Malley. "The night we arrived in New Orleans, Bernie and I hit Bourbon Street and stayed out all night and never came back to our room. It was a good thing because Baldy also told Joe Babish, the tax collector in South Fayette and the father of Melissa Babish, Miss Teenage America and the wife of Terry Bradshaw, that he and his friend Commissioner Desmet of South Fayette, could stay in our room. They were supposed to stay with Bradshaw's parents but they couldn't find their house. At least my dad wasn't lonely."

Tom O'Malley, Jim O'Brien and Hines Ward, left to right, are on Steelers' basketball team bench at Bethel Park High School.

Paul Tomasovich
"The Babe Ruth of Softball"

As I was writing the story about Art Rooney Jr. and Bernie Stein, I paused to call Paul Tomasovich on the telephone at his home in Greenfield.

His wife Jane answered the phone and told me Paul was taking a shower and that he would call me back in ten minutes. I could hear him screaming in the background.

Ten minutes later, my telephone rang. The caller ID said TOMASOVICH.

"Good morning, Brother," I said, doing my best imitation of his old buddy, Baldy Regan.

"This is a great day when I can talk to a big shot like you," replied Paul, doing his best imitation of his old buddy, Baldy Regan. "Only in America."

Then we both laughed. It's always been that way when I talk to Tomasovich, still regarded as the greatest slugger in Pittsburgh softball history—indeed, "The Babe Ruth of Softball"—and one of Pittsburgh's treasures.

Paul Tomasovich and Baldy Regan had that rare ability to make you feel like a big deal and brightened everyone's day with their cheerful repertoire.

Frank Thomas, third only to Ralph Kiner and Willie Stargell as home run hitters in Pirates' history, played some softball and supported Paul's claim to being the Babe Ruth of his sport.

Paul still has his membership card in the local sports officials' organization. "I've had a card since 1964, but I had a heart issue and I had to retire a few years back," he said. "I'd done football and basketball and baseball and softball and I was down to volleyball. If you can't officiate volleyball you better get suited for your funeral. Baldy always believed in having a spare black suit in your closet just in case. He bought two at a time when they were on sale, one to wear and one for the funeral."

I wanted to know if Paul had a phone number for Bernie Stein or remembered the name of Bernie's wife, or where they lived. Tomasovich struck out on three pitches.

He hit a home run or two, however, when it came to telling me some stories.

* * *

I mentioned to Tomasovich about what great Christmas parties Baldy used to host at his magistrate's office across from what is now called Perry Traditional Academy on Perry Avenue back in the '70s and '80s.

"Harold Betters would be there with his music group, playing 'Rambunctious' on his trombone, and the room would be wall-to-wall people," I said. "I remember one time that Larry Werner, an advertising and public relations executive at Ketchum, McLeod & Grove, said to me, 'This is the only party in town where you have bankers on one side of the room and bank-robbers on the other side of the room.'"

That was a cue for Tomasovich to tell me another tale. "What was that women's name who was married to the richest man in town?"

I told Tomasovich, "I think you're talking about Elsie Hillman."

"That's it," he came back. "She was *even* there talking to this one guy in the room and she comes and tells Baldy what a nice guy this man was, and Baldy says, 'That guy is about to do 20 years. He got caught robbing a bank here.' And Mrs. Hillman clutched her purse a bit. Baldy had a talent for putting people together who would never have met in their own social lives."

I told Tomasovich I remember being at one of Baldy's Christmas parties where he had Harold Betters

Photos by Jim O'Brien

**PAUL
TOMASOVICH**
Enjoys a seat in
press box at Heinz
Field

**BILLY CONN JR. AND
MARY LOUISE CONN**

**HAROLD
"MR. TROMBONE'
BETTERS**
Played his saxophone
before Steelers' games

and his group take a break while he married a young woman who looked to be about eight months pregnant. It was her and the groom and her dad. I don't think her dad was toting a rifle. They were probably hoping to get married on the sly before she had her baby. But they ended up getting married before a full house of Christmas revelers.

"That didn't bother Baldy," said Tomasovich. "He married them with great dignity, at least on his part. And he probably did it for free."

Baldy Regan was a fun guy. When I was a teenager I went to a night club he ran on the North Side. It looked like one of those two-decker western bars. "My mother told me to ask you to look after me while I was on the North Side," I told Regan that night.

"Where does your mother think you live?" roared Regan. "A lot of guys on the North Side are nervous about going to your hometown of Hazelwood!"

Baldy and I were both at the bachelor party for Paul Martha, a Pitt football star who was the No. 1 draft pick of the Steelers in 1964. Baldy brought a dozen chocolate pies to this place where the party was held. It got messy. And Martha was marrying Bobbie Gott, the beautiful blonde daughter of US Steel president and CEO, Edwin Gott. I was invited to the reception at one of the fancy clubs in Fox Chapel, maybe the Field Club. There was a nine-piece orchestra in black and gray tuxedos with tails.

Tomasovich told me how his seven daughters were doing. I was particularly interested in how Paula was doing because she was a student trainer for Foge Fazio's football team when I worked at Pitt as the assistant athletic director for Pitt athletics, and Paula helped out in our sports information office. She was just like Baldy Regan's kids, well-behaved and so respectful and pleasant. It was good to hear she got into sports physical therapy and has done well. "All my girls turned out well," said Paul, proudly. "Jane and I were blessed in that regard."

He told me something I didn't know. "You know Baldy had a limousine service for a while," said Tomasovich, "and he had me pick up Larry Holmes at the airport and bring him downtown."

Holmes was the heavyweight champion at the time, in November of 1981. A year earlier, he had TKOd Muhammad Ali in the 11th round of a title fight in Las Vegas. He retained his title with another 11th round TKO victory, this time over Renaldo Snipes, at the Civic Arena.

"I remember he asked me to stop somewhere and get him a Powerhouse candy bar," recalled Tomasovich. "Larry liked those Powerhouse candy bars, he told me."

Tomasovich was no one to mess with. He got tired of a guy heckling him from the stands at a high school basketball game. He went over to the guy with the basketball in his hands. The guy had been second guessing and hollering at him all night. Paul lofted the ball over his head—like for a tip-off—and when the guy's eyes followed the ball upward, Tomasovich leveled him with an overhand right. Billy Conn and Fritzie Zivic would have been proud of Paul.

My wife Kathie tells me all the time that I attract characters. Thank heavens. I couldn't make up these stories.

"I saw Paul Tomasovich play softball. He could pound it. I didn't know he became a sports official."
—Tom McGuire, South Strabane, Pennsylvania

Fritzie Zivic
The Croatian Comet

A friendly brown-uniformed UPS courier told me I could find photographs of Fritzie Zivic on the wall at Hambone's in the heart of Lawrenceville. "It's 4207 Butler Street," he said authoritatively, "just across from the parking lot."

Once inside the indistinctive door of Hambone's, I spotted two photographs in the first booth of Fritzie Zivic, flailing away at Beau Jack, Henry Armstrong or Lou Ambers, I'm not sure which, then a Terrible Towel was draped over a bar above the second booth, and then two photographs of Billy Conn over the third booth.

There were Terrible Towels everywhere in Hambone's. The Terrible Towel was my mentor Myron Cope's creation. Cope boxed a little as a young man and he loved the fight game. Cope would be proud to be represented between Billy Conn and Fritzie Zivic. He knew them both and wrote about them many times.

Conn and Zivic were both world champion boxers back in the early '40s. Conn came out of East Liberty and Zivic from Lawrenceville. Before them, there was Harry Greb of Garfield, which is in between East Liberty and Lawrenceville, and Greb is still considered one of the greatest fighters of all time.

Conn, who was much bigger than Zivic, won a split decision over his friend Fritzie when they fought in December of 1936 at Duquesne Garden in Oakland. They were both bloodied by the tenth round of what was reported to be an exciting fight. It was a fight that drew much interest in Pittsburgh because both were popular sports figures.

Before a big crowd at Forbes Field on July 18, 1951, Jersey Joe Walcott knocked out Ezzard Charles in the seventh round of one of Pittsburgh's most famous fights.

Zivic died in 1984 after a long battle with Alzheimer's disease and an 18-month stay at Veterans Hospital in

Aspinwall. He was inducted into the Boxing Hall of Fame in 1993.

His wife Helen said he heard from many boxing people during his stay at the Veterans Hospital, but none was more loyal in calling, she said, than Sugar Ray Robinson. That was good to hear. Robinson, considered by many to be "the greatest fighter pound for pound," scored a ten-round decision over Zivic at Madison Square Garden in 1941. There are pictures with Zivic and Robinson together at some saloons around town. I visited Helen Zivic at her home in Scott after Fritzie died and sat on a couch and talked to her for an hour.

Helen Stokan Zivic died at age 96 in mid-October 2010 in San Francisco, where she had lived the previous five years with her daughter Jan Zivic.

* * *

Zivic fought seven future Hall of Fame fighters and nine world champions. He defeated such men as Henry Armstrong, Charley Burley (once in three fights), Sammy Angott, Jake LaMotta and Red Cochrane.

Roy McHugh, a former columnist and sports editor at *The Pittsburgh Press*, wrote a farewell column to Zivic in which he reflected on the city's three greatest fighters, Greb, Conn and Zivic. The column contained this memorable line: "If you owned a saloon in Pittsburgh, photographs of the three were every bit as essential as a liquor license."

Just before it started to snow that afternoon—four to five inches worth—I went to the Heinz History Center on Smallman Street in The Strip and checked out the boxing display on the fourth floor of the old ice house in the Western Pennsylvania Sports Museum.

There are distinct black and white photographs of Greb, Conn and Zivic there, too, on a wall with other boxing champions who came out of the Pittsburgh area. There was a 16-month period, spanning 1939 to 1941, when five of the eight recognized boxing divisions were championed by boxers from Pittsburgh and Western Pennsylvania. That's when Pittsburgh first became known as "The City of Champions." The photographs are familiar to anyone who cares about the city's boxing history.

The boxers included Conn and Zivic, light heavyweight and welterweight champion respectively, and lightweight champion Sammy Angott of Washington, Pa., and featherweight champion Jackie Wilson of Homewood, middleweight champion Billy Soose of Farrell (who looks like a choir boy in his picture).

There's also a photo of Greb, a middleweight and light-heavyweight champion in the '20s and billed as "The Pittsburgh Windmill," and one of Charley Burley of The Hill District, regarded as one of the city's best boxers who never got the chance to compete for a championship because he was black and more so because his style made opposing boxers look bad.

I wondered why Teddy Yarosz of Monaca, a middleweight champion, was not included in the display, but no one on the Heinz staff could answer that question. Yarosz belongs there.

Yarosz is pictured, by the way, along with Conn, Greb and Zivic with Andy "Kid" DePaul of Green Tree, the late Pennsylvania boxing chairman, Don Alderson and a host of other lesser-known Pittsburgh prize fighters, in the back room of Atria's Restaurant & Tavern on Rt. 19 as Dormont gives way to Mt. Lebanon traveling south.

I was taking a photograph with my digital camera of a near life-size framed photo of Zivic at Atria's one afternoon in January, when a waitress, Deanna Hilligoss, spotted me doing so. She wanted to know what my interest was in Fritzie Zivic. When I told her I was doing a magazine piece on Zivic, she smiled and asked me if I had seen the green scrapbook high on a shelf over the doorway leading to the long bar at Atria's.

I had not. She summoned a tall waiter and had him take it down for me to see. It was professionally put together with photos of some of America's greatest fighters, and it included Greb, Conn and Zivic, along with Jess

Willard, Jack Dempsey, Gene Tunney, Gentleman Jim Corbett, James Braddock—"The Cinderella Man"—Rocky Marciano and Rocky Graziano. It was like being on a successful archaeological dig.

Billy Conn and Fritzie Zivic were two of the first Pittsburgh sports personalities I learned about as a child. When I was eight years old, I helped my older brother Dan to deliver the *Post-Gazette* in the morning before we went off to school. I'd devour the sports page of the *Post-Gazette* when we'd get home, starting with sports editor Al Abram's column, always on the far left side of the front page of the sports section.

His "Sidelights on Sports" column was must reading. He often mentioned Zivic and Conn in his column, along with other Pittsburgh sports personalities such as Ralph Kiner, "Bullet Bill" Dudley, Art Rooney and a host of characters he came by in his bar-hopping routine. John Deni, an Olympic heel-and-toe walker, was in there a lot, and a character he christened "The Japanese Ambassador." So was Archie "Tex" Litman, a local beer distributor and boxing and basketball promoter.

Conn was the first Pittsburgh Sportsman of the Year at the Dapper Dan Sports Dinner founded by Abrams and his associates. That was in 1939. Zivic was the award-winner the following year of 1940. If you fancy yourself a real Pittsburgh sports fan you must familiarize yourself with the story of Fritzie Zivic. There was a time when some referred to the Civic Arena as the Zivic Arena.

All told, Zivic had 231 fights that are in the record books and several more that didn't make it. His official record was 159-64-9, winning 80 fights by knockouts. Most of his losses came late in his career. Like most boxers, he didn't know when to quit. When he was ill toward the end of his life, doctors said he had suffered brain damage from all the blows he absorbed. His nose was broken so many times it was like putty, and he's get a rise out of fans by pushing his rubbery nose from side to side.

He had more than a few fights in his day in the streets of Lawrenceville.

There were five Zivic brothers who grew up in the 9th Ward, the "Irishtown" section of Lawrenceville, and four of them became boxers. They all had some main event fights on local cards. Pete and Jack Zivic were members of the 1920 Olympic team, with Jack bringing home a gold medal in the featherweight class. Eddie was also a boxer, and only Al refrained from fighting. The family was known as "The Fighting Zivics."

Talking about his tough boyhood neighborhood in Lawrenceville, Zivic once said, "You either had to fight or stay in the house. We went out."

Fritzie's birth name was Ferdinand Henry John Zivcich. His father was Croatian and his mother Mary Kepele was Slovenian and they settled in the mill town of Lawrenceville as did many ethnic groups who immigrated to this country from Europe.

Fritzie's biggest fight was when he won a 12-round TKO over the great Henry Armstrong to win the welterweight championship of the world before a record crowd at the old Madison Square Garden on October 4, 1040.

One of his champion opponents, Lew Jenkins, said of him, "Fritzie was the only guy I know who could start a fight in an empty room."

They called him "the Croat Comet" and they called him "the dirtiest fighter" in boxing. He succeeded Greb in that regard. "If you're going to fight you better fight dirty," said Zivic.

He was known to stick his thumb into an opponent's eye, scrape the laces on his gloves across the face of a foe, hit below the belt and on the break. The late Judge John Brosky, an AAU official for track and field events in the Allegheny Mountain Amateur Association, told me that he was recruited to ring the bell at one of Fritzie's fights. "Fritzie would slam an uppercut into the guy's gonads," recalled Brosky, "and then say, 'I'm sorry. I'm so sorry.' And then he would hit the guy below the belt again."

Zivic used his head, his elbows, his forearms and his knees, anything to hurt you. Yet he was proud to say he was never disqualified in 231 pro fights. Like the other fighters of his day, he trained at the Pittsburgh Lyceum, just across the street from Epiphany Church in the Lower Hill, or where Chatham Center is now located, across from the Consol Energy Center where the Penguins play.

One of the people who looked after him at the Pittsburgh Lyceum was Joe Luvara, who was a masseur, a cut man and a corner man in local boxing circles. His name often appeared in Al Abrams' column. Luvara's daughter, Denise Luvara Robinson, who is the catering director at Atria's, and her son, Devlin, brought me some scrapbooks their family had kept about Joe Luvara and it included many newspaper clippings with stories about Fritzie Zivic, Billy Conn and the Pittsburgh Golden Gloves. Denise handed me boxing gloves that Zivic had worn. They were soft and thin, I thought there wasn't much padding and you'd feel knuckles if someone hit you wearing those gloves. It felt strange to hold those gloves.

It was like a trip down memory lane, seeing all those stories written by Al Abrams, Myron Cope and Roy McHugh and Jimmy Jordan and Jimmy Miller. I'd met all those men in my teen years and they were all helpful to a young writer.

I first met Fritzie Zivic when I was about ten years old. My mother, Mary O'Brien, worked as a sales clerk at the State Store on Second Avenue in Hazelwood. Fritzie Zivic used to come there as a sales rep for a wine company. He was also a beer salesman, a boilermaker and a road worker for Allegheny County in his post-boxing career. You always wish you had visited these folks a few more times to get more of their stories.

The Zivics lived in the Irish Town section of Lawrenceville, which was good for a few fights right off the bat if you were a kid with parents from Croatia and Slovenia.

"I was from a fighting family," Zivic said. "We all liked boxing. The Fighting Zivics were a big hit in boxing circles. We'd fight anybody anytime."

Proof of that is Zivic's fight record. He fought 22 times in 1938 and 19 times in 1936 and 1939.

"When I was a kid my mom always sent me out of the house with the order— 'No fighting, hear? I don't want some neighbor yammering at my door about her son getting a black eye from you!'

"I had a reputation for being a dirty fighter, but I'm proud to say I never lost a fight on a foul."

FRITZIE ZIVIC
Zivic assumed a classic John L. Sullivan pose for picture taken in New York where the former welterweight champion was set to box Beau Jack, pride of the Stork Club sporting set, at Madison Square Garden on March 5, 1943. Zivic lost a 12-rounder that night.

DAPPER DANS—The Monroeville chapter of the Dapper Dan Club honored on November 18, 1968 the following, from left to right, Fritzie Zivic, Penn State's Ted Kwalick from McKees Rocks, the Steelers Dick Hoak from Jeannette, Zeke Shumaker, an assistant football coach at Pitt, the Panthers' Paul Martha from Wilkins Township, and Joe L. Brown, the general manager of the Pirates.

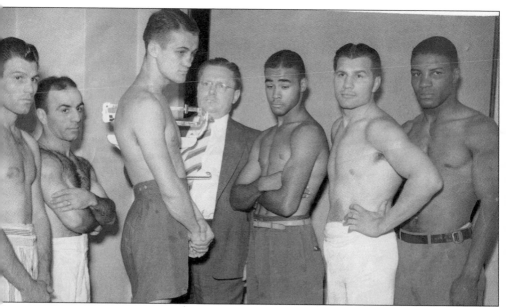

CHAMPION BOXERS -- An unidentified Pennsylvania Boxing Commission figure checks scales at weigh-in for, left to right, Sammy Angott, Pete Aaron, Fritzie Zivic, Charley Burley, Teddy Yarosz and Al Gainer on July 17, 1939.

Leah Smith
Olympic swimming medalist
has athletic bloodlines in Pittsburgh

L eah Smith, who will be a senior at the University of Virginia for the 2016-2017 academic calendar year, won two medals in the 2016 Summer Olympic Games in Rio. A native of Mt. Lebanon and a graduate of Oakland Catholic High School, she won a bronze medal in the 400-meter freestyle and was a member of the gold medal 4 x 200-meter relay team for the U.S.A.

She teamed with Kathie Ladecki, Allison Schmitt and Maya DiRado to win that event.

What made Smith's story even more compelling was that she is the great-granddaughter of "Greenfield Jimmy" Smith, who was a member of the New York Giants National League champion team of 1917. During Prohibition, he was also reputed for bringing bootleg alcohol into his Greenfield neighborhood from cities throughout the country. His daughter Mary Louise Smith married Billy Conn, the light heavyweight champion of the world who nearly dethroned heavyweight champion Joe Louis. So Leah Smith is the great-niece of Billy Conn.

Her challenge back at UVA is that Katie Ladecki will be a freshman at Stanford University and a favorite in NCAA championships.

LEAH SMITH

Book Review
"The Chief" is worth reading

By Edwin Pope
Sports Editor Emeritus,
The Miami Herald
September 2011

It's a lot more than coincidental that most of my all-time favorite sports people—Art Rooney and Dan Rooney, Dan Marino, Stan Musial and Billy Conn—are all Western Pennsylvanians.

It's more than coincidental because I've liked everybody I've ever met from there, from the late Froggy's proprietor Steve Morris, to all the guys who used to clean me out in midnight poker games at the old *Pittsburgh Press*.

And right now I'm reveling in the best book ever written about any sports figure from there—Jim O'Brien's "The Chief."

People have written lovingly about the late Art Rooney practically forever. No one has done it better than O'Brien in "The Chief." I first became aware of O'Brien when I judged a college writing contest back in the early '60s. I recall telling Beano Cook, the Pitt sports publicist and Jim's friend and co-conspirator with a lively establishment-tormenting tabloid called *Pittsburgh Weekly Sports* that it was no contest—O'Brien's work for the Pitt student newspaper was clearly the best in the competition.

Then O'Brien came to Miami in 1969 to cover the Dolphins for our rival newspaper, *The Miami News.*

He started frequenting my favorite after-hours watering hole, Julie's Pad, where he and Bill Braucher, our beat writer on the Dolphins, and Jack Mann, a noted newspaperman, talked shop long into the night and early morning. Even Larry King came by now and then when he was doing a popular radio talk show in Miami. O'Brien told me it was like going to grad school.

Before his first year was up, I had recommended him to our sister Knight-Ridder newspaper in Detroit. Frankly, I wanted to get him out of town because he beat us on a few good stories. He accepted a job there at the *Detroit Free Press*, where Joe Falls held forth, then changed his mind, and went to *The New York Post* instead. I'd run into Jim at Super Bowls and championship boxing events, Muhammad Ali and others of that time, and he once saved my butt when I took a bad fall at the media headquarters hotel in New Orleans.

He was always keeping the company of older out-of-town writers and always asking questions. I believe he looked up to us. I know he felt that way about Art Rooney. It's obvious by the way he wrote this book. I learned a lot of things I didn't know about Art Rooney and it only increased my regard for this great sportsman.

As a for-instance, I'd always understood The Chief bought the Steelers with the proceeds from a betting coup at Saratoga, New York.

Wrong.

He made plenty before that running juke boxes and slot machines in bars and restaurants all over Allegheny County. He was street smart and knew how to make a buck.

Besides, The Chief paid only $2,500 to the National Football League for the Steelers' franchise in 1933. And he called them the Pirates the first seven years because he was such a big baseball fan. He changed the name in 1940 to avoid confusion with the city's Major League Baseball team. I'm sure the sports editors and headline writers at the local newspapers appreciated that change. He won up to a hundred times that NFL entry fee in a two-day gambling spree in New York City and Saratoga.

As O'Brien tells the true story, Rooney ran a $300 stake up to $21,000 gambling in Manhattan. Then he set out for Saratoga and extended the spree by betting $2,000 at 8-1 odds on a horse named Quel Jeu.

He didn't stop there. As an old Pittsburgh friend of mine would say about a real plunger, "He bet what he weighed."

410

And Art Rooney kept winning until he had upwards of a quarter-million in his pockets.

The Steelers cost him many times that much before real football money started coming in after the NFL-AFL merger in 1970. Then, too, Art Rooney gave away what he won that day, many times over before he died in 1988.

You couldn't begin to list all the things that were right with Art Rooney and wrong with the Steelers in this relatively brief space. I used to kid the great Ed Kiely, Art's right-hand man for so long, about their judgments on both coaches and quarterbacks. But when they brought in Chuck Noll and then Terry Bradshaw, they hit a double gusher.

It isn't always the nicest people who get the big payoffs in football. Hey, even Al Davis has won Super Bowls. But it was the right thing happening to the right man when Art Rooney's Steelers finally zoomed into that wild and wonderful Super Bowl championship streak.

If you had to pick one attribute that made Art Rooney the most loved figure in the history of football, and I mean ALL football, it was the common touch.

In "The Chief," Dan Marino talks about working on a summer construction job at Three Rivers Stadium when he was at Pitt, and hearing "how well Mr. Rooney treated those guys on the ground crew." Marino also heard Rooney used to take two members of the ground crew on the plane to every Steelers' road game, and even to Super Bowls.

"He treated people like they were important," Marino said. "He touched people."

He sure touched me, and so did this book.

Art Rooney and his Pittsburgh Steelers

Art Rooney

Jim O'Brien

Dedication

It's never too late to say thank you. When friends suffer the loss of their mother I often assure them that their mother will always be with them. You will do something that would have pleased your mother, or you will watch your grandchildren at play, and think of how much your mother would have loved seeing them.

I was never more mindful of my mother, Mary O'Brien, than when I wrote this book during the spring and summer of 2016. She was with me all the way. She died in late February of 2003 at the age of 96. The staff at Asbury Heights Senior Care in Mt. Lebanon loved her because she always smiled at them and never forgot how to say "thank you."

My mother was a good speller. "Tell them, Jim, wasn't I smart?" she said one day when surrounded by other seniors in wheelchairs in the hallway at Asbury Heights. She made sure I was a good speller. She proofread my newspaper *Pittsburgh Weekly Sports* early in my career.

Later on, my mother kept meticulous scrapbooks filled with newspaper clippings from *The Miami News, The New York Post, The Pittsburgh Press* and *The Sporting News* over a 15-year period from 1969 to 1983. They are in surprisingly great shape.

I have about 30 of those scrapbooks in the basement of my home.

I went through them while working on this book, to find the stories I had written about the boxers I have met in my life, from Billy Conn to Joe Louis, to Muhammad Ali and Joe Frazier, and other great and not-so-great fighters. Like Augie Broudy, a boyhood neighbor on Sunnyside Street in Glenwood. They were all special in different ways.

I was able to draw from those stories for this book, to go with the stories I wrote especially for *From A to Z*. M is the 13th letter in the alphabet, right in the middle. For me, M is for my mother, Mary O'Brien. As Rocky Graziano, a champion boxer I met in my New York days, often said, "Somebody up there likes me."

Bill Jerome

Jim O'Brien's mother Mary seen proofreading his newspaper, *Pittsburgh Weekly Sports*, at Western Newspaper Printing in 1963.

About the Author

Pittsburgh sports author Jim O'Brien has written 24 books in his "Pittsburgh Proud" series. He is on the advisory board for the Western Pennsylvania Sports Museum at the Heinz History Center in Pittsburgh, and has been inducted into the Western Chapter of the Pennsylvania Sports Hall of Fame. He was given the Bob Prince Award for his journalism efforts and the David L. Lawrence Award for "promoting Pittsburgh in a positive manner on a national level" from Vectors. He was cited as a "Legend" by the Pittsburgh chapter of the Italian-American Sports Hall of Fame.

He teaches a class in "Pittsburgh's Rich Sports History" in the Osher Institute Lifelong Learning Institute at the University of Pittsburgh and was invited to teach the same course at Carnegie Mellon University. He has previously taught undergrad students at Point Park University and Robert Morris University, and mentored many student interns during his four-year stay in the mid-80s as assistant athletic director for public relations at the University of Pittsburgh. A half dozen of his proteges went on to big-time positions in television and radio, and pro and college and non-profit public relations.

He was the first Pittsburgher to be inducted into the U. S. Basketball Writers Association Hall of Fame at ceremonies at the Regency Hyatt in New Orleans on Monday, April 7, 2003. The event was held in conjunction with the NCAA Final Four men's basketball championship. During a three-year span, O'Brien also served on the nomination board for the Basketball Hall of Fame in Springfield, Massachusetts, and was responsible for promoting induction of Connie Hawkins of Brooklyn and Zigmund "Red" Mihalik of Ford City, Pennsylvania, a great referee. In 2012, he was given a "lifetime achievement" award and inducted into the Pittsburgh Basketball Hall of Fame. He voted for the Baseball Hall of Fame in Cooperstown, New York, and is an honorary member of the U.S. Baseball Writers Assn.

He writes a column for *The Valley Mirror* in the Steel Valley, and he wrote a column for 18 years in *The Almanac* in South Hills, and is a contributing writer for magazines in Mt. Lebanon and Upper St. Clair. O'Brien was the founding editor for 23 years for *Street & Smith's Basketball*, and a contributing writer and editor emeritus for an additional 14 years, and authored *The Complete Handbook of Pro Basketball* for three years. He wrote a column on pro basketball for *The Sporting News* for nine years. He was a staff writer for the *Philadelphia Evening Bulletin*, *The Miami News*, *The New York Post* and *The Pittsburgh Press*. He wrote stories for *SPORT* magazine, *Newsweek*, *Basketball Times*, *The Football News* and *The Washington Post*.

He has a degree in English from Pitt, and completed graduate-level courses in English Literature when he was working at his alma mater in the mid-80s.

He has been married for 49 years to Kathleen Churchman O'Brien and they live in the Pittsburgh suburb of North Strabane. They are the parents of Dr. Sarah O'Brien of Columbus, Ohio and Rebecca O'Brien of Woodland Hills, California. They are the grandparents of Margaret, Susannah, Jeffrey and Madeline of Columbus, Ohio.

Kathleen Churchman O'Brien

During a visit to the *Chicago Tribune* Authors' Row Book Fair in early June, 2007, Frank Deford, the finest sports author in America, shared some stories about Billy Conn and his wife, Mary Louise, whom he interviewed over a three-day visit to Pittsburgh to write the award-winning "The Boxer and the Blonde" story for *Sports Illustrated* in 1985. "We got more mail on that than any other piece in the history of the magazine," said Deford. "It was a love story about how Conn won the girl but lost the best fight ever."

"Jim O'Brien was one of a group of young sports writers of the 1970s in New York who were more than journalists. This new breed—Jim, along with Larry Merchant, Vic Ziegel, Stan Isaacs, Bob Lipsyte—treated the readers of The New York Times, The New York Post *and* Newsday *to a new investigative look at the total sports scene from ownership to management through the athletes on to the fans. It was great stuff."*
—LeRoy Neiman